BOOK OF REVELATION

BOOK OF REVELATION

THEORY OF THE TEXT: REARRANGED TEXT AND TRANSLATION: COMMENTARY

BY

JOHN OMAN

Principal, Westminster College Cambridge

CAMBRIDGE

AT THE UNIVERSITY PRESS

1923

CAMBRIDGE
UNIVERSITY PRESS

University Printing House, Cambridge CB2 8BS, United Kingdom

Cambridge University Press is part of the University of Cambridge.

It furthers the University's mission by disseminating knowledge in the pursuit of education, learning and research at the highest international levels of excellence.

www.cambridge.org
Information on this title: www.cambridge.org/9781107505391

First published 1923
First paperback edition 2015

A catalogue record for this publication is available from the British Library

ISBN 978-1-107-50539-1 Paperback

CONTENTS

PART I

THE TEXT AND ITS REARRANGEMENT

NOTES

PART II

TEXT AND TRANSLATION

PART III

COMMENTARY

PREFACE

A FITTING dedication would be, 'To the onlie begetter of the insuing book, Prof. Burkitt's Seminaar.' My presence at its deliberations on 'Revelation' was not due to any particular interest in the subject, but to a vague idea that, to think about religion, without knowing a little about its documents, is not much more use than to be a pundit on its documents, without doing a little thinking about religion. In the alembic of its learning, especially the Semitic erudition of the President, Dr Abrahams, Dr Stanley Cook and Canon Lukyn Williams, any ideas I had were evaporated, and only mere negations seemed to be left. The book could not be explained as composed of various documents; no known Jewish apocalyptic writing sheds much light on it; no method of interpretation—historical, allegorical, mythological, astrological—gives it any connected or reasonable meaning. This did not increase my interest in the book, but it stirred my antagonism to being baffled by a problem: so, having some leisure in a Christmas vacation, I set myself to a serious reading of the original. As I proceeded, the negations turned into three positive convictions. (1) The style and thought alike guarantee unity of authorship. (2) The literary sources are almost entirely the prophets, and most of all Daniel. (3) The visions are transparencies of what are for us abstractions, but were for the ancient world concrete, if ideal, realities, and not accounts of material supernatural happenings. There then seemed to run through the whole a view of the world which it might be possible to reconstruct. The greater clearness of some parts, when thus read, compared with the confusion of the rest suggested that there must be some other cause for so great a contrast than the incapacity of the author, and that the most probable cause was disarrangement of the text. The rearrangement was casual and uncertain, till the sudden discovery of the uniform length of the sections I was moving offered an objective and definite standard. Then, the sections rearranged themselves so simply and naturally that, in the first rapid ordering of them, a fuller consideration has only led to altering the position of one. The scholars, mentioned above, would probably not agree with all my inferences from their labours, but, as I could never have drawn them, with the same confidence from my own meagre Semitic learning, I trust they will allow me to acknowledge what I at least feel to be a debt. In this I have the greater confidence that, when an outline of the theory was submitted to the circle, it received enough approval to encourage further effort.

To my colleague, Dr Anderson Scott, the rearranged text and the explanation of it, so far as I had then mastered it, was first submitted. The equality of the sections impressed him as working out with astonishing accuracy, but he thought that, before the work could be wholly convincing, it would be necessary to show how the editor came to make so great confusion in the original work of his author. This, as will be seen, proved to be a fruitful line of inquiry.

From Prof. Burkitt I have had one or two useful references, and on some Old Testament points I have consulted Dr Abrahams, Prof. Kennett and our late Principal, Dr Skinner. Doubtless there are still mistakes, but they are fewer for their help. The acute, learned and critical mind of Dr Skinner has also helped to guard me against being satisfied with too easy solutions.

But the persons to whom I am most of all in debt are my old pupils, the Rev. Eric Philip and our tutor Mr T. W. Manson. They have carefully followed the work in all its later stages. Mr Manson, from the first, found the general theory beyond dubiety, and proceeded to make further investigations of his own on detail, especially in the LXX, which further strengthened his conviction, because he found in his work several confirmations of my conclusions. In the process he also discovered a few new interpretations, acknowledgment of which has been made in the notes. Mr Philip, being brought up on the classics, with strong prejudices against altering texts, was more difficult to convince, but the answers to his difficulties in every case strengthened the argument; and now he accepts, not only the theory in general, but practically all its applications. On one important point, however, it was he who did the convincing. Not having fully escaped from the influence of Dr Charles and certain German writers, I had made free with the text in several places, without any justification from the standard of length. These emendations Mr Philip called in question, giving good reasons for his opinion. The existing readings, I then discovered, could, with very few exceptions, be explained from the O. T.: and then it appeared that the evidence for the soundness of the text was one of the strongest proofs for the accuracy of the rearrangement. A critical study of the text requires a knowledge I do not possess. Yet, if the theory be right, it ought to be possible to test by the right order details of a text which has come down through centuries in a state of confusion. This would be the earliest known test of the transmission of any Christian document. That readings, which before seemed certainly corrupt, receive a clear and convincing meaning in the new order is itself important, but a more detailed study of what in the new order is the better text may also provide some evidence for the comparative value of the Eastern and Western texts.

The text used is, apart from the few alterations noted, merely a reproduction of Gebhardt's; and the printer has done his best, while omitting all paragraphs, to reproduce the exact length of Gebhardt's sections.

The only matter for which this is important is the smaller glosses, because the theory as a whole does not depend on any particular edition of the text. Within very narrow limits the equality of the sections appears from any carefully spaced edition; and all the glosses which affect the rearrangement and almost all those seriously affecting the interpretation are of a length which admits of no dubiety. But it may be questioned whether, granting that the original MS. consisted of equal sheets evenly written, any printed text can be relied on as reproducing this equality so precisely as to be a test for the shorter glosses. Of the evenness of Gebhardt's text there is fortunately a test in von Soden's, which is still more carefully printed in a still bolder type. The standard in von Soden is 26 lines, except that 26 is the lowest measure, save in two very slightly shorter instances, and the 33 of Gebhardt the highest. When Gebhardt is exactly 33, von Soden is usually about one-fifth of a line more. Then the two texts run parallel with quite astonishing precision. The only case in which the difference above 26 approaches half a line is where Gebhardt has only the Greek letters for the number of the beast, while in von Soden it is written in full, which is a remarkable confirmation of the text of Gebhardt.

Thus §§ I–IV are a little under 33 in Gebhardt and exactly 26 in von Soden; §§ XIII–XVI full 33 in Gebhardt, half a line more than 26 to be divided among four in von Soden. The broken sections all work out accurately, and § XIX shows a line too many and §§ XX, XXI nearly a line less as in Gebhardt.

The historical, religious and theological significance of Revelation lies outside the scope of the present work. The increased religious value may be left to speak for itself. But it surely is an additional argument for the present interpretation that it sheds light on the early development of Christianity by bringing into prominence the ideas which Primitive Christianity opposed to the imperial rule, and making it easier to understand how they were changed by annexing something of the idea of power from the might to which they had first been opposed.

JOHN OMAN.

WESTMINSTER COLLEGE,
Sept. 1923.

PART I

THE TEXT & ITS REARRANGEMENT

I

THE THEORY OF THE TEXT

THAT there is some disorder in the text of the Apocalypse is as near a certainty as a literary question can well be.

The evidence is plainest towards the end of the book. Nations need healing (xxii. 2) after pain and sorrow have passed for ever (xxi. 4); the unclean and idolaters and hypocrites must be kept out of the Holy City (xxi. 27) after they have all perished in the lake of fire (xxi. 8); this holy city comes (xxi. 9), but the saints already sit in it on thrones (xx. 4), and its 1000 years end with the loosing of Satan (xx. 7); the Last Judgment and the Eternal State must close the book.

Were the disorder confined to the end of the book, we might be persuaded by Dr Charles's view that John died or suffered martyrdom before finishing his work, leaving part of it on scraps of writing which the editor pieced together very badly.

How we are to conceive John composing in such disconnected clauses yet making his work so complete that Dr Charles can arrange it into a whole[1], we are not informed. Moreover, the result is stiff and formal and inferior to John's own writing, which is at least free and eloquent, and nowhere more than in this part. In fact nothing in the book seems to have been finished more carefully. But, throughout the whole book, from Ch. iv. onwards, evidences of disorder are easily discernible. The prophetic call is not immediately after the Messages to the Churches, as it ought to be, but in Ch. x. The earth suffers such disaster early in the book that nothing could well happen in it afterwards.

[1] Dr Charles's rearrangement is sufficient disproof of his contention. It is: xx. 1–3, xxi. 9—xxii. 2, 14–15, 17, xx. 4^{ch}, 4^{abl}, 5^{b}, 6–14, 15, xxi 5^{a}, 4^{d}, 5^{b}, 1–4^{c}, xxii. 3–5, xxi. 5^{c}, 6^{b}–8, xxii. 6–7, 18^{a}, 16, 13, 12, 10, 8–9, 20–21.

Satan is found working mischief on the earth in Ch. ix., while his fall to earth is not related till Ch. xii. Babylon has fallen in Ch. xiv., while the process which ends with her destruction does not begin till Ch. xvi.

In Dr Charles's view no transposition of leaves or any error which could have happened in transcription can possibly afford the explanation. And, in the sense of ordinary accidental errors, this is true, because the mere transcription seems to have been done with very special care. Yet the reconstruction here offered is based on transposition of pages which are found to be of exactly equal length, with the removal of certain glosses of which this equality affords a reliable, because a rigid, test. This theory can only approve itself by explaining the book, but it may be said beforehand in justification of its claim to a hearing, that what began as a vague impression wrought out with absolute precision and left no line over, that the same result seemed to be reached along quite different lines of inquiry, and that the reasons for the confusion became clearer as the right order was discovered.

The germ of the discovery—if it can be dignified by that name—upon which this reconstruction of the Apocalypse is based, was the view that the women of xii. 6 and xvii. 1 must be parallel conceptions. One sits in state in the wilderness, as her native dominion; the other flees into the wilderness, where she lives in exile from her heavenly home. One is a city, Babylon the Great; the other is at least related to the Holy Jerusalem. The seer is carried in spirit into the wilderness to see the former. This seems to be suggested by the temptation for which Jesus was carried by the Spirit into the wilderness, and to be interpreted by what He there saw—'the kingdoms of this world and the glory thereof.' In that case, Babylon the Great is the Rule of the World. Thereupon, the other woman is the Rule of God and His Christ. This would define the whole purpose of the book, in accord with xi. 15, as an account of how the Rule of the World is to become the Rule of our God and of His Christ.

On this interpretation we must distinguish between the Rule of the World and the World-empire. The former is the woman; the latter is the beast which carries her. If this distinction be correct, we seem to have some guide for the order of at least part of the book. The fall of the World-empire, of which Rome is the last great embodiment, and the fall of the whole worldly civilisation must be different events: and as the fall of the latter is a consequence of the fall of the former, the passages which describe the fall of Rome must go before the description of the end of the worldly civilisation which embodies the Rule of the World. This involves the transposition of xix. 11–21 and xvi. 17—xix. 9.

Further, if the trumpets (Chs. viii—ix) are reduced to three, as Dr Charles argues, they are merely a form of the last trump and must be towards the end of the book, and Ch. x, being the call to write the book, must be near the beginning.

While these sections were being transposed for the purpose of studying the result, it appeared that the length of the Greek text of each, in the Gebhardt edition which was being used, was always a little over a page or multiples of it. As the Gebhardt text is very carefully spaced and in a type imitating in width the ancient uncial writing, this singular fact seemed worth investigating.

The following passages were selected for the test because (*a*) they can be certainly distinguished from what precedes and what follows, and (*b*) the glosses are fairly evident.

I. Ch. i. 9—iii. 22. This is marked off (*a*) by its contents and (*b*) by the probability that it should be followed by Ch. x., which contains the prophetic call to write the rest of the book.

II. Ch. xvi. 17—xix. 9^a. Before it comes the abrupt ending of Har-magedon, when, after the most elaborate setting of the stage, nothing happens; and after it the doublet xix. 9^b, 10 which has no obvious connexion.

III. Chs. viii. and ix., the first six trumpets.

IV. Ch. xi. 1–13.

V. Ch. xii. 1—xiv. 5. Ch. xi. 14–19, which separates it from xi. 13, looks like an interpolation, and it is followed by the fall of Babylon, the causes of which are not related till xvi. 17 ff.

The result is:

I. Four sections of 33 lines each, minus about three words, when i. 20[b] and all the clauses, 'he that hath an ear, etc.' are omitted except the first and the last[1].

II. Four sections of 33 lines each, with two lines more. But 'earthquake' throughout the book means political upheaval, so 'then were there lightnings and thunders' in xvi. 18 must certainly be a gloss. 'Because he is king of kings and lord of lords' in xvii. 14 is a doublet of xix. 16, and interrupts the connexion, and 'it shall no more be' in xviii. 21[b] makes the description which follows superfluous. Omit and the result is exact.

III. Two sections of 33 lines each with two words over, when, as Dr Charles and others have maintained already, the first four trumpets are omitted as a gloss. As what follow are now the only voices, 'the rest' in viii. 13 is certainly one of the superfluous words.

IV. 'And gave glory to the God of heaven' in xi. 13 is a pious gloss, because they do not repent. This leaves exactly 33 lines.

V. Three sections as it stands, with only two or three words over. This is sufficiently near in itself, yet 'for they are virgins' (xiv. 4) is almost certainly a gloss, because the subject is idolatry, not celibacy. This makes them exact.

[1] If i. 20[b] is retained and all the repetitions of ii. 7[a] are omitted, the result is exactly four sections of 33 lines. But i. 20[b] (*a*) has the appearance of a typical explanatory gloss, (*b*) seems to explain τὸ μυστήριον as 'the secret,' a sense in which it is not used elsewhere by the author, (*c*) has four repetitions of ἑπτὰ, not even one being necessary, which is unlike the author and characteristic of the editor, (*d*) the stars in iii. 1 are parallel with and possibly identical with the seven spirits of God, and are, therefore, not probably the angels of the Churches. For retaining iii. 22 the reasons are: (*a*) While no section is longer than 33 lines, some are a word or two less. (*b*) The repetition is effective as a closing appeal. (*c*) Its position at the end of the message would explain why the repetitions on the same sheet as ii. 7 are, like it, before 'he that overcometh' and, on the other sheets, at the end of each message, which must be imitated from a genuine example in that position. (*d*) If the editor only filled in between the first and the last, it would be parallel with his action elsewhere.

So precise a result in so many instances seemed to justify an attempt to apply this measure to the whole text. Suppose it held good throughout, it might show some new divisions, but its certain value would be as a rigid standard of glosses. Therefore, the process was now reversed. Instead of determining the divisions and marking off glosses, and then counting the lines, the lines were counted and the glosses determined by the enumeration, while a watch was kept for possible new divisions.

In respect of divisions the important points were (1) That the two sections beginning with Ch. iv. 1 ended at vi. 1. This would not have been of any consequence by itself, but the omission of everything connecting the next section with these two left it exactly 33 lines. This singular fact is of the first importance for the interpretation of the book. (2) That of five shorter sections, three combined to make a section of the proper length, and two to make another. (3) That two passages, which made the section in which they stand too long, and which were irrelevant in their present connexion, fitted into two other sections and made them precisely the right length. Moreover, this process, though conducted without any regard to what would happen at the end, finished without leaving a line too many or too few.

In respect of glosses, practically all doublets went out, and the rest had a curious family likeness of dull comment, which, on being removed, left a length of a precision which, at first sight, seemed almost too exact to be credible.

The work was so full of surprises and unexpected confirmations, that, if the course of it could be reproduced, important evidence for the theory would appear. But this proved to be an impossible task without over-burdening the reader with detail. Therefore, we proceed at once to tabulate the result.

SECTIONS AND GLOSSES

Sections

I–IV. Ch. i. 9—iii. 22. Glosses i. 20^b, ii. 11^a, 17^a, 29, iii. 6, 13.

V–VI. Ch. iv. 1—vi. 1: 32 and 33 lines.

VII. Ch. vi. 2–17. Glosses *vv.* 3, 5^a, 7, 9^a, 12^a.

This will require more consideration, because it deeply affects the interpretation of the whole book. Meantime it is enough to note the singular fact that the omission of the opening of the second to the sixth seals leaves a section of exactly 33 lines.

VIII. Ch. vii. Glosses *vv.* 5–8 and *v.* 2 after 'angels.'

The enumeration of the tribes of Israel is irrelevant and contrary to the author's view of Israel as the true Elect of God—Christian as well as Jewish. The other is less certain, but the task of the angels is not to hurt the land and the sea but to prevent them from being hurt. 'Hurt not' which follows could mean, 'Let them not be hurt.'

IX–X. Chs. viii.—ix. Gloss viii. 7–12.

vv. 7–12 are a senseless destruction of thirds, out of harmony with the rest, and feeble in form. The other glosses are only three words, both 'sevens' in viii. 6 and 'rest' in *v.* 13.

XI. Ch. x. 1–10. Ch. xxii. 6–8ᵃ, Ch. x. 11.

xxii. 6–8ᵃ has no connexion where it stands, and 'he said' has no subject, but here we have a fitting connexion, because the scroll represents the faithful words, and the angel is a fitting speaker[1].

XII. Ch. xi. 1–13. Gloss *v.* 13, 'and gave glory to the God of heaven'—a repentance the author does not expect.

XIII–XV. Ch. xii. 1—xiv. 5. Gloss xiv. 4, 'for they are virgins,' the subject being freedom from idolatry not celibacy.

XVI–XVII. Ch. xi. 14–19 and Ch. xiv. 6—xv. 4. Ch. xiv. 19ᵇ–20 is out of place, being in conflict with the meaning of the passage.

XVIII. Ch. xv. 5—xvi. 16. Glosses xv. 8ᵇ, xvi. 2ᵇ after 'men,' 6, 9. Omit xvi. 15 as out of place, interrupting the connexion. The glosses are marked by repetition of phrases, crudeness of idea and feebleness of style.

[1] In the old context no plural subject for λέγουσιν (*v.* 11), the almost certain reading, can be found; in the new it might be οἱ λόγοι, but is more probably ταῦτα, considered as two sets—things seen and things heard. This is an important confirmation of the arrangement proposed.

XIX–XXII. Ch. xvi. 17—xix. 9ᵃ. Glosses: xvi. 18ᵃ, 'lightnings and voices and thunders,' because 'earthquake' here means 'political upheaval' and must stand alone; xvi. 21ᵇ, the usual commentary with the anti-climax 'very great'; xvii. 14ᵇ, a doublet of xix. 16; xviii. 21, last clause, because it deprives what follows of meaning, as it would include all the other things which are no more.

XXIII. Ch. xix. 11–16, xiv. 19ᵇ, 20, xix. 17–21.

This is the only place in the book where xiv. 19ᵇ–20 is appropriate. xix. 12ᵇ, 'having a name written which no one knew except himself' has been regarded as a gloss, but, on the test of length, it is genuine.

XXIV. Ch. xvi. 15, xix. 9ᵇ–10, xx. 1–10: 34 lines.

XXV. Ch. xx. 11—xxi. 8: 31 lines. The end of the book.

XXVI–XXVII. Ch. xxi. 9—xxii. 5, xxii. 10–17. Glosses 'the last' in xxi. 9 'and the height of it' in *v.* 16. Ch. xxii. 6–8ᵃ has already been accounted for.

This includes every word in the text except xxii. 8ᵇ, 9, which is a doublet of xix. 9–10, and i. 1–8, which is the editor's preface, and xxii. 18–21, which is the editor's epilogue.

The chief question regarding this result must concern the glosses. The best test is to put them all together and compare them with each other and with the editor's undoubted work in the prologue and epilogue. When this is done the marked family likeness becomes too obvious to be missed. This must be discussed more fully, but meantime we have to ask, how any series of glosses, however carefully selected, could be omitted and leave the rest, not approximately but so exactly 33 lines. Moreover, the astonishing precision of this result was not discovered till after the sections were made up with the glosses already marked off. The reckoning had been made with a Gebhardt Greek Testament, but the broken lines were difficult to estimate in that way, and it seemed as though the standard might vary by as much as half a line. Only when the sections had been made up separately from Gebhardt and the enumeration done with precision, was it discovered that 33 lines was so exact a standard that the sections were never more, and never above a word or two less. But three exceptions were discovered. §§ V–VI were found to be a line short; and the section which had been arranged before it, and which, being in three parts, was difficult to reckon accurately when they were apart, was found to be too long by precisely the amount that the section following it was short. This seemed too remarkable to be mere coincidence. The second was § XXIII. It was about a third of a line too short. The explanation is probably that 'and he gathered' in xiv. 19 belongs to both texts. Such a phrase seems necessary before 'and he cast,' and the existence of the same phrase in both passages would explain why the editor inserted the passage where he did. The third was § XXV, which is only 31 lines, but it is certainly the close of the book, and raises no question.

II

THE WORK OF THE EDITOR

WERE the book mere mysterious vaticination, it would be conceivable that the writer, especially if he had to find occupation for weary years of captivity, composed a work divided so exactly in equal sections. If we could believe that it is written in a kind of Hebrew metre, as Dr Charles supposes, this task might seem easier and more rational, though it is difficult to conceive what kind of metre would make sections so equal when written as prose. But the many changes Dr Charles has to introduce into the text to support his theory alter the length of the sections. This lands us in the still more perplexing theory, that the sections originally were not equal, but have been made so by the editor. To accomplish such a feat he ought surely to have been very clever, but Dr Charles has no such opinion of him: and in that he is not mistaken.

A simpler explanation is that we have to do with equal sheets of a MS. which have suffered disarrangement. This hypothesis we now proceed to consider. Only an arrangement in which the sections are made to fit naturally into each other would afford convincing proof, but, as the text stands and without any rearrangement, we have seen in it evidence of disorder, while the glosses show mistaken ideas about the meaning of the book likely to cause mistakes in its arrangement, and, when we proceed to consider the editor's own work in the preface and the epilogue, we shall discover some more misunderstandings of the same kind.

Our next task, therefore, must be to learn what we can of the editor, both of his ideas and of his capacity, by putting together and studying what he has added to his author.

In the editorial epilogue (xxii. 18, 19) the text may either be 'I testify' or 'we testify.' It is, therefore, impossible to be certain whether we ought to speak of editor or of editors. Possibly the careful transcribing and the incompetent editing may argue for a joint-stock responsibility, which is apt to be more efficient in small matters than in great. Yet, for the sake of convenience, we shall speak of the editor.

The strict numeration of lines of the original text, working out exactly at the end, shows that nothing has been omitted except one short doublet. It would, therefore, appear that the transcriber laid his own testimony about not taking from the words of the prophecy of this book very much to heart. But why he did not lay to heart equally his own warning about adding to the words of the prophecy is impossible to say, except that he undoubtedly thought his additions mere explanations and completions.

By his own work we can test the measure of his capacity for this task of interpretation and expansion.

The epilogue (xxii. 18, 19) is the nearest to original composition which he has achieved, because, even if he took the idea of such a testimony from the Gospel of John, he does manage to say what is in a measure new. Yet, even in this short paragraph, he repeats 'this book' four times, and twice with 'prophecy.' He also manages to show that he misunderstood his author's view of prophecy, of the plagues, of the tree of life, and of the Holy City. To him they are prediction, God's general judgments, eternal life, and heaven, while for our author they are declaring the mind of God, particular judgments on the world-empires, medicine for the healing of the nations, and the Millennial Kingdom.

Further, the threat shows an attitude towards the book impossible for the author, who wrote solely to the end that men should be warned and remain steadfast, or, if they had fallen, repent.

The only other section which the editor wrote as his own, and not as commentary on the work of his author, is the introduction (i. 1–8). Probably it was composed at the same time as the epilogue, because the epilogue is merely an expansion of Ch. xxii. 7, 'Blessed is he that keepeth the words of the prophecy of this book,' and in the introduction this is quoted in full.

In the first paragraph of the introduction (*vv.* 1–3) the book is called 'The Apocalypse of Jesus Christ.' In a sense this may be true of our author's work, but not in the sense of mere information about the future, as is here meant. John, instead of describing his message as 'the things which must shortly come to pass,' describes it as concerned with 'the things which are, and the things which shall come to pass hereafter.' From the contents of the book, this means the principles by which God governs the present and by which He will determine the future. Moreover, some of this future is not to be realised for at least a thousand years. Yet, with all this misunderstanding, the paragraph is made up almost entirely of phrases from the author.

The second paragraph (*vv.* 4–6) begins with 'John to the seven churches which are in Asia.' This may have been the destination of the book, but the phrase is a repetition from Ch. i. 11, with the characteristic tag of information, that the churches are in Asia. To John the essential point is their personal relation to him, and not probably their geographical position. This form of address is, moreover, an imitation of Paul's method of beginning his epistles. 'From Him which was and which is and which is to come,' twice repeated, with 'the Almighty' or 'All-Sovereign' in the last, is from Ch. iv. 8, where it is in place, as it is not here[1]. To the phrase 'From the seven spirits which are before the throne,' it is difficult to attach any meaning, and it certainly can have no

[1] 'Which is to come' is singular as a description of God even there, but was, is and is to come is probably merely a way of saying He is ruler of all in the past, the present and the future.

meaning consistent with the views of our author. Perhaps the editor took them to represent the Holy Spirit and regarded Him as the real source of the book. 'The faithful witness' is from Ch. iii. 14; 'the first born from the dead' from Col. i. 18; 'made us a kingdom and priests' from Rev. v. 10; 'washed us from our sins in his blood' an adaptation of Ch. vii. 14; 'to Him be the glory and the dominion for ever and ever' no doubt a current doxology, possibly suggested by v. 12; 'Behold he cometh with clouds' from Ch. xiv. 14. In the connexion here it is obviously meant to apply to the second coming, which is not its meaning in xiv. 14. The rest is an adaptation of Zech. xii. 10, a book suggested by Rev. vi. 3–8, but with a misunderstanding of the original meaning, such as our author never makes about an Old Testament passage.

This analysis has been made so fully in order to show how much our editor's idea of literary work is confined to piecing together quotations by their superficial resemblances.

The only additions of any length in the body of the work are Ch. vii. 5–7 and Ch. viii. 7–12. The first is a mere display of the editor's knowledge of the names of the twelve tribes of Israel, but it shows that he did not understand what the author meant by the true Israel. The second, which turns the three trumpets into seven, is an equally certain intrusion. (*a*) The first four angels will be shown afterwards to fulfil another task. (*b*) The senseless destruction of thirds, repeated in every verse of this passage, shows that 'three' existed in the text and that when the editor replaced it by 'seven,' he resolved to make good compensation. (*c*) The passage is marked by a feebleness of thought and expression unlike the resource and vigour of the author. Twice the editor resorts to 'blood,' introduced also by him unnecessarily elsewhere. Then he brings in a star called Wormwood[1], probably suggested by ix. 1, which would be immediately before him in his MS. Then he can only think of darkening thirds of the sun and moon with an anti-climax about the day not showing a third and the night similarly. (*d*) The

[1] Wormwood may have been suggested by Amos v. 7, 'who turn judgment to wormwood' with some influence from the waters of Marah. A torch is a figure inadequate enough to be his own.

four added woes are in no kind of harmony with the three genuine.

In the position he has given to these woes we have also a clear proof of the editor's lack of reasoning about what he was transcribing, because, if so great disasters befell the earth at this stage, how could the rest of the history as he arranges it have taken place upon it? When reduced to the real proportion of three woes, this section becomes plainly our author's presentation of the familiar conception of the Last Trumpet, and its place is just before the final judgment.

This is an important discovery resulting from the method of testing the text by the length of the pages, because it delivers us from the sense of meaningless destruction which haunts the book in its present order. Yet it is not so important as the discovery that there is no mention of any seals except the first and the last, because this changes both our conception of the sealed book and of the plan of the author from Ch. iv. onwards. Though the editor was unable to carry through his own conception of it, he so manifestly regards the whole prophecy as unfolded out of this mysterious writing by the breaking of the seals, that Dr Charles, though equally incapable of showing how it is to be done, believes that, in some way, it must be the scheme of the whole.

After discovering that the section beginning at Ch. iv. 1 ends with Ch. vi. 1, 'And I saw when the Lamb had opened one of the seals, and I heard one of the living creatures saying as a voice of thunder, Come and see,' and that the omission of all the references to the breaking of seals and the living creatures makes the section which begins with Ch. vi. 2 in the present order the right length, one is amazed at having been taken in so easily by the clumsiness of the treatment. No one can tell what, in the present context, the white horse can possibly mean, whereas, when the passage is restored to its right connexion, his rider is the victorious Word of God or His representative who sends out the other horses of war and famine and pestilence. There they are in place. But how can war and famine and pestilence be mysteries which only the Lamb could unseal, seeing they are objects of human experience only too appallingly evident? Again there is no kind of parallelism in the seals when thus divided, as we surely have a right to expect. The first four have living creatures and are of the same type. But the voice from the altar is wholly different from them, both in form and substance; and the great day of God's wrath has, in the present arrangement, had no preparation made for it, nor does it appear what it is to accomplish. Finally, the long interlude between the sixth and the seventh seals is a suspicious feature, seeing the first six follow in breathless haste. We can only conclude that the editor, finding one seal broken at the beginning and only the breaking of the last afterwards, concluded that the other five must be missing somehow: and, as he did not feel equal to composing them, he selected a page to dress up for the purpose. Finding one wherein 'a voice in the midst of the living creatures' (Ch. vi. 6) was mentioned, he selected it, because the opening of the first seal closed with a similar reference[1].

As soon as we are rid of the breaking of the five seals, we see that the sealed book is the Book of Life, and that the opening of it must be concerned with the manifestation of the sons of God, which could only take place towards the end. Then we are rid also of the idea, which undoubtedly the editor entertained, that the Apocalypse is a book of mysteries.

In all this we see how vast is the difference between the editor and his author. The Greek of the author is peculiar, showing by many traces that his native tongue was Semitic, but it is terse, rapid, vivid, full of colour and movement; whereas the editor is a mere copyist in both senses of the word. The author, moreover, has large resources both of knowledge and imagination, while the editor is helpless the moment he has to rely on himself. His misunderstanding of his author being profound, the constant result of his editing is confusion.

This, however, has one good result. When we have found the means for unravelling his tangled scheme, we can more easily distinguish his work from the work of the author than would have been possible had it been more ably done. It

[1] He may, however, have found the sheet in this place, and the mention of 'the living creature' may have suggested the use he makes of it.

also lets us see what misunderstandings determined his arrangement. Dr Charles, who has in part detected his work, declares that he never expands his author without misinterpreting him. But the misunderstandings are clear and explicable and they are mainly two, though these two branch out in several directions.

The first is the editor's conviction that he was dealing with a work of mysterious vaticination about the future which would only be clear when it came to pass. For this reason he interprets the sealed book as the book of these mysteries, and is led to put it as early as he can, though we shall see that he is also urged to this device by thc difficulties he had created for himself by the other misunderstanding.

This is the identifying of the Holy, the Millennial Jerusalem with the New, the Heavenly Jerusalem. It leads him to think that the coming of Christ is for the final end, whereas, for the author, it is only for the establishment of the Millennium. But after what seemed the end of all things the rest of the book could not follow: so the editor solved his problem by putting it at the beginning. This will have to be considered later. But the identification of the Millennial Jerusalem and the New Jerusalem also prevented him from seeing that there was a preparation for each; and, in consequence, he mixes both preparations together in a very tangled story. In view of his general conception of the book, this did not usually disturb him, but occasionally he found a sequence too impossible even for him to accept.

Yet the confusion is mainly due to a disorder in the sheets which, as an endeavour will be made to show, he found and did not make. Of the sheets themselves we shall see that there was only one which utterly baffled him, and that it accounts for almost all the deliberate transpositions.

In view of the extreme difficulty of arranging a book in any order which is not the right one, these are not greater liberties than we might reasonably expect.

Nor can we deny that the editor has managed to convey his own impression that the book consists of wholly mysterious prediction. And, without this success, it may be the book would never have found a place in the New Testament and, possibly, not have survived in any form. It might have passed with the passing of its millenarian view. If not, a still greater obstacle would have been the clear and full account in its original form of the destruction of the Roman Empire before the Eastern barbarian. Had it been in this form in their sacred book, it would have seemed to justify the charge against the Christians of disloyalty to the Empire, upon which all persecutions were based. Nor would this prophecy have been less disturbing when the Church no longer stood by the uncompromising attitude of the author, but, in time, became the official religion of the world-empire for which John had foreseen no end except destruction.

III

THE ORIGINAL TEXT

OUR next task, which is to discover the true order of the sheets, is made difficult mainly by the persistence of the impression of the book as arranged and expounded by the editor. When we are once rid of his ideas, the ideas of the author become reasonably clear and the main outlines at least of the order in which he has developed them reasonably certain. A summary of these differences between the ideas of the editor and the ideas of the author, therefore, is the first requirement.

1. Instead of the editor's account of the book as a mysterious apocalypse about what must shortly come to pass (Ch. i. 1), we must take the author's own account of it as a book of prophecy in the Old Testament sense of showing the Divine aspect of events—the principles of 'the things that are as well as the things that shall be' (Ch. i. 19 and x. 11).

2. For the editor's book of mysteries, which only the Lamb could open by His power, we must see the Book of Life, the opening of which is the manifestation of the sons of God, and which only the Lamb can open because He alone is the standard of the Divine righteousness (as Jn. v. 22 and viii. 16).

3. Instead of the editor's seven trumpets of warning, we have the author's three trumpets of the last woes, which we must relate to the traditional idea of the last trump.

4. Instead of considering, with the editor, only two Jerusalems—the actual city and the final state, we have to see that the author has, besides the actual city, two ideal Jerusalems—Mount Zion where Christ is with the 144,000 of the saints, which is also the Holy Jerusalem which is the millennial rule, and the New Jerusalem which is the heavenly state when material things have vanished and all evil has been done away forever.

5. Instead of the editor's confused chaos of destruction, we have to see two distinct preparations—the first for the Millennial Jerusalem and the second for the Heavenly; and in the first we have to distinguish between the overthrow of the seven world-empires and the fall of the Rule of the World which is incarnated in the worldly civilisation.

As Chs. iv. to ix., with the exception of the glossed sheet about the second to the sixth seal, are concerned with the end of the world and the preparation for the final judgment and the New Jerusalem, and Chs. x.—xxii., with the exception of three sheets, which ought to close the whole book, and one which comes between these two parts, are concerned with only the end of the World-rule and the preparation for the Millennial Jerusalem, the order of these parts, as a whole, must be reversed.

On the above ideas of the book the twenty-seven sections seem to rearrange themselves in the following order:

Previous order	New order	
I–IV	I–IV	Ch. i. 9—iii. 22.
XI–XV	V–IX	Ch. x. 1—xiv. 5, inserting xxii. 6–8[a] after x. 10 and omitting xi. 14–19.
XVIII	X	Ch. xv. 5—xvi. 16, omitting xvi. 15.
XXIII	XI	Ch. xix. 11–21, inserting xiv. 19[b]–20 after v. 16.
VII	XII	Ch. vi. 2–17.
XIX–XXII	XIII–XVI	Ch. xvi. 17—xix. 9[a].
XXVI–XXVII	XVII–XVIII	Ch. xxi. 9—xxii. 17, omitting xxii. 6–9.
XXIV	XIX	Ch. xvi. 15, xix. 9[b]–10, xx. 1–10.

Previous order	New order	
V–VI	XX–XXI	Ch. iv. 1—vi. 1.
VIII–X	XXII–XXIV	Ch. vii. 1—ix. 21.
XVI	XXV	Ch. xi. 14–19 and xiv. 6–11.
XVII	XXVI	Ch. xiv. 12—xv. 4, omitting xiv. 19[b], 20.
XXV	XXVII	Ch. xx. 11—xxi. 8.

This order was arrived at by putting the sections of the Greek text, as above explained, on separate sheets and arranging them purely by what seemed to be their natural sequence. No regard was paid to the order in the present text, because it then appeared as though the editor had found the MS. he copied in utter confusion. That such confusion in an ancient MS. is possible needs no demonstration, for an actual example of it exists[1].

Though arguments for this new order can be given when it is completed, the work did not depend upon arguments, but upon a general impression of the sequence of the book. To reduce an impression of this kind to bare statement in logical sequence largely robs it of its true character as an intuition, yet, there being no other way of conveying it, the attempt must be made.

1. John in exile is led to consider the situation in the Church and his duty concerning it. After warning his readers of their dangers, he thinks that, in accordance with the example of the prophets, he must threaten those who fail in the trial. But he is instructed that this is too hasty and narrow a conception of his task. Instead, he must show the persecuted Christians that the present conflict is only part of the age-long conflict between the Rule of the World and the Rule of God. To this end he must prophesy once more of the principles upon which God rules the present and determines the future, as the prophets had done before (§§ I–V).

2. In fulfilment of this task John sets forth two aspects of the Era of the World-empire, which, in dependence on Daniel, he regards as lasting three years and a half, or forty-two months, or 1260 days—the days being interpreted as years.

[1] See note, p. 36.

(*a*) The prophetic witness during this era (§ VI).

(*b*) The invisible conflict, which introduces and determines the struggle between good and evil in this era and calls up the forces which are in conflict (§§ VII–IX).

3. The time draws near for the overthrow of this World-Rule.

(*a*) Five of the empires in which it is embodied have already been destroyed, and now all World-empire is about to end with the fall of its present form in the Roman Empire (§§ X–XII).

(*b*) In the chaos which follows, the whole corrupt worldly civilisation is to be obliterated and with it the Rule of the World is to end (§§ XIII–XVI).

4. This judgment of the Rule of the World is in order to make room for the Rule of God and His Christ in the Holy Jerusalem: and a description of its thousand years' reign closes with a rapid summary of the events which follow it (§§ XVII–XIX).

5. He then goes back over this second period, and describes how the Millennial Rule ends with the separation between the saints and the sinners.

(*a*) The scene in Heaven, where the Book of Life is opened, after which the manifestation of the Sons of God takes place (§§ XX–XXI).

(*b*) The Roll-Call of the saints and the sealing of them against the Woes which are to follow (§ XXII).

6. The Woes, which are the disaster of sin wholly unredeemed by good, and the lesson of this future for the seer's contemporaries (§§ XXIII–XXV).

7. The end of the present order and the Final State.

(*a*) The reaping of the harvest of good from the earth. This is partly on the same sheet as the last and so must follow (§ XXVI).

(*b*) The Final Judgment and the Final State (§ XXVII).

When this order is examined, several remarkable connexions between the sections are found to confirm it.

When § V follows §§ I–IV, it is found not merely to be in sequence, but to be part of the same experience, which begins with 'I John was in the spirit on the Lord's Day' and ends with 'I John was seeing and hearing these things.'

The enlarging of his task in § V, from mere warning to a scheme of the whole Divine purpose, explains the abrupt termination of the Messages; while the seven trumpet voices of warning in §§ I–IV explain the voices of the seven thunders in § V. Moreover, the dependence of the visions in § V on the prophetic calls suggests that the first vision in § I depends on Isaiah's, and is in the Temple; and this gives a sequence for § VI which begins with measuring the Temple. §§ VI–IX follow in the present order, except that Ch. xi. 14–19 has been omitted.

§ X seems to start abruptly, but the Temple of Witness is the heavenly representative of the witness of the prophets and of Christ and the saints of the previous section; and the connexion further depends on Isaiah.

§§ XI–XII describe the battle of Har-magedon and its results, while in the present order we have an enormous setting of a stage upon which nothing happens.

'It is done' in § XIII is explained by what has taken place in § XII, because it means that the political disaster has already brought about the anarchy which is the seventh vial.

§ XVI ends with 'Blessed are they who are called to the marriage supper of the Lamb,' and § XVII continues with a description of the Bride.

At the beginning of § XIX it is obviously Jesus who is speaking, but He has only been introduced, if it follow § XVIII, where He introduces Himself as 'I Jesus.'

§ XX does not obviously follow, but there is a curious confirmation. It is short by one line and § XIX is long by exactly the same amount, which cannot be an accident, and suggests that, in this one case, a line was left behind on § XIX, when § XX was put in another connexion.

§ XXI ends with 'Come and see' and § XXII begins with 'Thereafter I saw.'

The four angels before the fifth who has the first trumpet in § XXIII are the four standing at the corners of the earth in § XXII.

§ XXV makes the woes follow in close sequence, and does away with the inexplicable break in them in the present order.

'The sea' in § XXVI probably explains 'the sea' in

§ XXVII which, in the first use of it at least, cannot mean the ordinary sea, as it must have vanished with the earth. Further, the sea is parallel with Hades[1]; and it is souls, not bodies, which are in Hades.

This rearrangement was made, as has been said, on the assumption that the sheets were in entire disorder, but a comparison of the new order with the old shows a remarkable amount of order in the old. Moreover, we have to explain the peculiar place which has been assigned in the new order to the material which interrupts the old.

In Chs. iv.—ix., one section (Ch. vi. 2–17) has been removed in the new arrangement, but the rest is in the old order. This section has been inserted in the other part (§§ X–XXII), and these parts (§§ IV–IX and §§ X–XXII) are transposed. From §§ X–XXII the passages xvi. 15, xix. 9^b–10, xx. 1–10 are omitted, and have become the sheet between the transposed parts. Also xi. 14–19, xiv. 6—xv. 4 and xx. 11—xxi. 8 have been omitted; and they now make up the three sheets which close the book. Then, apart from the transposition of a block of four sheets (xiii.—xvi. in the new order), the rest is in the old order. The problem, therefore, is to find an explanation, not for the confusion, but for the particular kind of confusion, which preserves so much of the original order, while disturbing so constantly the original sequence as to make it certain that the explanation is not the insight of the editor.

While the theory of the text here maintained does not depend on any particular view of the nature of the original document, it is some confirmation of the result that it can be explained on the hypothesis of a codex of seven quires of double sheets, with the last page left blank as a cover and protection for the writing, so that the last quire consists of three and the others of four sections. In such a codex one sheet was laid above another, then both were folded, then all the quires were sewn together through the fold.

That the quires should be seven adds an element of

[1] From § XIII onwards these connexions are so close as scarcely to admit of any dubiety about the true order of the sections, but in the earlier part the end of the sheet and the close of the paragraph several times coincide, which affords more room for question.

probability, because, while the author is not obsessed by the number seven as the editor is, he uses it with sufficient frequency to show that it is his usual unit of reckoning. Therefore it is a likely number of sheets to have been in his possession.

As the book was most exposed on the side of the blank sheet, damage to the last quire is the most likely. It now turns out that the most disturbing elements in the right order of what is in the present order the latter half of the book (from Ch. x. onwards) make up the last three sections, which, on this hypothesis, would be the last quire, with one blank page at the end. That the transcriber did not find this part of the MS. at the end is quite certain, because, if he had, he could not possibly have so confused the two Jerusalems. The present order would be explained, if the editor, finding this quire placed for safety inside quire 2, transcribed straight on till the sequence became impossible, and then entered the rest of the first two pages, as an appendix, at the first break in the thought, while the last page, being an account of the Last Judgment, he was forced by the subject to put near the close of the book, or it may have been in its present position.

The only other intrusions into this part are the three shorter passages which make up § XIX, but, as it is the sheet between the two parts of the book which have been transposed, we must leave this and the transposition to be considered together.

The next disturbing element is the placing of §§ XIII–XVI between §§ X and XI. This would be explained, if we suppose that quire 4 had come loose and been placed inside of quire 3.

One section only is restored to this part, the passage glossed for the opening of the seals, which has now become § XII. With this omission of six passages, the transposition of one block of four sections and the restoration of one, the whole reads straight on. This result is the more remarkable that the intrusions, the transposition and the omission have entirely obscured the original sequence.

The only disturbance in Chs. iv.—ix. is the insertion of § XII already mentioned. This might have been deliberately taken from its place, to supply what the editor thought an omission, because of the mention in it of one of the living creatures. But it is at least possible that the outside sheet of quire 3 was broken, and that he found the last page in its present position, and that the mention of the living creature suggested the use to which he put it. This is confirmed by the fact that the other half of this sheet, which would be § IX, follows § VIII and is separated by a long intrusion from § X.

All these changes from the original we may ascribe to a confusion in his MS., which the editor found and did not make, with some slight rearrangement which seemed necessary to give an appearance of connexion to the various parts.

The only other change is the transposition of §§ V–XVIII and §§ XX–XXIV, and with it we must take the division into three of § XIX, the section which now comes between these parts of the book.

We might suppose that the editor found quire 6 after quire 1, and that he put the relevant part of the previous section before it because of a connexion which could not be missed. This would be less arbitrary than a deliberate transposition and would make the editor's reading of the book easier to understand, as it would leave nothing in his MS. after what is now the end except § XIX, which would then be a mere perplexity to be distributed through the book as best he could.

But there is a reason which makes this hypothesis improbable. This is the insertion of a passage from § V (Ch. xxii. 6–8^{b}) into § XVIII, and after it of one from § XIX (xxii. 8^{b}, 9). This seems to show that he had all three sheets before him considering how he should proceed; and there seems to be no reason for selecting § XIX, unless it followed, and § V, unless it were in its right position in his MS. and he were already considering the transposition. Thus, while we must suppose a deliberate transposition, the confusion which he found and did not make explains the necessity for it; and it is difficult to see what other device, on his understanding of the book, he could have hit upon.

IV

THE VISIONS AND THE AUTHOR

THE whole question of how the book is to be interpreted must depend primarily on the nature of the visions. Are we to regard them as actual visions seen in some kind of ecstasy, or simply as a literary form? As the answer to this question must depend rather upon the general impression left by the study of the book as a whole than upon particular arguments, it may simplify matters to state at once what this impression seems to be.

It is that, except in §§ I–V, the book is too much reasoned out from Old Testament prophecy, too consistently the working out of one idea, and too consecutively constructed on a plan to be the result of any conceivable series of visions. Vision had become the accepted form of prophetic presentation, much in the same way as dialogue had become the form of philosophical exposition. Both forms have the same explanation. As philosophy began in public discussion, prophecy had its origin in states of ecstasy, wrought up as was done by the prophets who promised victory to Ahab or as it is still done by the dervish. And just as philosophy, when it freed itself from the heat of discussion and settled down to long reflexion and the calm expression of literature, retained the form of dialogue, prophecy, when it freed itself from the excitement of ecstasy and settled down to consider the application of eternal principles and spiritual appeal, retained the form of vision. As dialogue developed into the highest perfection of prose form, vision was constantly on the verge of poetic form and frequently became carefully constructed verse; and both alike were so much the fruit of reflexion that it is possible to render their meaning in a continuous exposition.

There are, however, three causes which gave peculiar intensity to the form of vision in the case of our author.

I. The influence of at least one intense experience.

The first visions are introduced by the statement that

John was in the spirit and close with the affirmation that he was seeing and hearing these things. This must mean that they were at least allied to ecstatic vision. The fact that he gives this testimony here and not later means that we are not to understand the rest in the same way, but a certain intensity may have flowed over into his whole way of realising his prophecy. This will be discussed more fully later.

II. The conditions under which the book was composed.

The visions, in any case, we can take to be the fruit of long solitary meditation in captivity. Indeed nothing less can explain their elaboration. And we can well believe that, in the loneliness of his spirit and the necessity of lifting his soul above the moral chaos and misery around, these visions of his inward eye were far more real to him than what presented itself to his outward vision, and that these lonely broodings may thus have given his visions almost objective form. Yet the fact that his thought does not follow them, but that they mirror the process of his thought shows it to have been an objectivity which did not deceive the author.

III. The writer's peculiar endowment and training.

The work bears the stamp of a mind with a type of imagination specially endowed for this form of embodying its thought, and which had long lived in a world where transparency and symbolism were in the air.

Tradition ascribes both the Apocalypse and the Gospel of John to a disciple of Jesus, called John the Elder, who lived at Ephesus to extreme old age. The striking difference in the style of these books would, by itself, be sufficient to prove that they cannot both be by the same author. Yet it is difficult to believe that so uniform a tradition about so late a period as the close of the first century and from such a centre of Church life, and even of literary activity, as Asia Minor is wholly baseless.

That the later identification of him with John the Apostle is mistaken is certain. Had he been John the son of Zebedee he would have been called John the Apostle, not John the Elder. Nor does anything we know of him agree with any idea we could form of a fisherman of Galilee. In the Gospel he is a friend of the high-priest and probably a householder in Jerusalem. This suggests a Jerusalem Jew of the learned priestly caste. If this were his origin, it would explain several things both in Revelation and in John's Gospel.

That he is the author of Revelation is probable from his simply calling himself John, as though he could assume that the persons for whom he wrote would not confuse him with any other John, and from his extremely Jewish way of writing Greek, his learning in the ancient Scriptures, his use of Jerusalem and the Temple, his view of true Christians as also of the true Israel, his intense monotheism, his way of relating Jesus to the likeness of the Son of Man and to the Lamb in the Old Testament, and possibly his careful method of writing, like the Scribes.

The proof that he is the author of Revelation would be the proof that he cannot be, at least in the same sense, the author of the Gospel, because, in addition to the difference in style, there are marked differences of view. Yet some kind of dependence upon his teaching and upon information which had its source in him would explain the tradition of the authorship of the Gospel. Further, this dependence would give a much needed explanation of two elements in it very difficult to regard as the unaided work of a Greek who lived in Asia Minor at the close of the century and who had a simple and generally rather colourless style and an abstract phraseology, which does not bespeak a vivid and original or even a concrete imagination.

1. The extremely vivid stories in the book, told in rapid flashes alive with the colours of the situation, are unlike the general style of the Gospel. Some of them are doubtless history, but some, such as the marriage at Cana, must be simply transparencies through which we are to see certain truths. That the author of the Gospel was capable of creating them seems little probable, and that the same person created them and told them as history is still less likely. But in the author of Revelation we have a mind for which such embodiment of his thought was as the breath of his nostrils and for which he was supremely endowed.

2. The accurate picture of the religious situation in Jerusalem at the time of our Lord, and some corrections of the synoptic narrative, as, for example, the time of the Crucifixion, which must be right. That the author of the Gospel

reached either by antiquarian research is extremely improbable. Moreover, if John lived in Jerusalem and knew little of the ministry of Jesus outside of it, we might also find an explanation of the concentration of the Gospel on the last part of His ministry, while the description of the Lamb as 'in the midst of the throne' in Revelation may have been the starting-point for the doctrine of Him as the Word[1].

John's habit of thinking in imagery and symbolism steeped in sacred lore may have been fixed in early years by taking part in the ritual of the Temple. Are they anything more than a ritual of religious thought? Even now we can find something similar in the Celt, whose religious oratory seeks in its ideas rather sublimity and spaciousness than precision and definiteness of plain fact and mere statement of truth. Entire absence of ritual in worship is thereby replaced by a ritual of imagery, which is fashioned in the same way from Scripture and phantasy.

The most frequent is the use of angels. Only in the post-Biblical Jewish literature do they, as here, play a large part. Yet our author's use of them embodies many Old Testament elements, some of which, however, had originally no such meaning as he gives them. One roars like a lion in accordance with the figure for prophecy in Amos and presents a roll as in Ezekiel. They blow trumpets and pour out vials and generally act as God's messengers and instruments. Michael is the special defender of the cause of the faithful (xii. 7) as in Daniel, but others are mere personifications of messages. Yet they fill the scene with life and movement, and, even when they are mere ways of announcing the doings of God, speak of a world conceived under ideas very different from the mechanical conceptions which we have so largely accepted from science.

But the clearest evidence is the symbolism, because it is

[1] The Semitic forms Dr Burney detects beneath some of the phraseology of John might also find here their explanation, and it would be a much more probable explanation than that the Fourth Gospel in a considerable part of it is a translation or that it reflects in any continuous way, even in translation, the style of the author of Revelation. Dr Burney's view that John is earlier than Revelation would come to grief on the different conceptions of the 'Word' alone, and is otherwise improbable.

used with a consistency which confirms its meaning as a kind of priestly ritual of thought[1].

The inference would seem to be that the spirit of the prophet was very much subject to the prophet; and that we have, not, as Dr Charles says, a mixture of vision and reflexion, but simply reflexion in the form of vision.

V

PLACE AND DATE

APPARENTLY Patmos was a convict settlement, so that, in one sense, John would not be solitary, but, in the deeper sense, he would be in great loneliness of spirit, with the sea around and the sky above and only the criminal and the victim of oppression around him.

That the book is deeply coloured by this experience scarcely admits of question. The sky, both by day and night, has a prominent place in his symbolism, and it is peopled by spirits good and bad. The references to the sea are largely drawn from the prophets, but they have an intensity which speaks of its prominence in his experience. His hatred of civilisation would be easy to explain, if he saw around him only the wrecks of its injustice.

That he received his call to write and saw the visions in which its purpose and scope were made clear to him in Patmos is plainly stated. That the general plan of his book was before him when he began to write is shown by the reference near the beginning to the days of the seventh angel (§ V), which time almost closes it (§ XXV). And this is borne out by the unbroken sequence as now arranged. This, we may believe, was the fruit of his long brooding in exile; and we can hardly explain the elaboration of his thought into such a series of transparencies on any other theory.

But it is a question whether we should not go still farther

[1] This is not the usual opinion, but an important confirmation of the present interpretation will appear in the consistency it gives to all the symbolism of the book.

and conceive the book to have been actually written in Patmos.

1. The usual English translation 'I was in the isle that is called Patmos' might seem to say that John was no longer there when he wrote, but the Greek word means 'I came to be' and is consistent with his being there still.

2. If the Messages to the Churches were written in Patmos we have an explanation of why they were sent to, or more probably by, their angels, and not, as with all other letters in the New Testament, direct to the churches themselves. It would mean that, while John had the means for writing, he had no means of communicating with the outside world. His only possible medium was the guardian angels: and his whole way of thinking of such beings proves that he would not question that in some way they would communicate what he had received. Of this he would be the more certain as he himself had received the messages when in the spirit. The definite command to write excludes the idea that they were merely composed in his mind. This would further explain how the messages could be specially for the churches yet be at the same time an integral part of the whole book, for, being only sent in the spirit, they remained as part of his writing. The connexion is so close that we can hardly question that a command to write which applies to them applies to the rest. This is confirmed by the command to write what he sees in a book, which would seem to mean the whole book, which he is to send, doubtless when opportunity offered, to the churches themselves.

3. If John received the command to write, it is natural to suppose that he had the means for obeying at the time, and not that he was to do it on some future occasion, but he could only have been provided with a limited supply of writing material, and there would probably be no means of obtaining more. This would explain why each sheet was so carefully and regularly filled, and possibly also why the earlier sheets so frequently end with the paragraph, while from § XIII onwards this method scarcely appears, because he might have been more anxious about getting his work into his material at the beginning than when he had advanced far enough to estimate the length of the whole. This might

also explain why, though 'book' in the text seems to be a roll, the original MS. seems to be a codex, for, by using the form of the codex, both sides could be written on and so twice as much be put on the parchment.

The literary sources of the book, moreover, are consistent with the view that it was written in exile. While the author was deeply influenced by the Judaism of the time, there is no certain evidence of dependence on any writings except the prophets and possibly Colossians and Luke, and only on vivid and memorable passages in them. Moreover, the way these passages are woven into the texture of the thought and style speaks rather of much brooding on the memory of them than on immediate reading. If there is any exception it is Daniel, and we might suppose that John had taken with him that treasured roll. But in view of his deep interest in the book and the more tenacious memory of an age when few people had private literary possessions, and the memorable nature of the passages he uses, even this is probably an unnecessary hypothesis.

The only remaining question is the date. On the present interpretation of the book the number of the Roman Emperors by which this used to be decided has disappeared. Nothing remains to judge from save the general situation.

So definite an opposition between the Church and the Empire could not be earlier than the declaration of Titus against Christianity. Moreover, the destruction of Rome outside Jerusalem probably means that the Holy City had been destroyed. But as no severe persecution had yet taken place, it cannot be so late as the persecution of Domitian. The limits are thus fixed between 70 A.D. and 95 A.D.

But the prominence of the imperial cult points to the reign of Domitian (81–96 A.D.): and though it was earlier, as well as more slavish, in the East than the West probably not before 85. The expectation of systematic ruthless persecution might show that the persecution which took place near the end of the reign was drawing near, but, on the other hand, the imperial cult was prominent in Asia Minor much earlier, and though death and banishment were not a general imperial policy before 95 A.D. a Christian might have been killed in a riot or even been put to death on some excuse by the authorities and a prominent leader removed at any time during this reign. The expectation of persecution was earlier still and certainly, during all the reign of Domitian, it would require no great foresight to see that some day it would be systematic and fierce.

Two facts in the book may indicate a more precise date. (1) The kings of the East who are to destroy Rome are probably the Parthians, and, if this were suggested by political events, the date would be fixed as 89 A.D. (2) The licence to buy and sell might be connected with an attempt to improve the imperial finances which took place about the same date. This date would also have some support from tradition, because, while it speaks of John as young at the time of the Crucifixion and old at the time of his death, and the state of his MS. and the need for someone else to edit it may mean that he ended his days in Patmos, he would even at that date be over 70. It seems improbable that he would be much older, because, while his work has something of the authority, of the detachment from life, of the reminiscence of age, it has a vividness, a force, a rapidity which is far from senile decay.

NOTES

I

THE PRESENT ARRANGEMENT OF THE TEXT

As the theory of deliberate alteration should not be introduced till the possibilities of accidental confusion are exhausted, Mr Manson has kindly wrought out for me a scheme of an order in which the editor might have found his MS. which seems as simple as can be conceived. The only damage to the sheets it assumes is that the outside sheets of quires 3 and 5 were broken and all the sheets of quire 7. As imperfectly prepared skins often broke at the fold, this is easy to accept. Then, by an ingenious method of placing sheets inside others in four bundles, the present arrangement of pages is achieved. The only resort to the long arm of coincidence is that the last sheet of quire 5 is in quire 1 and this is followed by quire 6, which, as both are out of place, is rather too happy an accident.

But no arrangement of sections accounts for the divided ones, and to assume that the pages were broken and that the editor could not fit them together involves a greater simplicity than his worst work entitles us to assume. § XXV would not be a difficulty, because, if § XXVI were where it now is, it would be obvious that the latter half of § XXV belonged to it, but no kind of explanation of the division of § XIX is forthcoming.

There are, moreover, positive reasons for assuming a deliberate rearrangement at § XIX.

1. This is the one place where the rearrangement does not appear to be by sheets. § XIX is 34 lines and § XX is 32. Each sheet apart might be capable of explanation. § XX has an unusual number of long words and in consequence few spaces, which spaces did not exist in the original. § XIX could be made the usual length by omitting Ch. xix. 9[b] as a doublet of xxii. 6. But in every other case the printed text faithfully reflects the length of the original, and the existence of similar phrases in both passages may be the explanation why the doublet of xix. 9 in xxii. 8[b] is put immediately after xxii. 6: and, when we take both together, it is difficult to believe that the one page was long by exactly the measure that the one following it was short through pure accident.

2. In § XVIII two passages are inserted, one from § V, and immediately after it, another from § XIX. This means that all three sheets were before the editor; and the natural conclusion is that § XIX was there because it followed, and § V because he was at least considering the question of putting the rest of his MS. before it. Probably he had already decided this with regard to §§ XX–XXIV, and was merely trying to establish some kind of connexion for § XIX, which obviously could not go so early in the book.

3. The difficulties which made the editor unable to follow in the order in which he found the sheets are plain.

(*a*) The Second Coming he identified with the Last

Judgment and the Holy Jerusalem with the final state. How could the letting loose of Satan follow: and what could be the meaning of the scene in heaven and the opening of the sealed book? Was not the sealed book the book out of which the whole mysterious prophecy was unfolded? In that case, should it not be as near the beginning as possible? This judgment he would find confirmed by discovering the original of 'the first voice that spake with me' in the Messages, which now came just before, and by finding the two other woes preceding the third which had already been entered.

(*b*) As the editor was no more a strongly monotheistic Jew than a millenarian, he could not believe that the prohibition against worshipping Him was spoken by Jesus. In spite of the impossibility of any other speaker in the book being John's fellow-witness, he was determined to regard it as directed against angel-worship. He takes the bold course, first of omitting the part wherein Jesus speaks and second of inserting from § V a passage wherein 'the angel which showed me these things' is mentioned, though in its original place the speaker in this passage too must be Jesus. Of this the editor must have been dimly aware, because he does not venture to complete the passage with the witness of Jesus. Having a tender conscience at least for omissions, he remained dissatisfied. Therefore he took the whole of the section, including the part already inserted in § XVIII, and tried to find a connexion for it. He started on § X; and the extensive glosses in this sheet, unlike anything else in the book, may show that he had it a long time before him considering how he could proceed. Christ coming quickly seemed to suit the plagues. But again he was faced by the difficulty that, if he copied straight on, Jesus seemed to forbid men to worship Him, which he was determined not to admit. He, therefore, changed his mind, and put in this passage on the first occasion where he found an angel speaking. But the letting loose of Satan obviously could not follow in this new connexion. Wherefore, he had to keep it, and simply enter it at the end of the next sheet, without any pretence of a connexion.

II

FIRST CENTURY BOOKS

It may be worth while to consider somewhat more fully how far our present knowledge of the method of writing and of making up books in the first century sheds light on our problem. Seeing that our author was both a Jew and a Christian, we must more particularly consider writings among the Jews and Christians.

The discovery of many ancient fragments of writing within recent years has made known some important facts. There is now such a large measure of certainty that only upon two points is there any essential disagreement among students of the subject. These points are (1) the relative cost of papyrus and parchment and the proportion of their employment as writing material, and (2) the exact period when this material was made up into a codex. But neither difference affects our question, because:

I. Papyrus is usually believed to have been more in fashion with the rich, and parchment, in all places except Egypt, to have been in common use, especially by poorer people. This has been questioned, but only to the extent of maintaining that some kinds of parchment were dearer than some kinds of papyrus. Two universally admitted facts make even this question irrelevant for us. (1) Our book was certainly written in Asia Minor: and in Asia Minor at this time some kind of preparation of skin was as much the ordinary writing material as papyrus was in Egypt. (2) Our author was a Jew, and skin was so exclusively the traditional writing material of the Jews that the rabbis strictly forbade the copying of sacred texts on papyrus.

II. The roll was the fashionable form of a book till a much later date than this. But the fastening of leaves together into a kind of notebook was an immemorial custom. The name 'codex' originally meant a number of wax tablets fastened together by a cord. As the name passed to any book made up of sheets fastened together, the original form of fastening may have been similar. It is now, however, known that as early as any date likely to be assigned to Revelation, the folded sheet was used, and even one sheet laid inside another, with these quires sewn together through the fold. Books even of ordinary literature were on sale by this time in this form. And, what is still more decisive for our purpose, is the fact that the codex was 'the book of humble people' and from the first the specially Christian form of a book.

As there are, therefore, no differences of opinion among students of the subject within the limits of our inquiry, we may proceed by the simple method of summing up in points the matters which seem to bear upon our problem, beginning with the roll and then considering how far there was anything special in the codex[1].

1. A writer in Asia Minor at this period—and still more certainly a Jewish writer learned in the Scriptures—would in all likelihood use some kind of parchment. Thus, even if the work were meant to be a roll, it would first be written in equal columns on equal strips, which would only afterwards be sewn together. This part of his work we can suppose the author was for some reason unable to complete. The book of the Gentile Christians, into whose hands it would come, being the codex not the roll, the sheets might simply have been fastened together as leaves, and the fastening have come loose by use, or the sheets might have been found useful for reading in parts by several people, and so have been mixed.

2. The size of the strip and the amount of writing on it varied considerably, and the ordinary size is uncertain. But in later writings the ordinary form is three columns of twenty-one lines with about twenty-seven letters to the line, and this may be traditional. This would mean something less than 100 letters more than the average number in our sections. But words were divided by syllables at the end of a line, so that every line could not have had the complete number of letters. Also the length of the book appears to

[1] T. Birt, *Das Antike Buchwesen*, 1882, and *Die Buchrolle in der Kunst*, 1907; W. Schubart, *Das Buch bei den Griechen und Römern*; Blau, *Studien zum Althebräischen Buchwesen*, 1902. There is a good summary of his results in E. N. Adler's *About Hebrew Manuscripts*, 1905; F. W. Hall, *A Companion to Classical Texts*, 1913; Sir Edward Maunde Thompson's articles on 'Manuscripts' and 'Parchment' in the *Encyclopaedia Britannica*.

be something like an average length of a roll. While it is difficult to compare a Greek text with a Hebrew, the book of Daniel must be somewhere about the same length[1]. Daniel is a book late enough to be affected by literary custom, and, moreover, the most likely of all books to have been a pattern for our author.

3. A custom spread from the Alexandrine school of Greek writers which required an author to make the main divisions of his work correspond with the end of the roll. This is the school most likely to have been affected by Jewish literary traditions; and the custom is more likely to have arisen with their parchment roll, which was bulky, than with the papyrus roll, which was both smaller and lighter[1]. This would require the author to control the proportion of his work throughout, which would most easily be done by the strips. Thus we may explain why our author so frequently ends a page with a sentence and occasionally with a paragraph. A roll had sufficient space unwritten to go round it for protection when rolled up. This would mean that he had 28 strips which being four times seven, may have been the number with which he had provided himself.

4. There was never any system of numbering either the columns or the sheets of a roll. This is the more important that the absence of numbering also applies at this period to the codex. In no early example are the pages regularly numbered. Apparently regularly numbered pages began with legal books which needed to be consulted and quoted. It was next introduced into the Christian sacred books, but not till they had become ecclesiastical authorities. From them it is thought to have passed into secular literature, yet not, as a regular practice, till the fourth century.

5. Several facts illustrate the evenness of the writing. Lines appear to have been counted carefully for three reasons: (1) to ensure accuracy in copying, (2) for the payment of the scribe, and (3) as the recognised measure of the length of a book. Josephus, for example, who was both a compatriot and a contemporary of our author, states at the end of his 'Jewish Antiquities' that it consists of 60,000 lines. In that case lines must have been of fairly equal

[1] This is merely a suggestion of my own.

length; and, as the length was based on the hexameter, it must have been somewhere about 35 letters. This is at least interesting because, so far as the letters have been counted, the sections of Revelation work out at 44 lines, some of 35 and some of 36 letters, with a few letters less in the sections with the longer line and a few more in those with the shorter. As this difference does not reflect itself in the print, it must be due to a difference of proportion in the size of the letters. This would work out at two columns of 22 lines to the strip, if a roll, or at two pages of the same length to the sheet, if a codex—a very likely length in both cases, as on the whole, the earlier the date, the smaller the sheet. As the sheet was equal in both cases, and the roll was written only on one side and the codex on both, our sections would be, in the former case, a sheet, and, in the latter, half a sheet or a leaf or two pages. Finally, while contractions were common in private letters, they do not seem to have been used in books in the first century. Later Christian books have a definite recognised set of contractions, but such a system would take a long time to develop.

That we may have here the explanation of the confusion all these facts confirm. Nor are we wholly left to conjecture as to the possibility of such an incident. The Bruce MS. at Oxford has been found to be made up of two quite distinct Gnostic treatises mixed in utter confusion. If this could happen at a later period, when we might have expected precautions against it to have grown up on the basis of experience, it is easy to suppose that it could happen at an earlier period before the danger had been realised. Thus we might have loose sheets of a roll which had been disarranged, in which case the difficulty is not to explain the confusion, but the peculiar nature and limits of it. There is no difficulty in supposing that the editor might have to do with a bundle of loose slips of equal size with equal writing on them, which, through passing from hand to hand, had been disarranged into utter confusion. Our real difficulty is to explain how so much of the book is in order.

We have seen that this may more easily be explained on the hypothesis of a damaged codex. Yet these facts about the roll are not irrelevant, because the same kind of regular writing was used in both cases. And this general resemblance is emphasised still more in the case of Revelation by the fact that its author would certainly have been most familiar with the roll and have formed his method of writing in copying sacred writings in the form of a roll.

As, however, the writer was a Christian as well as a Jew, we must also consider the possibilities of the codex.

Besides the cheapness and convenience we may find an additional reason for the early adoption of this form by the Christians in the fact that the earliest Christian writings were small and were written for the occasion and were not issued as books. The original Apostolic letters would have been written on sheets, the *membranae* mentioned by Paul, which may or may not have been fastened together. They would be copied on any kind of sheets which could be come by, and when a collection of them was made, it would be done by simply fastening them together. The Gospels and Acts alone were written as books, but, even if they were originally on rolls, they would be distributed as codices.

We have, therefore, to consider the possibility that the writer, being a Christian and writing for Gentile Christians, may have used the form familiar to them, or that, if he wrote a roll, the editor's original may have been a copy in the form of a codex.

This latter possibility raises the important question whether the editor's original was the author's MS. We can be certain that we have the author's own length of sheet, because, only if an author were half consciously determined by his writing material, could he have ended so many sentences with the sheet. A copyist, not following his divisions, could only have managed it by contracting or expanding the writing, which would not have given equal sections when printed evenly. Yet this does not settle the question, because the reproduction of an author line by line and column by column appears to have been a usual custom of scribes in those days.

Moreover, a book in the text probably means a roll, while, if the original text had been written as a codex, we might expect to find some trace of ending sentences with the page as well as with the leaf. Yet against these considerations two others may be set. (1) As the writer, as is certain, was familiar with the roll, the leaf and not the page would be his natural unit. (2) The fact that the copyist edits as well as transcribes would seem to suggest a first issue of the original. The misunderstandings of his author would not at first sight suggest that he had lived among the circle of the author's friends, but we have other evidence to show that humble converts brought up in paganism were unable to find their way into the inner mind of their Jewish teachers. To this we may add that the editor must have believed he was dealing with the one text then in existence, and that if the book had ever been current in the Church in its right order, the present confusion could not have happened.

A codex in those days was usually made up by folding the sheets, placing two together, one inside the other, and then sewing them all together through the fold. The writing material and the methods of writing differed so little from the roll that all that has been said of it applies here equally. But the codex developed alongside of the roll and in comparative independence of it. On the supposition, therefore, that the book was a codex, it would originally have been composed of seven sets of quires of two folded sheets or four leaves. This number of two sevens may also afford some confirmation of the view that the original was the author's own MS., because two sevens is more probable than four in the circumstances.

Finally, we have the important fact that, as time went on, it became the custom to fold more sheets together in the quire. Thus a transcriber, living even a few years after the author, would not have had his suspicion aroused by finding a quire of six or eight instead of four pages. Even an odd page might not disturb him, as such pages are found fastened into later books.

PART II

TEXT AND TRANSLATION

§ I

Ch. I. 9—II. 4

9 Ἐγὼ Ἰωάννης, ὁ ἀδελφὸς ὑμῶν καὶ συνκοινωνὸς ἐν τῇ
θλίψει καὶ βασιλείᾳ καὶ ὑπομονῇ ἐν Ἰησοῦ, ἐγενόμην ἐν τῇ νήσῳ
τῇ καλουμένῃ Πάτμῳ διὰ τὸν λόγον τοῦ θεοῦ καὶ διὰ τὴν
μαρτυρίαν Ἰησοῦ. 10 ἐγενόμην ἐν πνεύματι ἐν τῇ κυριακῇ ἡμέρᾳ,
καὶ ἤκουσα ὀπίσω μου φωνὴν μεγάλην ὡς σάλπιγγος 11 λεγούσης·
ὃ βλέπεις γράψον εἰς βιβλίον καὶ πέμψον ταῖς ἑπτὰ ἐκκλησίαις,
εἰς Ἔφεσον καὶ εἰς Ζμύρναν καὶ εἰς Πέργαμον καὶ εἰς Θυάτειρα
καὶ εἰς Σάρδεις καὶ εἰς Φιλαδελφίαν καὶ εἰς Λαοδικίαν. 12 καὶ
ἐπέστρεψα βλέπειν τὴν φωνὴν ἥτις ἐλάλει μετ’ ἐμοῦ· καὶ ἐπι-
στρέψας εἶδον ἑπτὰ λυχνίας χρυσᾶς, 13 καὶ ἐν μέσῳ τῶν λυχνιῶν
ὅμοιον υἱὸν ἀνθρώπου, ἐνδεδυμένον ποδήρη καὶ περιεζωσμένον
πρὸς τοῖς μασθοῖς ζώνην χρυσᾶν· 14 ἡ δὲ κεφαλὴ αὐτοῦ καὶ αἱ
τρίχες λευκαὶ ὡς ἔριον λευκὸν ὡς χιών, καὶ οἱ ὀφθαλμοὶ αὐτοῦ
ὡς φλὸξ πυρός, 15 καὶ οἱ πόδες αὐτοῦ ὅμοιοι χαλκολιβάνῳ ὡς
ἐν καμίνῳ πεπυρωμένῳ, καὶ ἡ φωνὴ αὐτοῦ ὡς φωνὴ ὑδάτων
πολλῶν, 16 καὶ ἔχων ἐν τῇ δεξιᾷ χειρὶ αὐτοῦ ἀστέρας ἑπτά, καὶ
ἐκ τοῦ στόματος αὐτοῦ ῥομφαία δίστομος ὀξεῖα ἐκπορευομένη,
καὶ ἡ ὄψις αὐτοῦ ὡς ὁ ἥλιος φαίνει ἐν τῇ δυνάμει αὐτοῦ. 17 καὶ
ὅτε εἶδον αὐτόν, ἔπεσα πρὸς τοὺς πόδας αὐτοῦ ὡς νεκρός, καὶ
ἔθηκεν τὴν δεξιὰν αὐτοῦ ἐπ’ ἐμὲ λέγων· μὴ φοβοῦ· ἐγώ εἰμι ὁ
πρῶτος καὶ ὁ ἔσχατος 18 καὶ ὁ ζῶν, καὶ ἐγενόμην νεκρὸς καὶ
ἰδοὺ ζῶν εἰμὶ εἰς τοὺς αἰῶνας τῶν αἰώνων, καὶ ἔχω τὰς κλεῖς
τοῦ θανάτου καὶ τοῦ ᾅδου. 19 γράψον οὖν ἃ εἶδες καὶ ἃ εἰσὶν
καὶ ἃ μέλλει γενέσθαι μετὰ ταῦτα, 20 τὸ μυστήριον τῶν ἑπτὰ
ἀστέρων οὓς εἶδες ἐπὶ τῆς δεξιᾶς μου, καὶ τὰς ἑπτὰ λυχνίας
τὰς χρυσᾶς. * 1 Τῷ ἀγγέλῳ τῆς ἐν Ἐφέσῳ ἐκκλησίας γράψον· τάδε
λέγει ὁ κρατῶν τοὺς ἑπτὰ ἀστέρας ἐν τῇ δεξιᾷ αὐτοῦ, ὁ περιπατῶν
ἐν μέσῳ τῶν ἑπτὰ λυχνιῶν τῶν χρυσῶν· 2 οἶδα τὰ ἔργα σου
καὶ τὸν κόπον καὶ τὴν ὑπομονήν σου, καὶ ὅτι οὐ δύνῃ βαστάσαι
κακούς, καὶ ἐπείρασας τοὺς λέγοντας ἑαυτοὺς ἀποστόλους καὶ
οὐκ εἰσίν, καὶ εὗρες αὐτοὺς ψευδεῖς· 3 καὶ ὑπομονὴν ἔχεις, καὶ
ἐβάστασας διὰ τὸ ὄνομά μου, καὶ οὐ κεκοπίακες. 4 ἀλλὰ ἔχω
κατὰ σοῦ ὅτι τὴν ἀγάπην σου τὴν πρώτην ἀφῆκες.

§ I

THE PROPHETIC CALL

I. 9 I John your brother and comrade both in oppression
and in dominion, by the patience which is in Jesus, came to
be in the island called Patmos on account of God's word and
the witness of Jesus. 10 I was in the spirit on the Lord's day
and heard behind me a great voice, as of a trumpet[1], 11 saying: What thou seest write in a book and send to the seven
churches—to Ephesus and to Smyrna and to Pergamum and
to Thyatira and to Sardis and to Philadelphia and to Laodicea.
12 And I turned to see the voice which spake with me. And
having turned I saw seven golden lampstands, 13 and amid
the lampstands one like a Son of Man, clothed to His feet, and
girded about the breasts with a golden girdle, 14 His head
and His hair white like snow-white wool, His eyes as a flame
of fire, 15 His feet like fine brass refined in a furnace; His
voice like the voice of many waters[2]. 16 And He was holding
in His right hand seven stars; from His mouth went out a
sharp two-edged sword; and His countenance was as the sun
shining in its might. 17 And when I saw Him I fell before
His feet as one dead. But He placed His right hand upon me,
saying: Fear not, I am the first and the last, 18 the living
one. I died, but behold I am the living one to ages of ages,
and have the keys of death and of hades. 19 Write what thou
hast seen—the things which are and the things about to be
hereafter, 20 even the mystery of the seven stars which thou
hast seen in my right hand, and the seven golden lampstands.
II. 1 To the angel of the church in Ephesus write: These
things says He who is holding the seven stars in His right hand,
He who is walking amid the seven golden lampstands: 2 I
know thy works and thy suffering and thy patience and that
thou canst not endure evil-doers, but hast tested those calling
themselves apostles, and they are not, and found them false.
3 And thou hast patience and hast endured on account of My
name and not grown weary. 4 But I have against thee that
thou hast left thy first love.

[1] Is. lviii. 1. Lift up thy voice like a trumpet. [2] Dan. vii. 9 and 13, 14. One that was ancient of days...his raiment was white as snow and the hair of his head like pure wool; his throne was fiery flame...one like unto a Son of man, and there was given him dominion and glory and a kingdom. x. 5, 6. A man clothed in linen, whose loins were girded with pure gold of Uphaz...his face as the appearance of lightning and his eyes as lamps of fire, his arms and feet like in colour to burnished brass, and the voice of his words as the voice of a multitude. Ez. i. 24. The noise of many waters.

§ II

Ch. ii. 5–19

5 μνημόνευε οὖν πόθεν πέπτωκες, καὶ μετανόησον καὶ τὰ πρῶτα
ἔργα ποίησον· εἰ δὲ μή, ἔρχομαί σοι καὶ κινήσω τὴν λυχνίαν
σου ἐκ τοῦ τόπου αὐτῆς, ἐὰν μὴ μετανοήσῃς. 6 ἀλλὰ τοῦτο ἔχεις,
ὅτι μισεῖς τὰ ἔργα τῶν Νικολαϊτῶν, ἃ κἀγὼ μισῶ. 7 ὁ ἔχων οὖς
ἀκουσάτω τί τὸ πνεῦμα λέγει ταῖς ἐκκλησίαις· τῷ νικῶντι δώσω
αὐτῷ φαγεῖν ἐκ τοῦ ξύλου τῆς ζωῆς, ὅ ἐστιν ἐν τῷ παραδείσῳ
τοῦ θεοῦ. 8 καὶ τῷ ἀγγέλῳ τῆς ἐν Ζμύρνῃ ἐκκλησίας γράψον·
τάδε λέγει ὁ πρῶτος καὶ ὁ ἔσχατος, ὃς ἐγένετο νεκρὸς
καὶ ἔζησεν· 9 οἶδά σου τὴν θλίψιν καὶ τὴν πτωχείαν, ἀλλὰ πλού-
σιος εἶ, καὶ τὴν βλασφημίαν ἐκ τῶν λεγόντων Ἰουδαίους εἶναι ἑαυ-
τούς, καὶ οὐκ εἰσὶν ἀλλὰ συναγωγὴ τοῦ σατανᾶ. 10 μηδὲν φοβοῦ
ἃ μέλλεις πάσχειν. ἰδοὺ μέλλει βάλλειν ὁ διάβολος ἐξ ὑμῶν εἰς
φυλακὴν ἵνα πειρασθῆτε, καὶ ἕξετε θλίψιν ἡμερῶν δέκα. γίνου πιστὸς ἄχρι θανάτου, καὶ δώσω σοι τὸν στέφανον τῆς ζωῆς.
11 * ὁ νικῶν οὐ μὴ ἀδικηθῇ ἐκ τοῦ θανάτου τοῦ δευτέρου.
12 καὶ τῷ ἀγγέλῳ τῆς ἐν Περγάμῳ ἐκκλησίας γράψον· τάδε
λέγει ὁ ἔχων τὴν ῥομφαίαν τὴν δίστομον τὴν ὀξεῖαν· 13 οἶδα ποῦ
κατοικεῖς· ὅπου ὁ θρόνος τοῦ σατανᾶ· καὶ κρατεῖς τὸ ὄνομά
μου, καὶ οὐκ ἠρνήσω τὴν πίστιν μου ἐν ταῖς ἡμέραις Ἀντείπας
ὁ μάρτυς μου ὁ πιστός μου, ὃς ἀπεκτάνθη παρ' ὑμῖν, ὅπου ὁ
σατανᾶς κατοικεῖ. 14 ἀλλ' ἔχω κατὰ σοῦ ὀλίγα, ὅτι ἔχεις ἐκεῖ
κρατοῦντας τὴν διδαχὴν Βαλαάμ, ὃς ἐδίδασκεν τῷ Βαλὰκ βαλεῖν
σκάνδαλον ἐνώπιον τῶν υἱῶν Ἰσραήλ, φαγεῖν εἰδωλόθυτα καὶ
πορνεῦσαι. 15 οὕτως ἔχεις καὶ σὺ κρατοῦντας τὴν διδαχὴν τῶν
Νικολαϊτῶν ὁμοίως. 16 μετανόησον· εἰ δὲ μή, ἔρχομαί σοι ταχὺ
καὶ πολεμήσω μετ' αὐτῶν ἐν τῇ ῥομφαίᾳ τοῦ στόματός μου. 17 * τῷ
νικοῦντι δώσω αὐτῷ τοῦ μάννα τοῦ κεκρυμμένου, καὶ δώσω αὐτῷ
ψῆφον λευκήν, καὶ ἐπὶ τὴν ψῆφον ὄνομα καινὸν γεγραμμένον,
ὃ οὐδεὶς οἶδεν εἰ μὴ ὁ λαμβάνων. 18 καὶ τῷ ἀγγέλῳ τῆς ἐν Θυατείροις ἐκκλησίας γράψον· τάδε λέγει ὁ υἱὸς τοῦ θεοῦ, ὁ ἔχων
τοὺς ὀφθαλμοὺς αὐτοῦ ὡς φλὸξ πυρός, καὶ οἱ πόδες αὐτοῦ ὅμοιοι
χαλκολιβάνῳ· 19 οἶδά σου τὰ ἔργα καὶ τὴν ἀγάπην καὶ
τὴν πίστιν καὶ τὴν διακονίαν καὶ τὴν ὑπομονήν,

§ II

The Prophetic Call

II. 5 Remember, therefore, whence thou hast fallen, and
repent and do the first works. If not, if thou repent not, I
am coming to thee and will remove thy lampstand from its
place. 6 Yet this thou hast that thou hatest the works of the
Nicolaitans, which I also hate. 7 He that hath an ear let him
hear what the Spirit says to the churches. To the victor I will
give to eat from the tree of life which is in the paradise of
God. 8 And to the angel of the church in Smyrna write:
These things says the first and the last[1], who was dead and
came to life. 9 I know thy oppression and thy poverty, yet
thou art rich; also the blasphemy of some calling themselves
Jews, and they are not, but are a synagogue of Satan. 10 Fear
not what thou art going to suffer. Behold the devil is going
to cast some of you into prison, that ye may be tried, and ye
shall have oppression ten days[2]. Be faithful unto death and
I will give thee the crown of life. 11 The victor shall not be
hurt of the second death. 12 And to the angel of the church
in Pergamum write: These things says He who has the sharp
two-edged sword. 13 I know where thou dwellest, where is
Satan's throne. Yet thou holdest fast My name, and didst
not deny My faith in the days of Antipas, My martyr, My
faithful one, who was put to death among you where Satan
dwells. 14 Yet I have somewhat against thee, that thou hast
there those holding the teaching of Balaam who taught Balak
to put a stumbling-block before the children of Israel, to eat
idol-offerings and commit fornication. 15 In like manner thou
too hast those holding the teaching of the Nicolaitans.
16 Repent: if not, I am coming to thee soon and will war
against them with the sword of My mouth[3]. 17 To the victor
I will give of the hidden manna; and I will give him a white
stone, and on the stone a new name written which no one
knows save the receiver. 18 And to the angel of the church
in Thyatira write: These things says the Son of God who has
His eyes as a flame of fire and His feet like fine brass. 19 I
know thy works, and thy love, and thy faith, and thy service,

[1] Is. xli. 4. I the Lord, the first, and with the last, I am he. [2] Dan. xi. 33. Yet they shall fall by the sword and by flame, by captivity and by spoil *for* days.
[3] Is. xlix. 2. He hath made my mouth like a sharp sword.

§ III

Ch. ii. 19—iii. 7

καὶ τὰ ἔργα σου τὰ ἔσχατα πλείονα τῶν πρώτων. 20 ἀλλ' ἔχω
κατὰ σοῦ ὅτι ἀφεῖς τὴν γυναῖκα Ἰεζάβελ, ἡ λέγουσα αὐτὴν προ-
φῆτιν καὶ διδάσκει καὶ πλανᾷ τοὺς ἐμοὺς δούλους πορνεῦσαι
καὶ φαγεῖν εἰδωλόθυτα. 21 καὶ ἔδωκα αὐτῇ χρόνον ἵνα μετα-
νοήσῃ, καὶ οὐ θέλει μετανοῆσαι ἐκ τῆς πορνείας αὐτῆς. 22 ἰδοὺ
βάλλω αὐτὴν εἰς κλίνην, καὶ τοὺς μοιχεύοντας μετ' αὐτῆς εἰς θλίψιν
μεγάλην, ἐὰν μὴ μετανοήσουσιν ἐκ τῶν ἔργων αὐτῆς. 23 καὶ τὰ
τέκνα αὐτῆς ἀποκτενῶ ἐν θανάτῳ, καὶ γνώσονται πᾶσαι αἱ ἐκκλησίαι ὅτι ἐγώ εἰμι ὁ ἐραυνῶν νεφροὺς καὶ καρδίας, καὶ δώσω
ὑμῖν ἑκάστῳ κατὰ τὰ ἔργα ὑμῶν. 24 ὑμῖν δὲ λέγω τοῖς λοιποῖς
τοῖς ἐν Θυατείροις, ὅσοι οὐκ ἔχουσιν τὴν διδαχὴν ταύτην, οἵτινες οὐκ ἔγνωσαν τὰ βαθέα τοῦ σατανᾶ, ὡς λέγουσιν· οὐ βάλλω
ἐφ' ὑμᾶς ἄλλο βάρος· 25 πλὴν ὃ ἔχετε κρατήσατε ἄχρι οὗ ἂν
ἥξω. 26 καὶ ὁ νικῶν καὶ ὁ τηρῶν ἄχρι τέλους τὰ ἔργα μου,
δώσω αὐτῷ ἐξουσίαν ἐπὶ τῶν ἐθνῶν, 27 καὶ ποιμανεῖ αὐτοὺς ἐν ῥάβδῳ σιδηρᾷ, ὡς τὰ σκεύη τὰ κεραμικὰ συντρίβεται,
ὡς κἀγὼ εἴληφα παρὰ τοῦ πατρός μου, 28 καὶ δώσω αὐτῷ
τὸν ἀστέρα τὸν πρωϊνόν. * 1 καὶ τῷ ἀγγέλῳ τῆς ἐν Σάρδεσιν
ἐκκλησίας γράψον· τάδε λέγει ὁ ἔχων τὰ ἑπτὰ πνεύματα τοῦ θεοῦ
καὶ τοὺς ἑπτὰ ἀστέρας· οἶδά σου τὰ ἔργα, ὅτι ὄνομα ἔχεις ὅτι
ζῇς, καὶ νεκρὸς εἶ. 2 γίνου γρηγορῶν, καὶ στήρισον τὰ λοιπὰ ἃ
ἔμελλον ἀποθανεῖν. οὐ γὰρ εὕρηκά σου τὰ ἔργα πεπληρωμένα
ἐνώπιον τοῦ θεοῦ μου. 3 μνημόνευε οὖν πῶς εἴληφας καὶ ἤκουσας,
καὶ τήρει καὶ μετανόησον. ἐὰν οὖν μὴ γρηγορήσῃς, ἥξω ὡς κλέπτης,
καὶ οὐ μὴ γνώσῃ ποίαν ὥραν ἥξω ἐπὶ σέ. 4 ἀλλὰ ἔχεις ὀλίγα
ὀνόματα ἐν Σάρδεσιν ἃ οὐκ ἐμόλυναν τὰ ἱμάτια αὐτῶν, καὶ περι-
πατήσουσιν μετ' ἐμοῦ ἐν λευκοῖς, ὅτι ἄξιοί εἰσιν. 5 ὁ νικῶν οὕτως
περιβαλεῖται ἐν ἱματίοις λευκοῖς, καὶ οὐ μὴ ἐξαλείψω τὸ ὄνομα
αὐτοῦ ἐκ τῆς βίβλου τῆς ζωῆς, καὶ ὁμολογήσω τὸ ὄνομα αὐτοῦ
ἐνώπιον τοῦ πατρός μου καὶ ἐνώπιον τῶν ἀγγέλων αὐτοῦ.*
7 καὶ τῷ ἀγγέλῳ τῆς ἐν Φιλαδελφίᾳ ἐκκλησίας γράψον· τάδε
λέγει ὁ ἅγιος ὁ ἀληθινός, ὁ ἔχων τὴν κλεῖν τοῦ Δαυείδ, ὁ
ἀνοίγων καὶ οὐδεὶς κλείσει, καὶ κλείων καὶ οὐδεὶς ἀνοίξει·

§ III

The Prophetic Call

II. 19 and thy patience and thy works, the last which are
more than the first. 20 But I have against thee that thou
permittest the woman Jezebel, who calls herself a prophetess,
while she teaches yea deludes My servants into committing
fornication and eating idol-offerings. 21 I gave her time that
she might repent: but she wishes not to repent of her fornication. 22 Lo I will cast her and those who commit fornication
with her into a bed, even into great trial, except they repent
of their works. 23 And her children I will slay with pestilence.
Thus all the churches shall know that it is I who am examining
reins and hearts, and I will award to each of you in accord
with your works. 24 I say to the rest of you in Thyatira, those
who have not this teaching, whosoever have not known the
depths of Satan as they say—I will not lay on you any other
burden: 25 only what you have hold fast till I shall come.
26 But to the victor who holds fast My works to the end
I will give power over the nations 27 and he shall rule them
with an iron rod, as earthenware vessels are shivered. As I
Myself have received of My Father, 28 I will give him the
morning star. III. 1 And to the angel of the church in Sardis
write: These things says He who has the seven spirits of God
and the seven stars. I know thy works, that thou hast a
reputation of being alive, but art dead. 2 Become awake and
brace up what remains and was about to die. For I have not
found thy tasks fulfilled before My God. 3 Recall then how
thou hast received and heard, and hold fast and repent. But,
if thou be not on watch, I will come as a thief, and thou shalt
not know what hour I will come on thee. 4 Yet thou hast a
few names in Sardis who have not defiled their garments, and
they shall walk with Me in white because they are worthy.
5 Thus the victor shall be clothed in white garments, and I
will never blot his name out of the book of life, but will
acknowledge his name before My Father and His angels.
7 And to the angel of the church in Philadelphia write: These
things saith the holy, the true, the possessor of the key of
David, He who opens and no one shall shut, and shuts and
no one shall open[1].

[1] Is. xxii. 22. And the key of David I will lay upon his shoulder; and he shall open and none shall shut; and he shall shut and none shall open. Mt. xvi. 18. For the relation of this to the gates of Hades (Rev. i. 18) and the keys of the kingdom of heaven.

§ IV

Ch. III. 8–22

8 οἶδά σου τὰ ἔργα· ἰδοὺ δέδωκα ἐνώπιόν σου θύραν ἠνεῳγμένην,
ἣν οὐδεὶς δύναται κλεῖσαι αὐτήν· ὅτι μικρὰν ἔχεις δύναμιν, καὶ
ἐτήρησάς μου τὸν λόγον καὶ οὐκ ἠρνήσω τὸ ὄνομά μου. 9 ἰδοὺ
διδῶ ἐκ τῆς συναγωγῆς τοῦ σατανᾶ τῶν λεγόντων ἑαυτοὺς Ἰουδαίους εἶναι, καὶ οὐκ εἰσὶν ἀλλὰ ψεύδονται· ἰδοὺ ποιήσω αὐτοὺς
ἵνα ἥξουσιν καὶ προσκυνήσουσιν ἐνώπιον τῶν ποδῶν σοῦ, καὶ
γνῶσιν ὅτι ἐγὼ ἠγάπησά σε. 10 ὅτι ἐτήρησας τὸν λόγον τῆς
ὑπομονῆς μου, κἀγώ σε τηρήσω ἐκ τῆς ὥρας τοῦ πειρασμοῦ τῆς
μελλούσης ἔρχεσθαι ἐπὶ τῆς οἰκουμένης ὅλης, πειράσαι τοὺς
κατοικοῦντας ἐπὶ τῆς γῆς. 11 ἔρχομαι ταχύ· κράτει ὃ ἔχεις, ἵνα
μηδεὶς λάβῃ τὸν στέφανόν σου. 12 ὁ νικῶν, ποιήσω αὐτὸν στῦλον
ἐν τῷ ναῷ τοῦ θεοῦ μου, καὶ ἔξω οὐ μὴ ἐξέλθῃ ἔτι, καὶ γράψω
ἐπ' αὐτὸν τὸ ὄνομα τοῦ θεοῦ μου καὶ τὸ ὄνομα τῆς πόλεως τοῦ
θεοῦ μου, τῆς καινῆς Ἱερουσαλὴμ ἡ καταβαίνουσα ἐκ τοῦ οὐρανοῦ
ἀπὸ τοῦ θεοῦ μου, καὶ τὸ ὄνομά μου τὸ καινόν. * 14 καὶ τῷ
ἀγγέλῳ τῆς ἐν Λαοδικίᾳ ἐκκλησίας γράψον· τάδε λέγει ὁ ἀμήν,
ὁ μάρτυς ὁ πιστὸς καὶ ἀληθινός, ἡ ἀρχὴ τῆς κτίσεως τοῦ
θεοῦ· 15 οἶδά σου τὰ ἔργα, ὅτι οὔτε ψυχρὸς εἶ οὔτε ζεστός.
ὄφελον ψυχρὸς ἦς ἢ ζεστός. 16 οὕτως ὅτι χλιαρὸς εἶ, καὶ οὔτε
ζεστὸς οὔτε ψυχρός, μέλλω σε ἐμέσαι ἐκ τοῦ στόματός μου. 17 ὅτι
λέγεις ὅτι πλούσιός εἰμι καὶ πεπλούτηκα καὶ οὐδὲν χρείαν ἔχω,
καὶ οὐκ οἶδας ὅτι σὺ εἶ ὁ ταλαίπωρος καὶ ἐλεεινὸς καὶ πτωχὸς καὶ
τυφλὸς καὶ γυμνός, 18 συμβουλεύω σοι ἀγοράσαι παρ' ἐμοῦ χρυσίον πεπυρωμένον ἐκ πυρὸς ἵνα πλουτήσῃς, καὶ ἱμάτια λευκὰ
ἵνα περιβάλῃ καὶ μὴ φανερωθῇ ἡ αἰσχύνη τῆς γυμνότητός σου,
καὶ κολλύριον ἔγχρισαι τοὺς ὀφθαλμούς σου ἵνα βλέπῃς. 19 ἐγὼ
ὅσους ἐὰν φιλῶ ἐλέγχω καὶ παιδεύω· ζήλευε οὖν καὶ μετανόησον.
20 ἰδοὺ ἕστηκα ἐπὶ τὴν θύραν καὶ κρούω· ἐάν τις ἀκούσῃ τῆς
φωνῆς μου καὶ ἀνοίξῃ τὴν θύραν, καὶ εἰσελεύσομαι πρὸς αὐτὸν
καὶ δειπνήσω μετ' αὐτοῦ καὶ αὐτὸς μετ' ἐμοῦ. 21 ὁ νικῶν, δώσω αὐτῷ καθίσαι μετ' ἐμοῦ ἐν τῷ θρόνῳ μου, ὡς κἀγὼ ἐνίκησα
καὶ ἐκάθισα μετὰ τοῦ πατρός μου ἐν τῷ θρόνῳ αὐτοῦ. 22 ὁ
ἔχων οὖς ἀκουσάτω τί τὸ πνεῦμα λέγει ταῖς ἐκκλησίαις.

§ IV

The Prophetic Call

III. 8 I know thy works. Lo, I have set an open door before
thee, which no one can shut, because thou hast some little
strength and hast held fast My word and not denied My
name. 9 Lo, I will give some from the synagogue of Satan,
of those who say they are Jews and are not, but are false—lo,
I will make them come and kneel before thy feet, that they
may know that I have loved thee. 10 Because thou hast kept
the word of My patience, I also will keep thee from the hour
of trial which is about to come on the whole civilised world
to try those dwelling on the earth. 11 I come soon. Hold
fast what thou hast that no one take away thy crown. 12 The
victor will I make a pillar in the temple of My God, and outside he shall never more go. And I will write on him the name
of My God and the name of the city of My God—the new
Jerusalem which comes down from heaven from My God,
and My name, the new one. 14 And to the angel of the church
in Laodicea write: These things says the Amen, the Witness,
the Faithful and True one, the beginning of the creation of
God. 15 I know thy works, that thou art neither cold nor hot.
Would thou wert cold or hot! 16 So, as thou art luke-warm,
and neither cold nor hot, I will spue thee out of My mouth.
17 Because thou sayest, I am rich, I have been enriched and
have no want, and dost not know that thou art miserable,
pitiable, poor, blind and naked, 18 I counsel thee to buy from
Me gold purified in the fire that thou mayest be rich, and
white raiment that thou mayest be clothed and the shame of
thy nakedness may not appear, and to anoint with eye-salve
thine eyes that thou mayest see. 19 Those I love I rebuke and
chasten. Have zeal then and repent. 20 Lo, I stand at the
door and knock. If any one hear My voice and open the door,
I will come in to him and sup with him, and he with Me.
21 To the victor I will grant to sit with Me on My throne,
even as I was victorious and sat down with My Father on His
throne. 22 He who has ears to hear, let him hear what the
Spirit says to the churches.

§ V

CH. X. 1–10, XXII. 6–8, X. 11

1 Καὶ εἶδον ἄλλον ἄγγελον ἰσχυρὸν καταβαίνοντα ἐκ τοῦ οὐρανοῦ, περιβεβλημένον νεφέλην, καὶ ἡ ἶρις ἐπὶ τὴν κεφαλὴν αὐτοῦ,
καὶ τὸ πρόσωπον αὐτοῦ ὡς ὁ ἥλιος, καὶ οἱ πόδες αὐτοῦ ὡς στῦλοι
πυρός, 2 καὶ ἔχων ἐν τῇ χειρὶ αὐτοῦ βιβλαρίδιον ἠνεῳγμένον.
καὶ ἔθηκεν τὸν πόδα αὐτοῦ τὸν δεξιὸν ἐπὶ τῆς θαλάσσης, τὸν δὲ
εὐώνυμον ἐπὶ τῆς γῆς, 3 καὶ ἔκραξεν φωνῇ μεγάλῃ ὥσπερ λέων
μυκᾶται. καὶ ὅτε ἔκραξεν, ἐλάλησαν αἱ ἑπτὰ βρονταὶ τὰς ἑαυτῶν
φωνάς. 4 καὶ ὅτε ἐλάλησαν αἱ ἑπτὰ βρονταί, ἔμελλον γράφειν,
καὶ ἤκουσα φωνὴν ἐκ τοῦ οὐρανοῦ λέγουσαν· σφράγισον ἃ ἐλάλησαν αἱ ἑπτὰ βρονταί, καὶ μὴ αὐτὰ γράψῃς. 5 καὶ ὁ ἄγγελος,
ὃν εἶδον ἑστῶτα ἐπὶ τῆς θαλάσσης καὶ ἐπὶ τῆς γῆς, ἦρεν τὴν
χεῖρα αὐτοῦ τὴν δεξιὰν εἰς τὸν οὐρανόν, 6 καὶ ὤμοσεν ἐν τῷ ζῶντι
εἰς τοὺς αἰῶνας τῶν αἰώνων, ὃς ἔκτισεν τὸν οὐρανὸν καὶ τὰ ἐν
αὐτῷ καὶ τὴν γῆν καὶ τὰ ἐν αὐτῇ καὶ τὴν θάλασσαν καὶ τὰ ἐν
αὐτῇ, ὅτι χρόνος οὐκέτι ἔσται, 7 ἀλλ' ἐν ταῖς ἡμέραις τῆς φωνῆς
τοῦ ἑβδόμου ἀγγέλου, ὅταν μέλλῃ σαλπίζειν, καὶ ἐτελέσθη τὸ
μυστήριον τοῦ θεοῦ, ὡς εὐηγγέλισεν τοὺς ἑαυτοῦ δούλους τοὺς
προφήτας. 8 καὶ ἡ φωνὴ ἣν ἤκουσα ἐκ τοῦ οὐρανοῦ πάλιν
λαλοῦσαν μετ' ἐμοῦ καὶ λέγουσαν· ὕπαγε λάβε τὸ βιβλαρίδιον τὸ ἠνεῳγμένον ἐν τῇ χειρὶ τοῦ ἀγγέλου τοῦ ἑστῶτος ἐπὶ
τῆς θαλάσσης καὶ ἐπὶ τῆς γῆς. 9 καὶ ἀπῆλθα πρὸς τὸν ἄγγελον,
λέγων αὐτῷ δοῦναί μοι τὸ βιβλαρίδιον. καὶ λέγει μοι· λάβε καὶ
κατάφαγε αὐτό, καὶ πικρανεῖ σου τὴν κοιλίαν, ἀλλ' ἐν τῷ στό-
ματί σου ἔσται γλυκὺ ὡς μέλι. 10 καὶ ἔλαβον τὸ βιβλαρίδιον ἐκ
τῆς χειρὸς τοῦ ἀγγέλου καὶ κατέφαγον αὐτό, καὶ ἦν ἐν τῷ στό-
ματί μου ὡς μέλι γλυκύ· καὶ ὅτε ἔφαγον αὐτό, ἐπικράνθη ἡ
κοιλία μου. 6 καὶ εἶπέν μοι· οὗτοι οἱ λόγοι πιστοὶ καὶ ἀληθινοί,
καὶ ὁ κύριος ὁ θεὸς τῶν πνευμάτων τῶν προφητῶν ἀπέστειλεν
τὸν ἄγγελον αὐτοῦ δεῖξαι τοῖς δούλοις αὐτοῦ ἃ δεῖ γενέσθαι ἐν
τάχει. 7 καὶ ἰδοὺ ἔρχομαι ταχύ. μακάριος ὁ τηρῶν τοὺς λόγους
τῆς προφητείας τοῦ βιβλίου τούτου. 8 κἀγὼ Ἰωάννης ὁ βλέπων
καὶ ἀκούων ταῦτα· 11 καὶ λέγουσίν μοι· δεῖ σε πάλιν προφητεῦσαι
ἐπὶ λαοῖς καὶ ἔθνεσιν καὶ γλώσσαις καὶ βασιλεῦσιν πολλοῖς.

§ V

The Prophetic Call

x. 1 Then I saw, coming down out of heaven, another angel
—one of strength. He was cloud enfolded, the rainbow over
his head[1], his face as the sun and his feet as pillars of fire[2],
2 and in his hand he held a small open roll[3]. He set his right
foot on the sea and his left on the land, 3 and he cried with
a great voice as a lion roars[4]. And, when he cried, the seven
thunders spake forth their voices[5]. 4 And, when the seven
thunders had spoken, I was about to write. But I heard a
voice from heaven saying: Seal up what things the seven
thunders have spoken and write them not. 5 And the angel
whom I saw standing on the sea and on the land lifted up his
right hand towards heaven, 6 and swore by him who lives to
ages of ages, who created the heavens and what is therein, the
earth and what is therein and the sea and what is therein, that
not yet is the time, 7 not till the days of the voice of the
seventh angel, when he is to sound his trumpet and God's
mystery is finished, as He has given His servants the prophets
the good-news. 8 Then the voice which I heard from heaven
was again speaking unto me, saying: Go, take the small roll
which is open in the hand of the angel standing on the sea
and on the land. 9 Then I went to the angel, saying to him:
Give me the small roll; and he says to me: Take and eat it;
and it will make bitter thy belly, though in thy mouth it will
be sweet as honey. 10 And I took the small roll from the hand
of the angel and ate it up. And it was in my mouth as honey
sweet, but when I ate it my belly was embittered[6]. xxii. 6 Then
he said to me: These are the reliable and true words[7]; and the
Lord, the God of the spirits of the prophets, sent His angel
to show to His servants what must come to pass soon.
7 Behold I come soon. Blessed is he who is keeping the sayings of the prophecy of this book. 8 And I, John, was he who
was seeing and hearing these things. x. 11 And they say to
me: It is required that thou also shouldest prophesy again
concerning many peoples and nations and tongues and kings.

[1] Ez. i. 28. As the appearance of the bow that is in the cloud in the day of rain, so was the appearance of the brightness round about. This was the appearance of the likeness of the glory of the Lord. [2] Ez. i. 27. And from the appearance of his loins downward I saw as it were the appearance of fire. [3] Ez. ii. 9. An hand was put forth unto me; and lo a roll of a book was therein. [4] Amos iii. 8. The lion roars, who will not fear? The Lord God hath spoken, who can but prophesy? [5] Ez. ii. 10. And there was written therein lamentations and mourning and woe. [6] Ez. iii. 1. Eat this roll and go speak unto the house of Israel....Fill thy bowels with this roll that I give thee. Then did I eat it; and it was in my mouth as honey for sweetness. *v.* 14. And I went in bitterness. [7] Jer. i. 9. I have put my words in thy mouth. *v.* 12. I watch over my word to perform it.

§ VI

Ch. xi. 1–13

1 Καὶ ἐδόθη μοι κάλαμος ὅμοιος ῥάβδῳ, λέγων· ἔγειρε καὶ
μέτρησον τὸν ναὸν τοῦ θεοῦ καὶ τὸ θυσιαστήριον καὶ τοὺς προσκυνοῦντας ἐν αὐτῷ. 2 καὶ τὴν αὐλὴν τὴν ἔξωθεν τοῦ ναοῦ ἔκβαλε
ἔξωθεν καὶ μὴ αὐτὴν μετρήσῃς, ὅτι ἐδόθη τοῖς ἔθνεσιν, καὶ τὴν
πόλιν τὴν ἁγίαν πατήσουσιν μῆνας τεσσεράκοντα δύο. 3 καὶ
δώσω τοῖς δυσὶν μάρτυσίν μου, καὶ προφητεύσουσιν ἡμέρας χιλίας
διακοσίας ἑξήκοντα περιβεβλημένοι σάκκους. 4 οὗτοί εἰσιν αἱ δύο
ἐλαῖαι καὶ αἱ δύο λυχνίαι αἱ ἐνώπιον τοῦ κυρίου τῆς γῆς ἑστῶτες·
5 καὶ εἴ τις αὐτοὺς θέλει ἀδικῆσαι, πῦρ ἐκπορεύεται ἐκ τοῦ στόματος αὐτῶν καὶ κατεσθίει τοὺς ἐχθροὺς αὐτῶν· καὶ εἴ τις
θελήσῃ αὐτοὺς ἀδικῆσαι, οὕτως δεῖ αὐτὸν ἀποκτανθῆναι. 6 οὗτοι
ἔχουσιν ἐξουσίαν κλεῖσαι τὸν οὐρανόν, ἵνα μὴ ὑετὸς βρέχῃ τὰς
ἡμέρας τῆς προφητείας αὐτῶν, καὶ ἐξουσίαν ἔχουσιν ἐπὶ τῶν
ὑδάτων στρέφειν αὐτὰ εἰς αἷμα καὶ πατάξαι τὴν γῆν ἐν πάσῃ
πληγῇ ὁσάκις ἐὰν θελήσωσιν. 7 καὶ ὅταν τελέσωσιν τὴν μαρτυρίαν αὐτῶν, τὸ θηρίον τὸ ἀναβαῖνον ἐκ τῆς ἀβύσσου ποιήσει μετ'
αὐτῶν πόλεμον καὶ νικήσει αὐτοὺς καὶ ἀποκτενεῖ αὐτούς. 8 καὶ
τὸ πτῶμα αὐτῶν ἐπὶ τῆς πλατείας τῆς πόλεως τῆς μεγάλης, ἥτις
καλεῖται πνευματικῶς Σόδομα καὶ Αἴγυπτος, ὅπου καὶ ὁ κύριος
αὐτῶν ἐσταυρώθη. 9 καὶ βλέπουσιν ἐκ τῶν λαῶν καὶ φυλῶν καὶ
γλωσσῶν καὶ ἐθνῶν τὸ πτῶμα αὐτῶν ἡμέρας τρεῖς καὶ ἥμισυ, καὶ
τὰ πτώματα αὐτῶν οὐκ ἀφίουσιν τεθῆναι εἰς μνῆμα. 10 καὶ οἱ
κατοικοῦντες ἐπὶ τῆς γῆς χαίρουσιν ἐπ' αὐτοῖς καὶ εὐφραίνονται,
καὶ δῶρα πέμπουσιν ἀλλήλοις, ὅτι οὗτοι οἱ δύο προφῆται ἐβασά-
νισαν τοὺς κατοικοῦντας ἐπὶ τῆς γῆς. 11 καὶ μετὰ τρεῖς ἡμέρας
καὶ ἥμισυ πνεῦμα ζωῆς ἐκ τοῦ θεοῦ εἰσῆλθεν ἐν αὐτοῖς, καὶ
ἔστησαν ἐπὶ τοὺς πόδας αὐτῶν, καὶ φόβος μέγας ἐπέπεσεν ἐπὶ
τοὺς θεωροῦντας αὐτούς. 12 καὶ ἤκουσαν φωνῆς μεγάλης ἐκ τοῦ
οὐρανοῦ λεγούσης αὐτοῖς· ἀνάβατε ὧδε· καὶ ἀνέβησαν εἰς τὸν
οὐρανὸν ἐν τῇ νεφέλῃ, καὶ ἐθεώρησαν αὐτοὺς οἱ ἐχθροὶ αὐτῶν.
13 καὶ ἐν ἐκείνῃ τῇ ὥρᾳ ἐγένετο σεισμὸς μέγας, καὶ τὸ δέκατον
τῆς πόλεως ἔπεσεν, καὶ ἀπεκτάνθησαν ἐν τῷ σεισμῷ ὀνόματα
ἀνθρώπων χιλιάδες ἑπτά, καὶ οἱ λοιποὶ ἔμφοβοι ἐγένοντο. *

§ VI

The Forces in Conflict

XI. 1 And a reed, like a measuring rod, was given me, saying: Rise and measure the temple of God, and the altar and
the worshippers at it[1]. 2 The court outside the temple omit
and measure it not[2], because it has been given over to the
Gentiles. And the Holy City they shall tread down forty-two
months[3]. 3 Yet I will endow my two witnesses that, clothed
in sackcloth[4], they shall prophesy one thousand two hundred
and sixty days. 4 These are the two olives with the two lights
which stand before the Lord of the earth[5]. 5 And if any one
would wrong them, fire goes out of their mouth and consumes
their enemies[6]; yea would any one wrong them, even so must
he be slain. 6 These have power to shut up the heavens that
rain fall not during the days of their prophesying[7]. And they
have power over the waters to turn them into blood; and, as
often as they will, to smite the earth with every plague[8].
7 But, when they shall have completed their witness, the beast
that comes up from the abyss shall make war with them and
conquer them and slay them, 8 and their corpse be on the
street of the city, the Great *City*, which allegorically is named
Sodom and Egypt, where also their Lord was crucified.
9 And from peoples, tribes, languages, nations, men look on
their corpses three days and a half and do not allow their
corpses to be laid in a tomb[9]. 10 And the dwellers on the
earth rejoice and exult over them and send presents to each
other, because these two prophets had put to the test those
dwelling on the earth. 11 But after three and a half days, the
spirit of life from God entered into them, and they stood on
their feet. Then great fear fell on those beholding. 12 And
I heard a great voice from heaven saying to them: Come up
hither. And they went up to heaven in the cloud, while their
enemies beheld them. 13 In that same hour a great earthquake befell; and the tenth of the city fell away, and there
were slain in the earthquake seven thousand men of name[10],
and the rest were terror-stricken.

[1] Ez. xl. 3 ff. [2] Ez. xlii. 15. Now when he had made an end of measuring the inner house, he brought me forth...and measured it round about. [3] Lk. xxi. 24. And Jerusalem shall be trodden down of the Gentiles, until the times of the Gentiles be fulfilled. Dan. xii. 7. And held up his right hand and his left hand unto heaven and sware by him that liveth forever that it shall be for a time and times and half a time (= 3½ years, 42 months, or 1260 days). [4] Is. xx. 2. Loose the sackcloth from thy loins. [5] Zech. iv. 11. Two olive trees upon the right side of the lampstand and on the left thereof. *v.* 14. These are the two sons of oil that stand by the Lord of the whole earth. [6] Jer. v. 14. I will make my words in thy mouth fire, and this people wood, and it shall devour them. [7] 1 K. xvii. 1. There shall not be dew nor rain these years, but according to my word (*i.e.* Elijah's). [8] Ex. vii. 19 ff. (Waters turned into blood and the other plagues of Egypt by Moses.) [9] Dan. ix. 27. And for the half of a week he shall cause the sacrifice and the oblation to cease. [10] Dan. viii. 24. And he shall destroy the mighty ones and the people of the saints.

§ VII

Ch. XII. 1–14

1 Καὶ σημεῖον μέγα ὤφθη ἐν τῷ οὐρανῷ, γυνὴ περιβεβλημένη
τὸν ἥλιον, καὶ ἡ σελήνη ὑποκάτω τῶν ποδῶν αὐτῆς, καὶ ἐπὶ τῆς
κεφαλῆς αὐτῆς στέφανος ἀστέρων δώδεκα, 2 καὶ ἐν γαστρὶ
ἔχουσα, καὶ κράζει ὠδίνουσα καὶ βασανιζομένη τεκεῖν. 3 καὶ ὤφθη
ἄλλο σημεῖον ἐν τῷ οὐρανῷ, καὶ ἰδοὺ δράκων πυρρὸς μέγας,
ἔχων κεφαλὰς ἑπτὰ καὶ κέρατα δέκα καὶ ἐπὶ τὰς κεφαλὰς αὐτοῦ
ἑπτὰ διαδήματα, 4 καὶ ἡ οὐρὰ αὐτοῦ σύρει τὸ τρίτον τῶν ἀστέρων τοῦ οὐρανοῦ, καὶ ἔβαλεν αὐτοὺς εἰς τὴν γῆν. καὶ ὁ δράκων
ἕστηκεν ἐνώπιον τῆς γυναικὸς τῆς μελλούσης τεκεῖν, ἵνα ὅταν
τέκῃ τὸ τέκνον αὐτῆς καταφάγῃ. 5 καὶ ἔτεκεν υἱὸν ἄρσεν, ὃς
μέλλει ποιμαίνειν πάντα τὰ ἔθνη ἐν ῥάβδῳ σιδηρᾷ· καὶ ἡρπάσθη
τὸ τέκνον αὐτῆς πρὸς τὸν θεὸν καὶ πρὸς τὸν θρόνον αὐτοῦ.
6 καὶ ἡ γυνὴ ἔφυγεν εἰς τὴν ἔρημον, ὅπου ἔχει ἐκεῖ τόπον ἡτοι-
μασμένον ἀπὸ τοῦ θεοῦ, ἵνα ἐκεῖ τρέφουσιν αὐτὴν ἡμέρας χιλίας
διακοσίας ἑξήκοντα. 7 καὶ ἐγένετο πόλεμος ἐν τῷ οὐρανῷ, ὁ
Μιχαὴλ καὶ οἱ ἄγγελοι αὐτοῦ πολεμῆσαι μετὰ τοῦ δράκοντος.
καὶ ὁ δράκων ἐπολέμησεν καὶ οἱ ἄγγελοι αὐτοῦ, 8 καὶ οὐκ ἴσχυ-
σαν, οὐδὲ τόπος εὑρέθη αὐτῶν ἔτι ἐν τῷ οὐρανῷ. 9 καὶ ἐβλήθη ὁ
δράκων ὁ μέγας, ὁ ὄφις ὁ ἀρχαῖος, ὁ καλούμενος διάβολος καὶ
ὁ σατανᾶς, ὁ πλανῶν τὴν οἰκουμένην ὅλην, ἐβλήθη εἰς τὴν γῆν,
καὶ οἱ ἄγγελοι αὐτοῦ μετ' αὐτοῦ ἐβλήθησαν. 10 καὶ ἤκουσα φωνὴν
μεγάλην ἐν τῷ οὐρανῷ λέγουσαν· ἄρτι ἐγένετο ἡ σωτηρία καὶ ἡ
δύναμις καὶ ἡ βασιλεία τοῦ θεοῦ ἡμῶν καὶ ἡ ἐξουσία τοῦ Χριστοῦ
αὐτοῦ, ὅτι ἐβλήθη ὁ κατήγωρ τῶν ἀδελφῶν ἡμῶν, ὁ κατηγορῶν
αὐτοὺς ἐνώπιον τοῦ θεοῦ ἡμῶν ἡμέρας καὶ νυκτός. 11 καὶ αὐτοὶ
ἐνίκησαν αὐτὸν διὰ τὸ αἷμα τοῦ ἀρνίου καὶ διὰ τὸν λόγον
τῆς μαρτυρίας αὐτῶν, καὶ οὐκ ἠγάπησαν τὴν ψυχὴν αὐτῶν ἄχρι
θανάτου. 12 διὰ τοῦτο εὐφραίνεσθε, οὐρανοὶ καὶ οἱ ἐν αὐτοῖς
σκηνοῦντες· οὐαὶ τὴν γῆν καὶ τὴν θάλασσαν, ὅτι κατέβη ὁ
διάβολος πρὸς ὑμᾶς ἔχων θυμὸν μέγαν, εἰδὼς ὅτι ὀλίγον καιρὸν
ἔχει. 13 καὶ ὅτε εἶδεν ὁ δράκων ὅτι ἐβλήθη εἰς τὴν γῆν, ἐδίωξεν
τὴν γυναῖκα ἥτις ἔτεκεν τὸν ἄρσενα. 14 καὶ ἐδόθησαν τῇ γυναικὶ
αἱ δύο πτέρυγες τοῦ ἀετοῦ τοῦ μεγάλου, ἵνα πέτηται εἰς τὴν

§ VII

The Forces in Conflict

xii. 1 A great sign appeared in the heavens, a woman clothed with the sun, the moon under her feet and on her head a crown of twelve stars. 2 And she was with child and cried out, being in labour and pain to bring forth[1]. 3 Then another sign appeared in the heavens: Lo, a great red dragon having seven heads and ten horns and on his heads seven diadems, 4 and his tail swept down a third of the stars of the heavens and cast them to earth[2]. And the dragon stood before the woman who was about to bring forth, that when she had brought forth, he might eat up her child. 5 And she brought forth a male child, who is hereafter to rule all the nations with an iron rod[3]. And her child was snatched up before God and before His throne. 6 Then the woman fled into the wilderness, where she had a place prepared for her by God that there they may nourish her one thousand two hundred and sixty days. 7 Then there was war in the heavens, Michael and his angels at war with the dragon and the dragon and his angels warred, 8 yet they could not prevail, nor was their place found any more in the heavens, 9 but the dragon, the great one, the serpent, the ancient one, he who is called devil and satan, the deceiver of the whole civilised world, was cast down. He was cast down to earth and his angels were cast down with him. 10 And I heard a great voice in the heavens saying, From henceforth is the salvation and the power and the dominion of our God and the authority of His Christ, because the accuser of our brethren, who accuses them day and night before our God, is cast down[4]; 11 and they have conquered him through the blood of the Lamb and through the word of their witness, and that they have not loved their lives even to death. 12 Wherefore, rejoice, O heavens, and ye who tabernacle in them. Woe to earth and sea, because the devil has come down to you, having great rage, knowing that he has only a little time. 13 Then, when the dragon saw that he was cast down to earth, he persecuted the woman who bare the male child. 14 And there were given to the woman the two wings of the great eagle that she might flee into the

[1] Mic. iv. 7–9. The Lord shall reign over them in mount Zion...unto thee shall it come; yea the former dominion shall come, the kingdom of the daughter of Jerusalem. Now why dost thou cry out aloud?...that pangs have taken hold of thee as of a woman in travail. Be in pain and labour to bring forth, O daughter of Zion. [2] Dan. viii. 10. And it waxed great even to the hosts of heaven; and some of the host and of the stars it cast down to the ground and trampled upon them, yea, it magnified itself even to the prince of the host...and it took away from him the continual burnt-offering, and the place of his sanctuary was cast down. And it cast down truth to the ground. [3] Dan. ix. 24. And to bring in everlasting righteousness. Ps. ii. 7–9. Thou art my son, this day have I begotten thee...I will give the nations for thine inheritance.... Thou shalt break them with a rod of iron (used also in Rev. ii. 27 and xix. 15). [4] Job i. Dan. vii. 7. (Some identification with the fourth beast) and it was diverse from all the beasts that were before it; and it had ten horns.

§ VIII

Ch. xii. 14—xiii. 10

ἔρημον εἰς τὸν τόπον αὐτῆς, ὅπου τρέφεται ἐκεῖ καιρὸν καὶ
καιροὺς καὶ ἥμισυ καιροῦ ἀπὸ προσώπου τοῦ ὄφεως. 15 καὶ
ἔβαλεν ὁ ὄφις ἐκ τοῦ στόματος αὐτοῦ ὀπίσω τῆς γυναικὸς ὕδωρ
ὡς ποταμόν, ἵνα αὐτὴν ποταμοφόρητον ποιήσῃ. 16 καὶ ἐβοή-
θησεν ἡ γῆ τῇ γυναικί, καὶ ἤνοιξεν ἡ γῆ τὸ στόμα αὐτῆς καὶ
κατέπιεν τὸν ποταμὸν ὃν ἔβαλεν ὁ δράκων ἐκ τοῦ στόματος
αὐτοῦ. 17 καὶ ὠργίσθη ὁ δράκων ἐπὶ τῇ γυναικί, καὶ ἀπῆλθεν
ποιῆσαι πόλεμον μετὰ τῶν λοιπῶν τοῦ σπέρματος αὐτῆς τῶν
τηρούντων τὰς ἐντολὰς τοῦ θεοῦ καὶ ἐχόντων τὴν μαρτυρίαν Ἰησοῦ.
18 καὶ ἐστάθην ἐπὶ τὴν ἄμμον τῆς θαλάσσης. 1 καὶ εἶδον ἐκ
τῆς θαλάσσης θηρίον ἀναβαῖνον, ἔχον κέρατα δέκα καὶ κεφαλὰς
ἑπτά, καὶ ἐπὶ τῶν κεράτων αὐτοῦ δέκα διαδήματα, καὶ ἐπὶ τὰς
κεφαλὰς αὐτοῦ ὀνόματα βλασφημίας. 2 καὶ τὸ θηρίον ὃ εἶδον ἦν
ὅμοιον παρδάλει, καὶ οἱ πόδες αὐτοῦ ὡς ἄρκου, καὶ τὸ στόμα αὐτοῦ
ὡς στόμα λεόντων· καὶ ἔδωκεν αὐτῷ ὁ δράκων τὴν δύναμιν αὐτοῦ
καὶ τὸν θρόνον αὐτοῦ καὶ ἐξουσίαν μεγάλην. 3 καὶ μίαν ἐκ τῶν
κεφαλῶν αὐτοῦ ὡς ἐσφαγμένην εἰς θάνατον, καὶ ἡ πληγὴ τοῦ
θανάτου αὐτοῦ ἐθεραπεύθη. καὶ ἐθαύμασεν ὅλη ἡ γῆ ὀπίσω τοῦ
θηρίου, 4 καὶ προσεκύνησαν τῷ δράκοντι, ὅτι ἔδωκεν τὴν ἐξουσίαν
τῷ θηρίῳ, καὶ προσεκύνησαν τῷ θηρίῳ λέγοντες· τίς ὅμοιος τῷ
θηρίῳ, καὶ τίς δύναται πολεμῆσαι μετ' αὐτοῦ; 5 καὶ ἐδόθη αὐτῷ
στόμα λαλοῦν μεγάλα καὶ βλασφημίας, καὶ ἐδόθη αὐτῷ ἐξουσία
ποιῆσαι μῆνας τεσσεράκοντα δύο. 6 καὶ ἤνοιξεν τὸ στόμα αὐτοῦ
εἰς βλασφημίας πρὸς τὸν θεόν, βλασφημῆσαι τὸ ὄνομα αὐτοῦ καὶ
τὴν σκηνὴν αὐτοῦ, τοὺς ἐν τῷ οὐρανῷ σκηνοῦντας. 7 καὶ ἐδόθη
αὐτῷ ποιῆσαι πόλεμον μετὰ τῶν ἁγίων καὶ νικῆσαι αὐτούς, καὶ
ἐδόθη αὐτῷ ἐξουσία ἐπὶ πᾶσαν φυλὴν καὶ λαὸν καὶ γλῶσσαν καὶ
ἔθνος. 8 καὶ προσκυνήσουσιν αὐτὸν πάντες οἱ κατοικοῦντες ἐπὶ τῆς
γῆς, οὗ οὐ γέγραπται τὸ ὄνομα αὐτοῦ ἐν τῷ βιβλίῳ τῆς ζωῆς τοῦ
ἀρνίου τοῦ ἐσφαγμένου ἀπὸ καταβολῆς κόσμου. 9 εἴ τις ἔχει οὖς,
ἀκουσάτω. 10 εἴ τις εἰς αἰχμαλωσίαν, εἰς αἰχμαλωσίαν ὑπάγει·
εἴ τις ἐν μαχαίρῃ ἀποκτενεῖ, δεῖ αὐτὸν ἐν μαχαίρῃ ἀποκτανθῆναι. ὧδέ
ἐστιν ἡ ὑπομονὴ καὶ ἡ πίστις τῶν ἁγίων. 11 καὶ εἶδον ἄλλο θηρίον

§ VIII

THE FORCES IN CONFLICT

XII. 14 wilderness, into her place, where she is sustained a time
and times and half a time out of reach of the serpent. 15 And
the serpent cast from his mouth after the woman water like a
river[1], that it might carry her away in flood. 16 But the earth
helped the woman, for the earth opened its mouth and
swallowed the river which the dragon cast out of his mouth.
17 Then the dragon was enraged at the woman and went
away to make war against the rest of her seed, even those who
hold fast the commandments of God and have the witness
of Jesus. 18 Then I stood on the shore of the sea, XIII. 1 and
I saw rising out of the sea a beast having ten horns, and seven
heads and on its horns ten diadems and on its heads names of
blasphemy. 2 The beast which I saw was like a leopard, with
his feet as a bear's and his mouth as the mouth of lions. To
him the dragon gave his power and his throne and great
authority[2]. 3 When one of his heads was as smitten unto
death, then the stroke of his death was healed. And all the
earth marvelled following the beast, 4 and they worshipped
the dragon, because he gave authority to the beast; and they
worshipped the beast, saying: Who is like the beast and who
is able to war with him? 5 There was given to him a mouth
speaking arrogancies and blasphemies[3], and there was given
him authority to act during forty-two months. 6 And he
opened his mouth in blasphemies against God, to blaspheme
His name and His dwelling-place, even those dwelling in
heaven. 7 And it was given him to make war with the saints
and to vanquish them; and authority was given him over
every tribe and people and language and nation. 8 And all
dwelling on the earth worshipped him, each one whose name
is not written, from the foundation of the world, in the roll
of life of the Lamb who was slain. 9 If any one has an ear,
let him hear. 10 If anyone goes into captivity, he brings into
captivity; if any slay with the sword, he must be slain by the
sword[4]. Herein is the patience and the faith of the saints.
11 And I saw another beast

[1] Is. lix. 7. They belch out with their mouth.... *v.* 12. For cursing and lying which they speak. [2] Dan. vii. 4–8. And four great beasts came up from the sea...the first was like a lion...a second like to a bear...and lo another like a leopard...the beast also had four heads: and dominion was given to it...and behold a fourth beast, terrible and powerful, and strong exceedingly. [3] Dan. vii. 8. And a mouth speaking great things. *v.* 25. And he shall speak words against the Most High, and shall wear out the saints of the Most High: and he shall think to change the times and the law; and they shall be given into his hands until a time and times and half a time. [4] Ps. lxviii. 18. Read as Eph. iv. 8. He leadeth captivity captive. Mt. xxvi. 52. For all they that take the sword shall perish with the sword.

§ IX

Ch. XIII. 11—XIV. 5

ἀναβαῖνον ἐκ τῆς γῆς, καὶ εἶχεν κέρατα δύο ὅμοια ἀρνίῳ καὶ
ἐλάλει ὡς δράκων. 12 καὶ τὴν ἐξουσίαν τοῦ πρώτου θηρίου πᾶσαν
ποιεῖ ἐνώπιον αὐτοῦ. καὶ ποιεῖ τὴν γῆν καὶ τοὺς ἐν αὐτῇ κατοικοῦντας ἵνα προσκυνήσουσιν τὸ θηρίον τὸ πρῶτον, οὗ ἐθεραπεύθη
ἡ πληγὴ τοῦ θανάτου αὐτοῦ. 13 καὶ ποιεῖ σημεῖα μεγάλα, ἵνα
καὶ πῦρ ποιῇ καταβαίνειν ἐκ τοῦ οὐρανοῦ εἰς τὴν γῆν ἐνώπιον τῶν
ἀνθρώπων. 14 καὶ πλανᾷ τοὺς κατοικοῦντας ἐπὶ τῆς γῆς διὰ τὰ
σημεῖα ἃ ἐδόθη αὐτῷ ποιῆσαι ἐνώπιον τοῦ θηρίου, λέγων τοῖς
κατοικοῦσιν ἐπὶ τῆς γῆς ποιῆσαι εἰκόνα τῷ θηρίῳ, ὃς ἔχει τὴν
πληγὴν τῆς μαχαίρης καὶ ἔζησεν. 15 καὶ ἐδόθη αὐτῷ δοῦναι πνεῦμα
τῇ εἰκόνι τοῦ θηρίου, ἵνα καὶ λαλήσῃ ἡ εἰκὼν τοῦ θηρίου, καὶ
ποιήσῃ ὅσοι ἐὰν μὴ προσκυνήσουσιν τῇ εἰκόνι τοῦ θηρίου ἀπο-
κτανθῶσιν. 16 καὶ ποιεῖ πάντας, τοὺς μικροὺς καὶ τοὺς μεγάλους,
καὶ τοὺς πλουσίους καὶ τοὺς πτωχούς, καὶ τοὺς ἐλευθέρους
καὶ τοὺς δούλους, ἵνα δῶσιν αὐτοῖς χάραγμα ἐπὶ τῆς χειρὸς
αὐτῶν τῆς δεξιᾶς ἢ ἐπὶ τὸ μέτωπον αὐτῶν, 17 ἵνα μή τις δύνηται
ἀγοράσαι ἢ πωλῆσαι εἰ μὴ ὁ ἔχων τὸ χάραγμα τὸ ὄνομα τοῦ
θηρίου ἢ τὸν ἀριθμὸν τοῦ ὀνόματος αὐτοῦ. 18 ὧδε ἡ σοφία ἐστίν.
ὁ ἔχων νοῦν ψηφισάτω τὸν ἀριθμὸν τοῦ θηρίου· ἀριθμὸς γὰρ ἀνθρώπου ἐστίν. καὶ ὁ ἀριθμὸς αὐτοῦ χξσ'[1]. 1 καὶ ἴδον, καὶ ἰδοὺ
τὸ ἀρνίον ἑστὸς ἐπὶ τὸ ὄρος Σιών, καὶ μετ' αὐτοῦ ἑκατὸν τεσσεράκοντα τέσσαρες χιλιάδες ἔχουσαι τὸ ὄνομα αὐτοῦ καὶ τὸ ὄνομα
τοῦ πατρὸς αὐτοῦ γεγραμμένον ἐπὶ τῶν μετώπων αὐτῶν. 2 καὶ
ἤκουσα φωνὴν ἐκ τοῦ οὐρανοῦ ὡς φωνὴν ὑδάτων πολλῶν καὶ
ὡς φωνὴν βροντῆς μεγάλης, καὶ ἡ φωνὴ ἣν ἤκουσα ὡς κιθα-
ρῳδῶν κιθαριζόντων ἐν ταῖς κιθάραις αὐτῶν· 3 καὶ ᾄδουσιν ᾠδὴν
καινὴν ἐνώπιον τοῦ θρόνου καὶ ἐνώπιον τῶν τεσσάρων ζώων
καὶ τῶν πρεσβυτέρων· καὶ οὐδεὶς ἐδύνατο μαθεῖν τὴν ᾠδὴν εἰ
μὴ αἱ ἑκατὸν τεσσεράκοντα τέσσαρες χιλιάδες, οἱ ἠγορασμένοι
ἀπὸ τῆς γῆς. 4 οὗτοί εἰσιν οἳ μετὰ γυναικῶν οὐκ ἐμολύνθησαν.
* οὗτοι οἱ ἀκολουθοῦντες τῷ ἀρνίῳ ὅπου ἂν ὑπάγῃ. οὗτοι ἠγο-
ράσθησαν ἀπὸ τῶν ἀνθρώπων ἀπαρχὴ τῷ θεῷ καὶ τῷ ἀρνίῳ,
5 καὶ ἐν τῷ στόματι αὐτῶν οὐχ εὑρέθη ψεῦδος· ἄμωμοι γάρ εἰσιν.

[1] Text ϛ.

§ IX

The Forces in Conflict

XIII. 11 coming up out of the earth, and he had two horns
like a lamb[1], but he spoke like a dragon. 12 All the authority
of the first beast he exercises before him. And he works on the
earth and those dwelling on it that they should worship the
first beast the stroke of whose death was healed. 13 He does
great signs, even to making fire come down from heaven to
earth in the sight of men. 14 And he deceives the dwellers
on the earth through the signs which were given him to do
before the beast, telling those who dwell on the earth to make
an image to the beast which had the stroke of the sword, yet
came to life. 15 And it was given to him to give a spirit to
the image of the beast, so that the image of the beast might
speak and might cause as many as would not worship the
image of the beast to be put to death. 16 And he causes all
—small and great, rich and poor, freemen and slaves—that
there be given them a mark on their right hand or on their
forehead, 17 and that no one be able to buy or sell unless he
have the mark, the name of the beast or the number of his
name. 18 Herein is the wisdom. Let him who has understanding count up the number of the beast, for it is the
number of a man; and the number of it is 1000 + 60 + 200[2].
XIV. 1 Then I beheld and lo the Lamb standing on Mount
Zion and with him a hundred and forty-four thousand having
the name of his Father written on their foreheads[3]. 2 And I
heard a sound from heaven as a sound of many waters, as a
sound of great thunder. The sound which I heard was as of
harpers harping with their harps. 3 And they sing a new song
before the Throne and before the four living creatures and
the elders. And no one could learn the song save the hundred
and forty and four thousand, the redeemed from the earth.
4 These are they who have not been defiled with women,
those following the Lamb wherever he may go. These have
been redeemed from among men, first-fruits to God and to
the Lamb, 5 and in whose mouth is found no guile, for they
are blameless[4].

[1] Dan. viii. 3. A ram which had two horns. [2] Dan. xii. 7–10. It shall be for a time, times and a half....And I heard, but I understood not...but the wicked shall do wickedly; and none of the wicked shall understand, but they that be wise shall understand. [3] Is. xiv. 22. The Lord hath founded Zion, and in her shall the afflicted of his people take refuge. (This connects the 144,000 with the holy remnant.) [4] Is. liii. 9. Although he had done no violence, neither was any deceit in his mouth. (Last transferred to saints.)

§ X

Ch. xv. 5—xvi. 16.

5 Καὶ μετὰ ταῦτα ἴδον, καὶ ἠνοίγη ὁ ναὸς τῆς σκηνῆς τοῦ
μαρτυρίου ἐν τῷ οὐρανῷ, 6 καὶ ἐξῆλθον οἱ ἑπτὰ ἄγγελοι οἱ ἔχοντες τὰς ἑπτὰ πληγὰς ἐκ τοῦ ναοῦ, ἐνδεδυμένοι λίνον καθαρὸν
λαμπρὸν καὶ περιεζωσμένοι περὶ τὰ στήθη ζώνας χρυσᾶς. 7 καὶ
ἓν ἐκ τῶν τεσσάρων ζώων ἔδωκεν τοῖς ἑπτὰ ἀγγέλοις ἑπτὰ φιάλας
χρυσᾶς γεμούσας τοῦ θυμοῦ τοῦ θεοῦ τοῦ ζῶντος εἰς τοὺς αἰῶνας
τῶν αἰώνων. 8 καὶ ἐγεμίσθη ὁ ναὸς καπνοῦ ἐκ τῆς δόξης τοῦ θεοῦ
καὶ ἐκ τῆς δυνάμεως αὐτοῦ. * 1 καὶ ἤκουσα μεγάλης φωνῆς ἐκ
τοῦ ναοῦ λεγούσης τοῖς ἑπτὰ ἀγγέλοις· ὑπάγετε καὶ ἐκχέετε τὰς
ἑπτὰ φιάλας τοῦ θυμοῦ τοῦ θεοῦ εἰς τὴν γῆν. 2 καὶ ἀπῆλθεν ὁ
πρῶτος καὶ ἐξέχεεν τὴν φιάλην αὐτοῦ εἰς τὴν γῆν· καὶ ἐγένετο
ἕλκος κακὸν καὶ πονηρὸν ἐπὶ τοὺς ἀνθρώπους. * 3 καὶ ὁ δεύτερος
ἐξέχεεν τὴν φιάλην αὐτοῦ εἰς τὴν θάλασσαν· καὶ ἐγένετο * ὡς
νεκροῦ. * 4 καὶ ὁ τρίτος ἐξέχεεν τὴν φιάλην αὐτοῦ εἰς τοὺς
ποταμοὺς καὶ τὰς πηγὰς τῶν ὑδάτων. 5 καὶ ἤκουσα τοῦ ἀγγέλου
τῶν ὑδάτων λέγοντος· δίκαιος εἶ, ὁ ὢν καὶ ὁ ἦν, ὁ ὅσιος,
ὅτι ταῦτα ἔκρινας, 6 ὅτι αἷματα ἁγίων καὶ προφητῶν ἐξέχεαν·
ἄξιοί εἰσιν. 7 καὶ ἤκουσα τοῦ θυσιαστηρίου λέγοντος· ναί,
κύριε ὁ θεὸς ὁ παντοκράτωρ, ἀληθιναὶ καὶ δίκαιαι αἱ κρίσεις σου.
8 καὶ ὁ τέταρτος ἐξέχεεν τὴν φιάλην αὐτοῦ ἐπὶ τὸν ἥλιον, καὶ
ἐδόθη αὐτῷ καυματίσαι τοὺς ἀνθρώπους ἐν πυρί. * 10 καὶ ὁ
πέμπτος ἐξέχεεν τὴν φιάλην αὐτοῦ ἐπὶ τὸν θρόνον τοῦ θηρίου·
καὶ ἐγένετο ἡ βασιλεία αὐτοῦ ἐσκοτωμένη, καὶ ἐμασῶντο τὰς
γλώσσας αὐτῶν ἐκ τοῦ πόνου. * 12 καὶ ὁ ἕκτος ἐξέχεεν τὴν
φιάλην αὐτοῦ ἐπὶ τὸν ποταμὸν * τὸν Εὐφράτην· καὶ ἐξηράνθη τὸ
ὕδωρ αὐτοῦ, ἵνα ἑτοιμασθῇ ἡ ὁδὸς τῶν βασιλέων τῶν ἀπὸ ἀνατολῆς ἡλίου. 13 καὶ ἴδον ἐκ τοῦ στόματος τοῦ δράκοντος καὶ ἐκ
τοῦ στόματος τοῦ θηρίου καὶ ἐκ τοῦ στόματος τοῦ ψευδοπροφήτου
πνεύματα τρία ἀκάθαρτα ὡς βάτραχοι· 14 εἰσὶν γὰρ πνεύματα
δαιμονίων ποιοῦντα σημεῖα, ἃ ἐκπορεύεται ἐπὶ τοὺς βασιλεῖς τῆς
οἰκουμένης ὅλης, συναγαγεῖν αὐτοὺς εἰς τὸν πόλεμον τῆς ἡμέρας
τῆς μεγάλης τοῦ θεοῦ τοῦ παντοκράτορος. * 16 καὶ συνήγαγεν
αὐτοὺς εἰς τὸν τόπον τὸν καλούμενον Ἑβραϊστὶ Ἁρμαγεδών.

§ X

The Fall of the Monarchies

xv. 5 Thereupon I saw that the temple of the tent of witness
in heaven was opened: 6 and from the temple came out the
seven angels having the seven plagues, clothed in linen pure
and bright and girt about the breasts with golden girdles.
7 Then one of the four living creatures gave to the seven
angels seven golden vials full of the wrath of God, the living
one unto ages of ages. 8 Then was the temple filled with
smoke from God's glory and His might[1]. xvi. 1 Then I heard
a great voice from the temple saying to the seven angels: Go
and pour out the seven vials of God's wrath on the earth.
2 The first went and poured his vial on the land; and there
was a sore, foul and grievous, upon men. 3 The second angel
poured his vial on the sea; and it became as of one dead.
4 The third angel poured out his vial on the rivers and the
springs of waters. 5 Then I heard the angel of the waters
saying: Righteous art Thou O Lord, who art and who wast,
the holy one, because Thou hast judged these things, 6 because
they poured out the blood of saints and prophets. Worthy
are they! 7 And I heard *the angel* of the altar replying: Yea
Lord, all sovereign God, true and righteous are Thy judgments. 8 The fourth angel poured out his vial on the sun,
and there was given to it to burn men with fire. 10 The fifth
angel poured his vial on the throne of the beast, and his
kingdom became darkened, and men gnawed their tongues
from pain. 12 The sixth angel poured out his vial on the river,
the Euphrates. And the water of it was dried up that the way
of the kings of the East might be made ready. 13 Then I saw
from the mouth of the dragon and from the mouth of the
beast and from the mouth of the false prophet three unclean
spirits like frogs, 14 which are spirits of demons working
miracles, which go out to the kings of the whole civilised
world to gather them unto the battle of the great day of the
all-sovereign God[2], 16 and they gathered them to the place
which is called in Hebrew Har-magedon[3].

[1] Is. vi. 4. And the house was filled with smoke. [2] 1 K. xxii. 23. I will go forth and will be a lying spirit in the mouth of all his prophets...thou shalt entice him. [3] Dan. xi. 45. And he shall plant the tents of his palace between the sea and the glorious holy mountain; yet he shall come to an end and none shall help him.

§ XI

Ch. xix. 11–16, xiv. 19–20, xix. 17–21

11 καὶ εἶδον τὸν οὐρανὸν ἠνεῳγμένον, καὶ ἰδοὺ ἵππος λευκός,
καὶ ὁ καθήμενος ἐπ' αὐτὸν καλούμενος πιστὸς καὶ ἀληθινός, καὶ
ἐν δικαιοσύνῃ κρίνει καὶ πολεμεῖ. 12 οἱ δὲ ὀφθαλμοὶ αὐτοῦ φλὸξ
πυρός, καὶ ἐπὶ τὴν κεφαλὴν αὐτοῦ διαδήματα πολλά, ἔχων ὄνομα
γεγραμμένον ὃ οὐδεὶς οἶδεν εἰ μὴ αὐτός, 13 καὶ περιβεβλημένος
ἱμάτιον περιρεραμμένον αἵματι, καὶ κέκληται τὸ ὄνομα αὐτοῦ
ὁ λόγος τοῦ θεοῦ. 14 καὶ τὰ στρατεύματα ἐν τῷ οὐρανῷ ἠκολούθει αὐτῷ ἐφ' ἵπποις λευκοῖς, ἐνδεδυμένοι βύσσινον λευκὸν
καθαρόν. 15 καὶ ἐκ τοῦ στόματος αὐτοῦ ἐκπορεύεται ῥομφαία
ὀξεῖα, ἵνα ἐν αὐτῇ πατάξῃ τὰ ἔθνη· καὶ αὐτὸς ποιμανεῖ αὐτοὺς
ἐν ῥάβδῳ σιδηρᾷ, καὶ αὐτὸς πατεῖ τὴν ληνὸν τοῦ οἴνου τοῦ
θυμοῦ τῆς ὀργῆς τοῦ θεοῦ τοῦ παντοκράτορος. 16 καὶ ἔχει ἐπὶ τὸ
ἱμάτιον καὶ ἐπὶ τὸν μηρὸν αὐτοῦ ὄνομα γεγραμμένον· βασιλεὺς
βασιλέων καὶ κύριος κυρίων. 19 καὶ ἐτρύγησεν καὶ ἔβαλεν εἰς
τὴν ληνὸν τοῦ θυμοῦ τοῦ θεοῦ τὸν μέγαν. 20 καὶ ἐπατήθη ἡ ληνὸς
ἔξωθεν τῆς πόλεως, καὶ ἐξῆλθεν αἷμα ἐκ τῆς ληνοῦ ἄχρι τῶν
χαλινῶν τῶν ἵππων, ἀπὸ σταδίων χιλίων ἑξακοσίων. 17 καὶ εἶδον
ἕνα ἄγγελον ἑστῶτα ἐν τῷ ἡλίῳ, καὶ ἔκραξεν ἐν φωνῇ μεγάλῃ
λέγων πᾶσιν τοῖς ὀρνέοις τοῖς πετομένοις ἐν μεσουρανήματι· δεῦτε
συνάχθητε εἰς τὸ δεῖπνον τὸ μέγα τοῦ θεοῦ, 18 ἵνα φάγητε σάρκας βασιλέων καὶ σάρκας χιλιάρχων καὶ σάρκας ἰσχυρῶν καὶ
σάρκας ἵππων καὶ τῶν καθημένων ἐπ' αὐτῶν, καὶ σάρκας πάντων
ἐλευθέρων τε καὶ δούλων καὶ μικρῶν καὶ μεγάλων. 19 καὶ ἴδον
τὸ θηρίον καὶ τοὺς βασιλεῖς τῆς γῆς καὶ τὰ στρατεύματα αὐτῶν
συνηγμένα ποιῆσαι τὸν πόλεμον μετὰ τοῦ καθημένου ἐπὶ τοῦ
ἵππου καὶ μετὰ τοῦ στρατεύματος αὐτοῦ. 20 καὶ ἐπιάσθη τὸ
θηρίον καὶ μετ' αὐτοῦ ὁ ψευδοπροφήτης ὁ ποιήσας τὰ σημεῖα
ἐνώπιον αὐτοῦ, ἐν οἷς ἐπλάνησεν τοὺς λαβόντας τὸ χάραγμα τοῦ
θηρίου καὶ τοὺς προσκυνοῦντας τῇ εἰκόνι αὐτοῦ· ζῶντες ἐβλήθησαν οἱ δύο εἰς τὴν λίμνην τοῦ πυρὸς τῆς καιομένης ἐν θείῳ.
21 καὶ οἱ λοιποὶ ἀπεκτάνθησαν ἐν τῇ ῥομφαίᾳ τοῦ καθημένου
ἐπὶ τοῦ ἵππου τῇ ἐξελθούσῃ ἐκ τοῦ στόματος αὐτοῦ, καὶ πάντα
τὰ ὄρνεα ἐχορτάσθησαν ἐκ τῶν σαρκῶν αὐτῶν.

§ XI

The Fall of the Monarchies

xix. 11 Then I saw the heaven opened, and lo, a white
horse. The one sitting on him, called Faithful and True,
judges and wars in righteousness[1], 12 his eyes a flame of fire
and on his head many diadems, having a name written which
no one knew except himself, 13 and clothed in a garment
dripping with blood. And his name was called The Word of
God. 14 The armies which are in heaven followed him on
white horses, clothed in fine linen white and pure. 15 From
his mouth goes out a sharp sword that with it he should smite
the nations, and it is he who will rule them with an iron rod.
He too treads the wine-press of the wine of the anger of the
wrath of God, the all-sovereign. 16 On his garment and on
his thigh he has a name inscribed, King of kings and Lord of
lords. xiv. 19 And he gathered and cast into the great wine-
press of the anger of God; 20 and the wine-press was trodden
without the city, and from the wine-press blood went out up
to the bridles of the horses and out for one thousand six
hundred stadia[2]. xix. 17 Then I saw an angel standing in the
sun, and he cried with a great voice, calling to all the birds
that fly in the sky: Come and be gathered together to God's
great supper, 18 that ye may eat the flesh of kings and the
flesh of captains and the flesh of mighty men and the flesh of
horses and their riders and the flesh of all—freemen and slaves,
small and great[3]. 19 Then I saw the beast and the kings of
the earth and their armies gathered to make war with the rider
on the horse and with his army. 20 Then was mastered the
beast and with him the false prophet, the worker of miracles
before him, with which he deceived those who received the
mark of the beast and worshipped his image. Alive the two
were cast into the lake of fire burning with brimstone[4].
21 The rest were slain with the sword of him who sits on the
horse—the sword which comes out of his mouth; and all the
birds were gorged with their flesh[5].

[1] Is. xi. 4, 5. And he shall smite the earth with the rod of his mouth, and with the breath of his lips shall he slay the wicked. And righteousness shall be the girdle of his loins and faithfulness the girdle of his reins. [2] Is. lxiii. 3–6. I trod the wine-press alone,...their life-blood is sprinkled upon my garments, and I have stained all my raiment. For the day of vengeance was in my heart, and the year of my redeemed is come....I poured out their life-blood on the earth. [3] Lk. xvii. 37. Where the body is, thither will the vultures be gathered together. [4] Dan. vii. 11. I beheld even till the beast was slain, and his body destroyed, and he was given to be burned with fire. [5] Ez. xxxix. 4. Thou shalt fall upon the mountains of Israel, thou, and all thy hordes, and of the peoples that are with thee: I will give thee unto the ravenous birds of every sort, and to the beasts of the field to be devoured.

§ XII

Ch. vi. 2–17

2 καὶ ἴδον, καὶ ἰδοὺ ἵππος λευκός, καὶ ὁ καθήμενος ἐπ' αὐτὸν
ἔχων τόξον, καὶ ἐδόθη αὐτῷ στέφανος, καὶ ἐξῆλθεν νικῶν καὶ ἵνα
νικήσῃ. * 4 καὶ ἐξῆλθεν ἄλλος ἵππος πυρρός, καὶ τῷ καθημένῳ ἐπ'
αὐτὸν ἐδόθη αὐτῷ λαβεῖν τὴν εἰρήνην ἐκ τῆς γῆς καὶ ἵνα ἀλλήλους
σφάξουσιν, καὶ ἐδόθη αὐτῷ μάχαιρα μεγάλη. 5 * καὶ ἴδον, καὶ
ἰδοὺ ἵππος μέλας, καὶ ὁ καθήμενος ἐπ' αὐτὸν ἔχων ζυγὸν ἐν τῇ
χειρὶ αὐτοῦ. 6 καὶ ἤκουσα ὡς φωνὴν ἐν μέσῳ τῶν τεσσάρων
ζώων λέγουσαν· χοῖνιξ σίτου δηναρίου, καὶ τρεῖς χοίνικες κρι-
θῶν δηναρίου· καὶ τὸ ἔλαιον καὶ τὸν οἶνον μὴ ἀδικήσῃς. * 8 καὶ
ἴδον, καὶ ἰδοὺ ἵππος χλωρός, καὶ ὁ καθήμενος ἐπάνω αὐτοῦ,
ὄνομα αὐτῷ θάνατος, καὶ ὁ ᾅδης ἠκολούθει μετ' αὐτοῦ, καὶ ἐδόθη
αὐτοῖς ἐξουσία ἐπὶ τὸ τέταρτον τῆς γῆς, ἀποκτεῖναι ἐν ῥομφαίᾳ
καὶ ἐν λιμῷ καὶ ἐν θανάτῳ καὶ ὑπὸ τῶν θηρίων τῆς γῆς. 9 * καὶ
ἴδον ὑποκάτω τοῦ θυσιαστηρίου τὰς ψυχὰς τῶν ἐσφαγμένων
διὰ τὸν λόγον τοῦ θεοῦ καὶ διὰ τὴν μαρτυρίαν ἣν εἶχον. 10 καὶ
ἔκραξαν φωνῇ μεγάλῃ λέγοντες· ἕως πότε, ὁ δεσπότης ὁ ἅγιος
καὶ ἀληθινός, οὐ κρίνεις καὶ ἐκδικεῖς τὸ αἷμα ἡμῶν ἐκ τῶν κατοι-
κούντων ἐπὶ τῆς γῆς; 11 καὶ ἐδόθη αὐτοῖς ἑκάστῳ στολὴ λευκή, καὶ
ἐρρέθη αὐτοῖς ἵνα ἀναπαύσωνται ἔτι χρόνον μικρόν, ἕως πληρώσωσιν
καὶ οἱ σύνδουλοι αὐτῶν καὶ οἱ ἀδελφοὶ αὐτῶν οἱ μέλλοντες ἀπο-
κτέννεσθαι ὡς καὶ αὐτοί. 12 * καὶ ἴδον, καὶ σεισμὸς μέγας ἐγένετο,
καὶ ὁ ἥλιος μέλας ἐγένετο ὡς σάκκος τρίχινος, καὶ ἡ σελήνη
ὅλη ἐγένετο ὡς αἷμα, 13 καὶ οἱ ἀστέρες τοῦ οὐρανοῦ ἔπεσαν
εἰς τὴν γῆν, ὡς συκῆ βάλλουσα τοὺς ὀλύνθους αὐτῆς ὑπὸ ἀνέμου
μεγάλου σειομένη, 14 καὶ ὁ οὐρανὸς ἀπεχωρίσθη ὡς βιβλίον ἑλισ-
σόμενον, καὶ πᾶν ὄρος καὶ νῆσος ἐκ τῶν τόπων αὐτῶν ἐκινήθησαν.
15 καὶ οἱ βασιλεῖς τῆς γῆς καὶ οἱ μεγιστᾶνες καὶ οἱ χιλίαρχοι
καὶ οἱ πλούσιοι καὶ οἱ ἰσχυροὶ καὶ πᾶς δοῦλος καὶ ἐλεύθερος
ἔκρυψαν ἑαυτοὺς εἰς τὰ σπήλαια καὶ εἰς τὰς πέτρας τῶν ὀρέων,
16 καὶ λέγουσιν τοῖς ὄρεσιν καὶ ταῖς πέτραις· *πέσετε ἐφ' ἡμᾶς
καὶ κρύψατε ἡμᾶς* ἀπὸ προσώπου τοῦ καθημένου ἐπὶ τῷ θρόνῳ
καὶ ἀπὸ τῆς ὀργῆς τοῦ αὐτοῦ[1]. 17 ὅτι ἦλθεν ἡ ἡμέρα
ἡ μεγάλη τῆς ὀργῆς αὐτῶν, καὶ τίς δύναται σταθῆναι;

[1] Geb. ἀρνίου.

§ XII

THE FALL OF THE MONARCHIES

VI. 2 Then I saw and lo, a white horse and one sitting on
him having a bow. And a crown was given him, and as a conqueror he went forth to conquer. 3 Then came forth another,
a red horse; and to the rider on him was it given to take peace
from the earth, 4 that men might slay each other. To him
was given a great sword. 5 Then I saw and lo, a black horse,
the rider on him having a balance in his hand. 6 And I heard
a voice in the midst of the four living creatures saying: A
quart of wheat for a day's wage and three quarts of barley for
a day's wage. But the olive and the vine injure not. 8 Then
I saw and lo, a pale horse, and his rider's name was Pestilence. And with him followed Hades. To these authority was
given over a quarter of the earth to kill with sword, famine and
pestilence, and by the wild beasts of the earth[1]. 9 Then I
saw under the altar the souls of those slain on account of the
word of God and for the witness which they held. 10 And
they cried with a great voice saying: How long, O Sovereign,
the holy and true, dost Thou not judge and take retribution
for our blood from those dwelling on the earth? 11 But to
each of them a white robe was given, and it was told them
that they must wait yet a little time until the number of their
fellow servants and brethren, who are to be slain even as they,
shall be full. 12 Then I saw, and there was a great earthquake
and the sun became black as sackcloth of hair and the whole
moon became as blood[2], 13 and the stars of the heavens fell
to earth like a fig-tree shaken by a great wind casting its
winter figs, 14 and the heavens were removed as a scroll
being rolled up[3], and every mountain and island were removed
from their places[4]. 15 The kings of the earth, and the nobles
and the captains and the rich and the powerful, and slave and
free-man alike, hid themselves in caves and rocks of the
mountains[5]; 16 and say to the mountains and to the rocks:
Fall on us and hide us from before Him, who sits on the throne,
and from His wrath, 17 because the day, the great day of His
wrath has come; and who is able to stand[6].

[1] Zech. i. 8. A man riding on a red horse...and behind him there were horses, red, sorrel and white. [2] Joel ii. 30, 31. And I will show wonders in the heavens and the earth, blood and fire and pillars of smoke. The sun shall be turned into darkness and the moon into blood before the great and terrible day of the Lord come. [3] Is. xxxiv. 4. The heavens shall be rolled together as a scroll. [4] Is. xl. 4. Every mountain and hill shall be made low. [5] Is. ii. 9. And the mean man is bowed down and the great man is brought low. *v.* 19. And men shall go into the caves of the rocks and into the holes of the earth. [6] Lk. xxiii. 30. Then shall they begin to say to the mountains, fall on us, and to the hills, cover us.

§ XIII

CH. XVI. 17—XVII. 9

17 Καὶ ὁ ἕβδομος ἐξέχεεν τὴν φιάλην αὐτοῦ ἐπὶ τὸν ἀέρα·
καὶ ἐξῆλθεν φωνὴ μεγάλη ἐκ τοῦ ναοῦ ἀπὸ τοῦ θρόνου λέγουσα·
γέγονεν. 18 * καὶ σεισμὸς ἐγένετο μέγας, οἷος οὐκ ἐγένετο ἀφ' οὗ
ἄνθρωπος ἐγένετο ἐπὶ τῆς γῆς, τηλικοῦτος σεισμὸς οὕτω μέγας.
19 καὶ ἐγένετο ἡ πόλις ἡ μεγάλη εἰς τρία μέρη, καὶ αἱ πόλεις
τῶν ἐθνῶν ἔπεσαν. καὶ Βαβυλὼν ἡ μεγάλη ἐμνήσθη ἐνώπιον τοῦ
θεοῦ δοῦναι αὐτῇ τὸ ποτήριον τοῦ οἴνου τοῦ θυμοῦ τῆς ὀργῆς αὐτοῦ.
20 καὶ πᾶσα νῆσος ἔφυγεν, καὶ ὄρη οὐχ εὑρέθησαν. 21 καὶ χάλαζα
μεγάλη ὡς ταλαντιαία καταβαίνει ἐκ τοῦ οὐρανοῦ ἐπὶ τοὺς ἀνθρώπους. * 1 καὶ ἦλθεν εἷς ἐκ τῶν ἑπτὰ ἀγγέλων τῶν ἐχόντων τὰς
ἑπτὰ φιάλας, καὶ ἐλάλησεν μετ' ἐμοῦ λέγων· δεῦρο, δείξω σοι τὸ
κρίμα τῆς πόρνης τῆς μεγάλης τῆς καθημένης ἐπὶ ὑδάτων πολλῶν,
2 μεθ' ἧς ἐπόρνευσαν οἱ βασιλεῖς τῆς γῆς, καὶ ἐμεθύσθησαν οἱ
κατοικοῦντες τὴν γῆν ἐκ τοῦ οἴνου τῆς πορνείας αὐτῆς. 3 καὶ
ἀπήνεγκέν με εἰς ἔρημον ἐν πνεύματι. καὶ εἶδον γυναῖκα καθη-
μένην ἐπὶ θηρίον κόκκινον, γέμοντα ὀνόματα βλασφημίας, ἔχοντα
κεφαλὰς ἑπτὰ καὶ κέρατα δέκα. 4 καὶ ἡ γυνὴ ἦν περιβεβλημένη
πορφυροῦν καὶ κόκκινον, καὶ κεχρυσωμένη χρυσῷ καὶ λίθῳ τιμίῳ
καὶ μαργαρίταις, ἔχουσα ποτήριον χρυσοῦν ἐν τῇ χειρὶ αὐτῆς
γέμων βδελυγμάτων καὶ τὰ ἀκάθαρτα τῆς πορνείας αὐτῆς, 5 καὶ
ἐπὶ τὸ μέτωπον αὐτῆς ὄνομα γεγραμμένον· μυστήριον, Βαβυλὼν
ἡ μεγάλη, ἡ μήτηρ τῶν πορνῶν καὶ τῶν βδελυγμάτων τῆς γῆς.
6 καὶ εἶδα τὴν γυναῖκα μεθύουσαν ἐκ τοῦ αἵματος τῶν ἁγίων
καὶ ἐκ τοῦ αἵματος τῶν μαρτύρων Ἰησοῦ, καὶ ἐθαύμασα ἰδὼν
αὐτὴν θαῦμα μέγα. 7 καὶ εἶπέν μοι ὁ ἄγγελος· διατί ἐθαύμασας;
ἐγώ σοι ἐρῶ τὸ μυστήριον τῆς γυναικὸς καὶ τοῦ θηρίου τοῦ
βαστάζοντος αὐτὴν τοῦ ἔχοντος τὰς ἑπτὰ κεφαλὰς καὶ τὰ δέκα
κέρατα. 8 τὸ θηρίον ὃ εἶδες ἦν καὶ οὐκ ἔστιν, καὶ μέλλει ἀναβαί-
νειν ἐκ τῆς ἀβύσσου καὶ εἰς ἀπώλειαν ὑπάγειν· καὶ θαυμάσονται
οἱ κατοικοῦντες ἐπὶ τῆς γῆς, ὧν οὐ γέγραπται τὸ ὄνομα ἐπὶ τὸ
βιβλίον τῆς ζωῆς ἀπὸ καταβολῆς κόσμου, βλεπόντων τὸ θηρίον
ὅτι ἦν καὶ οὐκ ἔστιν καὶ παρέσται. 9 ὧδε ὁ νοῦς ὁ ἔχων σοφίαν.
αἱ ἑπτὰ κεφαλαὶ ἑπτὰ ὕδατα[1] εἰσίν, ὅπου ἡ γυνὴ κάθηται ἐπ'

[1] Geb. ὄρη.

§ XIII

END OF THE WORLD-RULE

XVI. 17 The seventh poured out his vial on the air. Then went forth a great voice out of the temple, from the throne, saying: It is done *already*. 18 Then was there a great earthquake: so great an earthquake never was since man was on the earth[1]; 19 and the great city parted into three[2], and the cities of the nations fell away. So Babylon the Great was remembered before God to give her the cup of the wine of the anger of His wrath. 20 Every island fled and hills were not found[3]. 21 And great hail, about a talent weight, came down from the heavens upon men. XVII. 1 Then came one of the seven angels who had the seven vials and spake with me saying: Come, I will show thee the judgment of the great harlot, who sits on many waters, 2 with whom the kings of the earth committed fornication, while the inhabitants of the earth were made drunk by the wine of her fornication. 3 Then he carried me in spirit into the wilderness, and I saw a woman sitting on a scarlet beast full of names of blasphemy and having seven heads and ten horns[4]. 4 The woman was clothed in purple and scarlet, glittering with gold and precious stone and pearls, holding a golden cup in her hand full of abominations—the unclean things of her fornication. 5 On her forehead was a name inscribed, a mystery: 'Babylon the Great, the mother of harlots and of earth's abominations.' 6 I saw the woman drunk from the blood of the saints and the blood of the witnesses of Jesus; and seeing her I was amazed with a great amazement. 7 But the angel said to me: Why art thou amazed? I will tell thee the mystery of the woman and of the beast having the seven heads and ten horns that carries her. 8 The beast which thou sawest, was and is not, yet is about to come up out of the abyss and to subject unto destruction[5]. Then it shall be the inhabitants of the earth—each one whose name has not been written from the foundation of the world in the book of life—who shall be amazed seeing the beast 9 that was and is not, yet is to be. Thus is the meaning whosoever has wisdom![6] The seven heads are seven rivers upon which the woman is seated.

[1] Dan. xii. 1. And there shall be a time of trouble, such as never was since there was a nation even to that time. [2] Dan. vii. 8. Another horn, a little one, before which three of the first horns were plucked up by the roots. [3] Is. ii. 12, 14. A day of the lord of Hosts...upon the hills that are lifted up. [4] Lk. iv. 1–5. And was led by the Spirit into the wilderness...and he showed him all the kingdoms of the world. [5] Dan. viii. 24. And he shall destroy wonderfully. ix. 27. One that maketh desolate [6] Dan. xii. 10. They that be wise shall understand.

§ XIV

CH. XVII. 10—XVIII. 6

αὐτῶν, 10 καὶ βασιλεῖς ἑπτά εἰσιν· οἱ πέντε ἔπεσαν, ὁ εἷς ἔστιν,
ὁ ἄλλος οὔπω ἦλθεν, καὶ ὅταν ἔλθῃ ὀλίγον αὐτὸν δεῖ μεῖναι.
11 καὶ τὸ θηρίον ὃ ἦν καὶ οὐκ ἔστιν, καὶ αὐτὸς ὄγδοός ἐστιν, καὶ
ἐκ τῶν ἑπτά ἐστιν, καὶ εἰς ἀπώλειαν ὑπάγει. 12 καὶ τὰ δέκα
κέρατα ἃ εἶδες δέκα βασιλεῖς εἰσίν, οἵτινες βασιλείαν οὔπω ἔλαβον,
ἀλλὰ ἐξουσίαν ὡς βασιλεῖς μίαν ὥραν λαμβάνουσιν μετὰ τοῦ
θηρίου. 13 οὗτοι μίαν γνώμην ἔχουσιν, καὶ τὴν δύναμιν καὶ τὴν
ἐξουσίαν αὐτῶν τῷ θηρίῳ διδόασιν. 14 οὗτοι μετὰ τοῦ ἀρνίου πο-
λεμήσουσιν καὶ τὸ ἀρνίον νικήσει αὐτούς, * καὶ οἱ μετ᾽ αὐτοῦ κλητοὶ
καὶ ἐκλεκτοὶ καὶ πιστοί. 15 καὶ λέγει μοι· τὰ ὕδατα ἃ εἶδες, οὗ
ἡ πόρνη κάθηται, λαοὶ καὶ ὄχλοι εἰσὶν καὶ ἔθνη καὶ γλῶσσαι.
16 καὶ τὰ δέκα κέρατα ἃ εἶδες καὶ τὸ θηρίον, οὗτοι μισήσουσιν
τὴν πόρνην, καὶ ἠρημωμένην ποιήσουσιν αὐτὴν καὶ γυμνήν, καὶ
τὰς σάρκας αὐτῆς φάγονται, καὶ αὐτὴν κατακαύσουσιν πυρί· 17 ὁ
γὰρ θεὸς ἔδωκεν εἰς τὰς καρδίας αὐτῶν ποιῆσαι τὴν γνώμην αὐτοῦ
καὶ ποιῆσαι μίαν γνώμην καὶ δοῦναι τὴν βασιλείαν αὐτῶν τῷ
θηρίῳ, ἄχρι τελεσθήσονται οἱ λόγοι τοῦ θεοῦ. 18 καὶ ἡ γυνὴ ἣν
εἶδες ἔστιν ἡ πόλις ἡ μεγάλη ἡ ἔχουσα βασιλείαν ἐπὶ τῶν βασιλέων τῆς γῆς. 1 Μετὰ ταῦτα εἶδον ἄλλον ἄγγελον καταβαίνοντα
ἐκ τοῦ οὐρανοῦ, ἔχοντα ἐξουσίαν μεγάλην, καὶ ἡ γῆ ἐφωτίσθη ἐκ
τῆς δόξης αὐτοῦ. 2 καὶ ἔκραξεν ἐν ἰσχυρᾷ φωνῇ λέγων· ἔπεσεν
ἔπεσεν Βαβυλὼν ἡ μεγάλη, καὶ ἐγένετο κατοικητήριον δαιμονίων καὶ φυλακὴ παντὸς πνεύματος ἀκαθάρτου καὶ φυλακὴ παντὸς
ὀρνέου ἀκαθάρτου καὶ μεμισημένου, 3 ὅτι ἐκ τοῦ οἴνου τοῦ θυμοῦ
τῆς πορνείας αὐτῆς πέπωκαν πάντα τὰ ἔθνη, καὶ οἱ βασιλεῖς
τῆς γῆς μετ᾽ αὐτῆς ἐπόρνευσαν, καὶ οἱ ἔμποροι τῆς γῆς ἐκ τῆς
δυνάμεως τοῦ στρήνους αὐτῆς ἐπλούτησαν. 4 καὶ ἤκουσα ἄλλην
φωνὴν ἐκ τοῦ οὐρανοῦ λέγουσαν· ἐξέλθατε ὁ λαός μου ἐξ αὐτῆς,
ἵνα μὴ συνκοινωνήσητε ταῖς ἁμαρτίαις αὐτῆς, καὶ ἐκ τῶν πληγῶν
αὐτῆς ἵνα μὴ λάβητε, 5 ὅτι ἐκολλήθησαν αὐτῆς αἱ ἁμαρτίαι
ἄχρι τοῦ οὐρανοῦ καὶ ἐμνημόνευσεν ὁ θεὸς τὰ ἀδικήματα αὐτῆς.
6 ἀπόδοτε αὐτῇ ὡς καὶ αὐτὴ ἀπέδωκεν, καὶ διπλώσατε τὰ διπλᾶ
κατὰ τὰ ἔργα αὐτῆς· ἐν τῷ ποτηρίῳ ᾧ ἐκέρασεν

§ XIV

End of the World-rule

XVII. 10 And they are seven monarchies. The five have fallen,
the one still is, the other has not yet come; and, when it is come,
it is to endure a short time. 11 The beast which was and is
not is also the eighth. It is from the seven, and it subjects to
destruction[1]. 12 The ten horns which thou hast seen are ten
kings who have not yet received dominion, but they shall receive as kings authority with the beast for one hour[2]. 13 These
have one mind, which is to give their power and authority to
the beast. 14 These shall fight with the Lamb, and the Lamb
shall vanquish them and the elect, chosen and faithful with
Him[3]. 15 Then he says to me: The waters which thou hast
seen, where the harlot is seated, are peoples and multitudes
and nations and languages. 16 The ten horns which thou
hast seen and the beast alike will hate the harlot and will
make her waste and naked, and eat her flesh and burn her
with fire[2]. 17 For God has put it into their hearts to work
His purpose, to give with one mind their rule to the beast,
till God's words shall be fulfilled. 18 And the woman whom
thou hast seen is the Great City which has dominion over
the kings of the earth. XVIII. 1 Thereafter I saw another angel
coming down from heaven, having great authority, and the
earth was lighted up by his glory. 2 And he cried with a
strong voice saying: Fallen, fallen is Babylon the Great! and
is become a habitation of demons, a post of every unclean
spirit and a post of every unclean and hateful bird[4]; 3 for
from the wine of the anger of her fornication all the nations
have drunk, and the kings of the earth have committed
fornication with her, and the merchants of the earth been
enriched from the wealth of her wantoning. 4 Then I heard
another voice from heaven saying: Come out of her, my
people, that ye do not participate in her sins and receive
of her plagues, 5 for her sins have been piled up to heaven,
and God has called to remembrance her iniquities. 6 Render to her as she rendered, yea doubling twofold according
to her works. In the cup which she mingled

[1] vii. 23. The fourth beast shall be a fourth kingdom upon earth, which shall be diverse from all the kingdoms, and shall devour the whole earth and tread it down and break it in pieces. [2] vii. 24. And as for the ten horns, out of this kingdom shall ten kings arise. [3] vii. 21. The same horn made war with the saints, and prevailed against them until the ancient of days came. [4] Is. xxxiv. 8–15.

§ XV

Ch. xviii. 6–19

κεράσατε αὐτῇ διπλοῦν· 7 ὅσα ἐδόξασεν αὐτὴν καὶ ἐστρηνίασεν,
τοσοῦτον δότε αὐτῇ βασανισμὸν καὶ πένθος. ὅτι ἐν τῇ καρδίᾳ
αὐτῆς λέγει ὅτι κάθημαι βασίλισσα καὶ χήρα οὐκ εἰμὶ καὶ πένθος
οὐ μὴ ἴδω, 8 διὰ τοῦτο ἐν μιᾷ ἡμέρᾳ ἥξουσιν αἱ πληγαὶ αὐτῆς,
θάνατος καὶ πένθος καὶ λιμός, καὶ ἐν πυρὶ κατακαυθήσεται· ὅτι
ἰσχυρὸς κύριος ὁ θεὸς ὁ κρίνας αὐτήν. 9 καὶ κλαύσονται καὶ
κόψονται ἐπ' αὐτὴν οἱ βασιλεῖς τῆς γῆς οἱ μετ' αὐτῆς πορνεύ-
σαντες καὶ στρηνιάσαντες, ὅταν βλέπωσιν τὸν καπνὸν τῆς πυρώσεως αὐτῆς, 10 ἀπὸ μακρόθεν ἑστηκότες διὰ τὸν φόβον τοῦ
βασανισμοῦ αὐτῆς, λέγοντες· οὐαὶ οὐαί, ἡ πόλις ἡ μεγάλη,
Βαβυλὼν ἡ πόλις ἡ ἰσχυρά, ὅτι μιᾷ ὥρᾳ ἦλθεν ἡ κρίσις σου.
11 καὶ οἱ ἔμποροι τῆς γῆς κλαίουσιν καὶ πενθοῦσιν ἐπ' αὐτήν, ὅτι
τὸν γόμον αὐτῶν οὐδεὶς ἀγοράζει οὐκέτι, 12 γόμον χρυσοῦ καὶ
ἀργύρου καὶ λίθου τιμίου καὶ μαργαριτῶν καὶ βυσσίνου καὶ πορ-
φύρας καὶ σιρικοῦ καὶ κοκκίνου, καὶ πᾶν ξύλον θύϊνον καὶ πᾶν
σκεῦος ἐλεφάντινον καὶ πᾶν σκεῦος ἐκ ξύλου τιμιωτάτου καὶ
χαλκοῦ καὶ σιδήρου καὶ μαρμάρου, 13 καὶ κιννάμωμον καὶ ἄμωμον
καὶ θυμιάματα καὶ μύρον καὶ λίβανον καὶ οἶνον καὶ ἔλαιον καὶ
σεμίδαλιν καὶ σῖτον καὶ κτήνη καὶ πρόβατα, καὶ ἵππων καὶ ῥεδῶν
καὶ σωμάτων, καὶ ψυχὰς ἀνθρώπων, 14 καὶ ἡ ὀπώρα σου τῆς
ἐπιθυμίας τῆς ψυχῆς ἀπῆλθεν ἀπὸ σοῦ, καὶ πάντα τὰ λιπαρὰ καὶ
τὰ λαμπρὰ ἀπώλοντο ἀπὸ σοῦ, καὶ οὐκέτι οὐ μὴ αὐτὰ εὑρήσουσιν.
15 οἱ ἔμποροι τούτων, οἱ πλουτήσαντες ἀπ' αὐτῆς, ἀπὸ μακρόθεν
στήσονται διὰ τὸν φόβον τοῦ βασανισμοῦ αὐτῆς κλαίοντες καὶ
πενθοῦντες, 16 λέγοντες· οὐαὶ οὐαί, ἡ πόλις ἡ μεγάλη, ἡ περιβεβλημένη βύσσινον καὶ πορφυροῦν καὶ κόκκινον, καὶ κεχρυσωμένη ἐν χρυσῷ καὶ λίθῳ τιμίῳ καὶ μαργαρίτῃ, ὅτι μιᾷ ὥρᾳ ἠρημώθη
ὁ τοσοῦτος πλοῦτος. 17 καὶ πᾶς κυβερνήτης καὶ πᾶς ὁ ἐπὶ τόπον
πλέων καὶ ναῦται καὶ ὅσοι τὴν θάλασσαν ἐργάζονται, ἀπὸ μακρόθεν ἔστησαν 18 καὶ ἔκραζον βλέποντες τὸν καπνὸν τῆς πυρώσεως
αὐτῆς λέγοντες· τίς ὁμοία τῇ πόλει τῇ μεγάλῃ; 19 καὶ ἔβαλον
χοῦν ἐπὶ τὰς κεφαλὰς αὐτῶν καὶ ἔκραζον κλαίοντες καὶ πενθοῦντες, λέγοντες· οὐαὶ οὐαί, ἡ πόλις ἡ μεγάλη, ἐν ᾗ ἐπλούτησαν

§ XV

End of the World-rule

xviii. 6 mix to her double[1]. 7 According as she glorified
herself and wantoned give to her trial and grief, for in her
heart she says: I am seated as a queen, I am no widow and
grief shall I never see. 8 For this shall her plagues come in
one day—pestilence and grief and famine. And with fire
shall she be burned, because strong is the Lord God who
judges her. 9 Then shall the kings of the earth, who committed fornication and wantoned with her, weep and wail over
her, when they see the smoke of her burning. 10 Having
taken their stand afar off for fear of her trial, they shall say:
Woe, woe, the Great City, Babylon the strong city! for in
one hour thy judgment has come. 11 Over her the merchants
of the earth weep and grieve, because no one any more buys
their lading—12 lading of gold and silver and precious stone
and pearls and fine linen and purple and silk and scarlet. No
one buys any thyine wood, any ivory vessel, any vessel of
precious wood or brass or iron or marble, 13 or cinnamon
or spice or incense or perfume, or frankincense or wine or
oil, or fine flour or wheat, or cattle or sheep, nor of horses or
chariots or bodies, that is lives of men. 14 The fruit of thy
soul's desire has gone from thee. All that gives softness and
all that gives brightness are lost utterly from thee, never any
more shall they be found. 15 The merchants of these things
who became rich by her shall stand far away from fear of her
trial, weeping and grieving, 16 saying: Woe, woe, the Great
City, once arrayed in fine linen and purple and scarlet, decked
in gold and precious stone and pearl. For in one hour wealth
so great has been reft away. 17 Every steersman and every
one sailing towards a place, and sailors, yea whosoever live by
the sea, stood afar off, 18 and seeing the smoke of her burning
cried out saying: What *city* is like the Great City! 19 And
they cast dust on their heads and cried out, weeping and
grieving, saying: Woe, woe the city, the Great City whereby
were enriched

[1] Jer. xvi. 18. I will recompense their iniquity and their sin double. xvii. 18. And destroy them with double destruction.

§ XVI

Ch. xviii. 19—xix. 9

πάντες οἱ ἔχοντες τὰ πλοῖα ἐν τῇ θαλάσσῃ ἐκ τῆς τιμιότητος
αὐτῆς, ὅτι μιᾷ ὥρᾳ ἠρημώθη. 20 εὐφραίνου ἐπ' αὐτῇ, οὐρανὲ καὶ
οἱ ἅγιοι καὶ οἱ ἀπόστολοι καὶ οἱ προφῆται, ὅτι ἔκρινεν ὁ θεὸς τὸ
κρίμα ὑμῶν ἐξ αὐτῆς. 21 καὶ ἦρεν εἷς ἄγγελος ἰσχυρὸς λίθον ὡς
μῦλον μέγαν, καὶ ἔβαλεν εἰς τὴν θάλασσαν λέγων· οὕτως ὁρμή-
ματι βληθήσεται Βαβυλὼν ἡ μεγάλη πόλις. * 22 καὶ φωνὴ κιθα-
ρῳδῶν καὶ μουσικῶν καὶ αὐλητῶν καὶ σαλπιστῶν οὐ μὴ ἀκουσθῇ
ἐν σοὶ ἔτι, καὶ πᾶς τεχνίτης πάσης τέχνης οὐ μὴ εὑρεθῇ ἐν σοὶ
ἔτι, καὶ φωνὴ μύλου οὐ μὴ ἀκουσθῇ ἐν σοὶ ἔτι, 23 καὶ φῶς
λύχνου οὐ μὴ φάνῃ ἐν σοὶ ἔτι, καὶ φωνὴ νυμφίου καὶ νύμφης οὐ
μὴ ἀκουσθῇ ἐν σοὶ ἔτι, ὅτι οἱ ἔμποροί σου ἦσαν οἱ μεγιστᾶνες
τῆς γῆς, ὅτι ἐν τῇ φαρμακίᾳ σοῦ ἐπλανήθησαν πάντα τὰ ἔθνη,
24 καὶ ἐν αὐτῇ αἵματα προφητῶν καὶ ἁγίων εὑρέθη καὶ πάντων
τῶν ἐσφαγμένων ἐπὶ τῆς γῆς. 1 Μετὰ ταῦτα ἤκουσα ὡς φωνὴν
μεγάλην ὄχλου πολλοῦ ἐν τῷ οὐρανῷ λεγόντων· ἀλληλούϊα,
ἡ σωτηρία καὶ ἡ δόξα καὶ ἡ δύναμις τοῦ θεοῦ ἡμῶν, 2 ὅτι
ἀληθιναὶ καὶ δίκαιαι αἱ κρίσεις αὐτοῦ, ὅτι ἔκρινεν τὴν πόρνην τὴν
μεγάλην ἥτις ἔφθειρεν τὴν γῆν ἐν τῇ πορνείᾳ αὐτῆς, καὶ ἐξε-
δίκησεν τὸ αἷμα τῶν δούλων αὐτοῦ ἐκ χειρὸς αὐτῆς. 3 καὶ δεύτερον εἴρηκαν· ἀλληλούϊα, καὶ ὁ καπνὸς αὐτῆς ἀναβαίνει εἰς τοὺς
αἰῶνας τῶν αἰώνων. 4 καὶ ἔπεσαν οἱ πρεσβύτεροι οἱ εἴκοσι τέσσαρες καὶ τὰ τέσσερα ζῷα, καὶ προσεκύνησαν τῷ θεῷ τῷ καθημένῳ ἐπὶ τῷ θρόνῳ λέγοντες· ἀμὴν ἀλληλούϊα. 5 καὶ φωνὴ
ἐκ τοῦ θρόνου ἐξῆλθεν λέγουσα· αἰνεῖτε τῷ θεῷ ἡμῶν, πάντες
οἱ δοῦλοι αὐτοῦ, οἱ φοβούμενοι αὐτόν, οἱ μικροὶ καὶ οἱ μεγάλοι.
6 καὶ ἤκουσα ὡς φωνὴν ὄχλου πολλοῦ καὶ ὡς φωνὴν ὑδάτων
πολλῶν καὶ ὡς φωνὴν βροντῶν ἰσχυρῶν, λεγόντων· ἀλληλούϊα,
ὅτι ἐβασίλευσεν κύριος ὁ θεὸς ἡμῶν ὁ παντοκράτωρ. 7 χαί-
ρωμεν καὶ ἀγαλλιῶμεν, καὶ δῶμεν τὴν δόξαν αὐτῷ, ὅτι ἦλθεν ὁ
γάμος τοῦ ἀρνίου καὶ ἡ γυνὴ αὐτοῦ ἡτοίμασεν ἑαυτήν, 8 καὶ ἐδόθη
αὐτῇ ἵνα περιβάληται βύσσινον λαμπρὸν καθαρόν. τὸ γὰρ βύσσινον τὰ δικαιώματα τῶν ἁγίων ἐστίν. 9 καὶ λέγει μοι· γράψον·
μακάριοι οἱ εἰς τὸ δεῖπνον τοῦ γάμου τοῦ ἀρνίου κεκλημένοι.

§ XVI

END OF THE WORLD-RULE

XVIII. 19 all having ships on the sea, even from her cost-
liness! For in one hour she has been laid waste. 20 Rejoice
over her O heaven and ye saints and apostles and prophets,
because God has judged your judgment on her. 21 Then
a strong angel raised a stone like a great mill-stone and
cast it into the sea, saying: Thus, with an impulsion shall
Babylon the Great City be hurled down. 22 Note of harpers
shall never more be heard in thee, nor of minstrels or flute-
players or trumpeters, nor in thee ever more be found any
craftsman of any trade. Never in thee again shall sound of
mill-stone be heard, 23 nor light of lamp ever shine, nor voice
of bridegroom or bride ever again be heard[1]. For thy merchants were the magnates of the earth, and by thy enchant-
ment all nations were deceived. 24 In her the blood of prophets and saints was found, yea of all slain upon the earth.
XIX. 1 Thereafter I heard as it were a great voice of a vast
multitude saying: Hallelujah, the salvation and the glory and
the power of our God! 2 for true and righteous are His judgments. For He has judged the great harlot who has destroyed
the earth with her fornication, and exacted at her hand justice
for the blood of His servants. 3 And once again they said:
Hallelujah. Her smoke goes up for ages of ages[2]. 4 Then the
twenty-four elders and the four living creatures fell down and
worshipped the God who sits on the throne, saying: Amen,
Hallelujah. 5 Then a voice came forth from the throne, saying: Praise our God, all His servants, those who fear Him,
small and great. 6 Then, like the sound of a vast multitude,
like the sound of many waters, like the sound of heavy
thunders, I heard them saying: Hallelujah! for the All-
sovereign Lord our God now reigns. 7 Let us rejoice and
exult and give Him the glory, because the marriage of the
Lamb has come, and His wife has made herself ready, 8 and
it has been granted her that she be clothed in fine linen, bright
and pure, the linen being the righteous doings of the saints[3].
9 And he said to me, write: Blessed are those who are called
to the marriage-supper of the Lamb[4].

[1] Jer. xxv. 10. Moreover I will take from them the voice of mirth, etc. [2] Is. xxxiv. 10. It shall not be quenched night nor day; the smoke thereof shall go up for ever: from generation to generation it shall lie waste. [3] Is. lii. 1. Awake, awake, put on thy strength, O Zion: put on thy beautiful garments, O Jerusalem, the holy city; for henceforth there shall no more come into thee the uncircumcised and the unclean. lx. i. Arise, shine; for thy light has come, and the glory of the Lord is risen upon thee. [4] Lk. xiv. 15. Blessed is he that shall eat bread in the kingdom of God...a certain man made a great supper, and he bade many. Mt. xxii. 2. The kingdom of heaven is likened unto a certain king, who made a marriage feast for his son.

§ XVII

Ch. XXI. 9–23

9 Καὶ ἦλθεν εἷς ἐκ τῶν ἑπτὰ ἀγγέλων τῶν ἐχόντων τὰς ἑπτὰ
φιάλας τῶν γεμόντων τῶν ἑπτὰ πληγῶν, * καὶ ἐλάλησεν μετ' ἐμοῦ
λέγων· δεῦρο, δείξω σοι τὴν νύμφην τὴν γυναῖκα τοῦ ἀρνίου.
10 καὶ ἀπήνεγκέν με ἐν πνεύματι ἐπὶ ὄρος μέγα καὶ ὑψηλόν, καὶ
ἔδειξέν μοι τὴν πόλιν τὴν ἁγίαν Ἱερουσαλὴμ καταβαίνουσαν ἐκ
τοῦ οὐρανοῦ ἀπὸ τοῦ θεοῦ, 11 ἔχουσαν τὴν δόξαν τοῦ θεοῦ· ὁ
φωστὴρ αὐτῆς ὅμοιος λίθῳ τιμιωτάτῳ, ὡς λίθῳ ἰάσπιδι κρυσταλ-
λίζοντι· 12 ἔχουσα τεῖχος μέγα καὶ ὑψηλόν, ἔχουσα πυλῶνας
δώδεκα, καὶ ἐπὶ τοῖς πυλῶσιν ἀγγέλους δώδεκα, καὶ ὀνόματα
ἐπιγεγραμμένα, ἅ ἐστιν τῶν δώδεκα φυλῶν υἱῶν Ἰσραήλ. 13 ἀπὸ
ἀνατολῆς πυλῶνες τρεῖς, καὶ ἀπὸ βορρᾶ πυλῶνες τρεῖς, καὶ ἀπὸ
νότου πυλῶνες τρεῖς, καὶ ἀπὸ δυσμῶν πυλῶνες τρεῖς. 14 καὶ τὸ
τεῖχος τῆς πόλεως ἔχων θεμελίους δώδεκα, καὶ ἐπ' αὐτῶν δώδεκα
ὀνόματα τῶν δώδεκα ἀποστόλων τοῦ ἀρνίου. 15 καὶ ὁ λαλῶν μετ'
ἐμοῦ εἶχεν μέτρον κάλαμον χρυσοῦν, ἵνα μετρήσῃ τὴν πόλιν καὶ
τοὺς πυλῶνας αὐτῆς καὶ τὸ τεῖχος αὐτῆς. 16 καὶ ἡ πόλις τετρά-
γωνος κεῖται, καὶ τὸ μῆκος αὐτῆς ὅσον τὸ πλάτος. * καὶ ἐμέτρησεν
τὴν πόλιν τῷ καλάμῳ ἐπὶ σταδίων δώδεκα χιλιάδων· τὸ μῆκος
καὶ τὸ πλάτος αὐτῆς ἴσα ἐστίν. 17 καὶ ἐμέτρησεν τὸ τεῖχος
αὐτῆς ἑκατὸν τεσσεράκοντα τεσσάρων πηχῶν, μέτρον ἀνθρώπου,
ὅ ἐστιν ἀγγέλου. 18 καὶ ἡ ἐνδώμησις τοῦ τείχους αὐτῆς ἴασπις,
καὶ ἡ πόλις χρυσίον καθαρὸν ὅμοιον ὑάλῳ καθαρῷ. 19 οἱ θεμέλιοι
τοῦ τείχους τῆς πόλεως παντὶ λίθῳ τιμίῳ κεκοσμημένοι· ὁ θεμέ-
λιος ὁ πρῶτος ἴασπις, ὁ δεύτερος σάπφειρος, ὁ τρίτος χαλκηδών,
ὁ τέταρτος σμάραγδος, 20 ὁ πέμπτος σαρδόνυξ, ὁ ἕκτος σάρδιον,
ὁ ἕβδομος χρυσόλιθος, ὁ ὄγδοος βήρυλλος, ὁ ἔνατος τοπάζιον,
ὁ δέκατος χρυσόπρασος, ὁ ἑνδέκατος ὑάκινθος, ὁ δωδέκατος ἀμέ-
θυστος. 21 καὶ οἱ δώδεκα πυλῶνες δώδεκα μαργαρῖται· ἀνὰ εἷς
ἕκαστος τῶν πυλώνων ἦν ἐξ ἑνὸς μαργαρίτου. καὶ ἡ πλατεῖα
τῆς πόλεως χρυσίον καθαρὸν ὡς ὕαλος διαυγής. 22 καὶ ναὸν
οὐκ εἶδον ἐν αὐτῇ· ὁ γὰρ κύριος ὁ θεὸς ὁ παντοκράτωρ ναὸς αὐτῆς
ἐστίν, καὶ τὸ ἀρνίον. 23 καὶ ἡ πόλις οὐ χρείαν ἔχει τοῦ ἡλίου
οὐδὲ τῆς σελήνης, ἵνα φαίνωσιν αὐτῇ· ἡ γὰρ δόξα τοῦ θεοῦ

§ XVII

The Millennial Rule

XXI. 9 Then came to me one of the seven angels who had
the seven vials full of the seven plagues and spake with me
saying: Come, I will show thee the bride, the Lamb's wife.
10 Then he carried me in spirit to a mountain, great and high,
and showed me the city, the Holy Jerusalem, coming down
out of heaven from God, 11 having the glory of God. Her
light was like a most precious stone, as a jasper stone clear as
crystal[1]. 12 She had a wall great and high. Her gates were
twelve and at the gates twelve angels[2]. And names were
inscribed on them, those of the twelve tribes of the children
of Israel. 13 Three gates were on the east, three on the north,
three on the south and three on the west. 14 The wall of the
city had twelve foundations, and on them were the twelve
names of the twelve apostles of the Lamb[3]. 15 He who spake
with me had a golden measuring reed that he might measure
the city, her gates and her wall. 16 The city lies four-square,
her length the same as the breadth. And he measured the
city with the reed, twelve thousand furlongs—the length and
the breadth of it are equal. 17 Then he measured her wall, a
hundred and forty-four cubits—man's measure, which is *also*
angel's. 18 The material of her wall was jasper, and the city
herself pure gold, like pure glass. 19 The foundations of the
wall of the city were embellished with every kind of precious
stone—the first foundation jasper, the second sapphire, the
third chalcedony, the fourth emerald, 20 the fifth sardonyx,
the sixth sardius, the seventh chrysolite, the eighth beryl, the
ninth topaz, the tenth chrysoprase, the eleventh jacynth, the
twelfth amethyst. 21 The twelve gates were twelve pearls,
each gate of one pearl. The street of the city was pure gold
like transparent glass[4]. 22 Temple in her I saw none, for the
All-sovereign God is her temple, and the Lamb. 23 Nor had
the city need of the sun or of the moon to shine for her, because
the glory of God[1]

[1] Num. xiv. 21. And as all the earth shall be filled with the glory of the Lord. Is. lx. 18–21. Violence shall no more be heard in thy land, desolation nor destruction within thy borders; but thou shalt call thy walls Salvation and thy gates Praise. The sun shall be no more thy light by day; neither for brightness shall the moon give light unto thee; but the Lord shall be unto thee an everlasting light, and thy God thy glory. Thy sun shall no more go down, nor shall thy moon withdraw itself; for the Lord shall be thine everlasting light, and the days of thy mourning shall be ended. Thy people also shall be all righteous. [2] lxii. 6. I have set watchmen upon thy walls, O Jerusalem. [3] Ex. xxviii. 29. The names of the children of Israel on the breastplate. [4] Is. liv. 11, 12, 14. I will set thy stones in fair colours and lay thy foundations with sapphires...and all thy border of pleasant stones....In righteousness shalt thou be established. Is. lx. 17. For brass I will bring gold.

§ XVIII

Ch. xxi. 23—xxii. 17

ἐφώτισεν αὐτήν, καὶ ὁ λύχνος αὐτῆς τὸ ἀρνίον. 24 καὶ περιπατή-
σουσιν τὰ ἔθνη διὰ τοῦ φωτὸς αὐτῆς, καὶ οἱ βασιλεῖς τῆς γῆς
φέρουσιν τὴν δόξαν αὐτῶν εἰς αὐτήν, 25 καὶ οἱ πυλῶνες αὐτῆς οὐ
μὴ κλεισθῶσιν ἡμέρας, νὺξ γὰρ οὐκ ἔσται ἐκεῖ, 26 καὶ οἴσουσιν
τὴν δόξαν καὶ τὴν τιμὴν τῶν ἐθνῶν εἰς αὐτήν. 27 καὶ οὐ μὴ
εἰσέλθῃ εἰς αὐτὴν πᾶν κοινὸν καὶ ὁ ποιῶν βδέλυγμα καὶ ψεῦδος,
εἰ μὴ οἱ γεγραμμένοι ἐν τῷ βιβλίῳ τῆς ζωῆς τοῦ ἀρνίου. 1 Καὶ
ἔδειξέν μοι ποταμὸν ὕδατος ζωῆς λαμπρὸν ὡς κρύσταλλον, ἐκ-
πορευόμενον ἐκ τοῦ θρόνου τοῦ θεοῦ καὶ τοῦ ἀρνίου. 2 ἐν μέσῳ
τῆς πλατείας αὐτῆς καὶ τοῦ ποταμοῦ ἐντεῦθεν καὶ ἐκεῖθεν ξύλον
ζωῆς ποιῶν καρποὺς δώδεκα, κατὰ μῆνα ἕκαστον ἀποδιδοὺς τὸν
καρπὸν αὐτοῦ, καὶ τὰ φύλλα τοῦ ξύλου εἰς θεραπείαν τῶν ἐθνῶν.
3 καὶ πᾶν κατάθεμα οὐκ ἔσται ἔτι. καὶ ὁ θρόνος τοῦ θεοῦ καὶ τοῦ
ἀρνίου ἐν αὐτῇ ἔσται, καὶ οἱ δοῦλοι αὐτοῦ λατρεύσουσιν αὐτῷ
4 καὶ ὄψονται τὸ πρόσωπον αὐτοῦ, καὶ τὸ ὄνομα αὐτοῦ ἐπὶ τῶν
μετώπων αὐτῶν. 5 καὶ νὺξ οὐκ ἔσται ἔτι, καὶ οὐκ ἔχουσιν χρείαν
φωτὸς λύχνου καὶ φωτὸς ἡλίου, ὅτι κύριος ὁ θεὸς φωτιεῖ ἐπ᾽
αὐτούς, καὶ βασιλεύσουσιν εἰς τοὺς αἰῶνας τῶν αἰώνων. * 10 καὶ
λέγει μοι· μὴ σφραγίσῃς τοὺς λόγους τῆς προφητείας τοῦ βιβλίου
τούτου· ὁ καιρὸς γὰρ ἐγγύς ἐστιν. 11 ὁ ἀδικῶν ἀδικησάτω ἔτι,
καὶ ὁ ῥυπαρὸς ῥυπανθήτω ἔτι, καὶ ὁ δίκαιος δικαιοσύνην ποιησάτω
ἔτι, καὶ ὁ ἅγιος ἁγιασθήτω ἔτι. 12 ἰδοὺ ἔρχομαι ταχύ, καὶ ὁ
μισθός μου μετ᾽ ἐμοῦ, ἀποδοῦναι ἑκάστῳ ὡς τὸ ἔργον ἐστὶν
αὐτοῦ. 13 ἐγὼ τὸ ἄλφα καὶ τὸ ω, ὁ πρῶτος καὶ ὁ ἔσχατος,
ἡ ἀρχὴ καὶ τὸ τέλος. 14 μακάριοι οἱ πλύνοντες τὰς στολὰς
αὐτῶν, ἵνα ἔσται ἡ ἐξουσία αὐτῶν ἐπὶ τὸ ξύλον τῆς ζωῆς καὶ τοῖς
πυλῶσιν εἰσέλθωσιν εἰς τὴν πόλιν. 15 ἔξω οἱ κύνες καὶ οἱ φαρ-
μακοὶ καὶ οἱ πόρνοι καὶ οἱ φονεῖς καὶ οἱ εἰδωλολάτραι καὶ πᾶς
ποιῶν καὶ φιλῶν ψεῦδος. 16 ἐγὼ Ἰησοῦς ἔπεμψα τὸν ἄγγελόν
μου μαρτυρῆσαι ὑμῖν ταῦτα ἐπὶ ταῖς ἐκκλησίαις. ἐγώ εἰμι ἡ ῥίζα
καὶ τὸ γένος Δαυείδ, ὁ ἀστὴρ ὁ λαμπρὸς ὁ πρωϊνός. 17 καὶ τὸ
πνεῦμα καὶ ἡ νύμφη λέγουσιν· ἔρχου. καὶ ὁ ἀκούων εἰπάτω· ἔρχου.
καὶ ὁ διψῶν ἐρχέσθω, ὁ θέλων λαβέτω ὕδωρ ζωῆς δωρεάν.

§ XVIII

THE MILLENNIAL RULE

XXI. 23 illumined her and the Lamb is her lamp. 24 In her
light shall the nations walk, and into her the kings of the earth
bring their glory. 25 Her gates shall not be shut by day, for
night is not there. 26 And they will bring into her the glory
and the honour of the Gentiles[1]. 27 Nothing profane shall
enter her, no one doing abomination or falsehood, none save
those written in the Lamb's book of life. XXII. 1 Then he
showed me a river of water of life, bright like crystal, issuing
forth from the throne of God and of the Lamb. 2 In the
middle of her street and on both sides of the river was a tree
of life, bearing twelve fruitings, producing its fruit each month.
And the leaves of the tree are for the healing of the nations[2].
3 Nothing dedicated to evil shall any more be, but the throne
of God and of the Lamb shall be in her, and His servants shall
serve Him 4 and shall see His face, having His name on their
foreheads. 5 And there shall be no night there, nor have they
need of light of lamp or light of sun, for the Lord God shall
shine on them[3]. And they shall reign to ages of ages[4]. 10 Then
he says to me: Do not seal up the words of the prophecy of
this roll for the time is near. 11 Let the unjust be unjust still
and the filthy be filthy still, but let the righteous do righteousness still and the holy be holy still[5]. 12 Lo I come quickly
and my reward is with me, to render to each as his work is.
13 I am the alpha and the omega, the first and the last, the
beginning and the end. 14 Blessed are those washing their
robes, that their authority may be over the tree of life when
they have entered by the gates into the city. 15 Without are
the shameless, the sorcerers, the fornicators, the murderers,
the idolaters, and everyone making and loving falsehood.
16 I Jesus sent my angel to testify to you these things concerning the churches. I am the root and the descendant of
David, the bright, the morning star. 17 The Spirit and the
bride say, come. And whosoever hears let him say, come.
And whosoever thirsts, let him come. Whosoever will, let
him take the water of life freely.

[1] Is. lx. 11. Thy gates shall be open continually; they shall not be shut day nor night; that men may bring unto thee the wealth of the nations, and their kings led with them. [2] Jer. ii. 13. They have forsaken me the fountain of living waters. Ez. xlvii. 12. And by the river upon the bank thereof, on this side and on that side, shall grow every tree for food, whose leaf shall not wither, neither shall the fruit thereof fail; it shall bring forth new fruit every month, because the waters thereof issue out of the sanctuary: and the fruit thereof shall be for food, and the leaf thereof for healing. [3] Is. lx. 20. Thy sun shall no more go down...for the Lord shall be thine everlasting light. [4] Dan. vii. 18. But the saints of the Most High shall receive the kingdom, and possess the kingdom for ever, even for ever and ever. [5] Dan. xii. 10. Many shall purify themselves...but the wicked shall do wickedly.

§ XIX

CH. XVI. 15, XIX. 9, 10, XX. 1–10

15 ἰδοὺ ἔρχομαι ὡς κλέπτης· μακάριος ὁ γρηγορῶν καὶ τηρῶν τὰ
ἱμάτια αὐτοῦ, ἵνα μὴ γυμνὸς περιπατῇ καὶ βλέπωσιν τὴν ἀσχη-
μοσύνην αὐτοῦ. XIX. 9 καὶ λέγει μοι· οὗτοι οἱ λόγοι ἀληθινοὶ τοῦ
θεοῦ εἰσίν. 10 καὶ ἔπεσα ἔμπροσθεν τῶν ποδῶν αὐτοῦ προσκυνῆσαι
αὐτῷ. καὶ λέγει μοι· ὅρα μή· σύνδουλός σου εἰμὶ καὶ τῶν ἀδελφῶν
σου τῶν ἐχόντων τὴν μαρτυρίαν τῶν προφήτων[1]· τῷ θεῷ προσκύνησον. ἡ γὰρ μαρτυρία Ἰησοῦ ἐστὶν τὸ πνεῦμα τῆς προφητείας.
XX. 1 καὶ ἴδον ἄγγελον καταβαίνοντα ἐκ τοῦ οὐρανοῦ, ἔχοντα τὴν
κλεῖν τῆς ἀβύσσου καὶ ἅλυσιν μεγάλην ἐπὶ τὴν χεῖρα αὐτοῦ.
2 καὶ ἐκράτησεν τὸν δράκοντα, ὁ ὄφις ὁ ἀρχαῖος, ὅ ἐστιν ὁ διάβολος καὶ ὁ σατανᾶς, καὶ ἔδησεν αὐτὸν χίλια ἔτη, 3 καὶ ἔβαλεν
αὐτὸν εἰς τὴν ἄβυσσον, καὶ ἔκλεισεν καὶ ἐσφράγισεν ἐπάνω αὐτοῦ,
ἵνα μὴ πλανήσῃ ἔτι τὰ ἔθνη, ἄχρι τελεσθῇ τὰ χίλια ἔτη· μετὰ
ταῦτα δεῖ αὐτὸν λυθῆναι μικρὸν χρόνον. 4 καὶ ἴδον θρόνους, καὶ
ἐκάθισαν ἐπ' αὐτούς, καὶ κρίμα ἐδόθη αὐτοῖς, καὶ τὰς ψυχὰς τῶν
πεπελεκισμένων διὰ τὴν μαρτυρίαν Ἰησοῦ καὶ διὰ τὸν λόγον τοῦ
θεοῦ, καὶ οἵτινες οὐ προσεκύνησαν τὸ θηρίον οὐδὲ τὴν εἰκόνα
αὐτοῦ καὶ οὐκ ἔλαβον τὸ χάραγμα ἐπὶ τὸ μέτωπον καὶ ἐπὶ τὴν
χεῖρα αὐτῶν· καὶ ἔζησαν καὶ ἐβασίλευσαν μετὰ τοῦ Χριστοῦ
χίλια ἔτη. 5 οἱ λοιποὶ τῶν νεκρῶν οὐκ ἔζησαν ἄχρι τελεσθῇ
τὰ χίλια ἔτη. αὕτη ἡ ἀνάστασις ἡ πρώτη. 6 μακάριος καὶ
ἅγιος ὁ ἔχων μέρος ἐν τῇ ἀναστάσει τῇ πρώτῃ· ἐπὶ τούτων ὁ
δεύτερος θάνατος οὐκ ἔχει ἐξουσίαν, ἀλλὰ ἔσονται ἱερεῖς τοῦ
θεοῦ καὶ τοῦ Χριστοῦ, καὶ βασιλεύσουσιν μετ' αὐτοῦ τὰ χίλια
ἔτη. 7 καὶ ὅταν τελεσθῇ τὰ χίλια ἔτη, λυθήσεται ὁ σατανᾶς ἐκ
τῆς φυλακῆς αὐτοῦ, 8 καὶ ἐξελεύσεται πλανῆσαι τὰ ἔθνη τὰ ἐν
ταῖς τέσσαρσιν γωνίαις τῆς γῆς, τὸν Γὼγ καὶ Μαγώγ, συναγαγεῖν
αὐτοὺς εἰς τὸν πόλεμον, ὧν ὁ ἀριθμὸς αὐτῶν ὡς ἡ ἄμμος τῆς
θαλάσσης. 9 καὶ ἀνέβησαν ἐπὶ τὸ πλάτος τῆς γῆς, καὶ ἐκύκλευ-
σαν τὴν παρεμβολὴν τῶν ἁγίων καὶ τὴν πόλιν τὴν ἠγαπημένην·
καὶ κατέβη πῦρ ἐκ τοῦ οὐρανοῦ καὶ κατέφαγεν αὐτούς· 10 καὶ
ὁ διάβολος ὁ πλανῶν αὐτοὺς ἐβλήθη εἰς τὴν λίμνην τοῦ πυρὸς
καὶ τοῦ θείου, ὅπου καὶ τὸ θηρίον καὶ ὁ ψευδοπροφήτης, καὶ

[1] Geb. Ἰησοῦ.

§ XIX

The Millennial Rule

xvi. 15 Lo I come as a thief. Blessed is he who is watching
and keeping his garments[1], that he walk not naked and men
behold his shame. xix. 9 And he says to me: These are the
true words of God. 10 Then I fell before his feet to worship
him, but he says to me: See thou do it not. I am thy fellow-
servant and of thy brethren who hold the witness of the
prophets. Worship God. For the witness of Jesus is the spirit
of prophecy. xx. 1 Then I saw an angel coming down out of
heaven, having the key of the abyss and a great chain in his
hand. 2 And he mastered the dragon, the serpent, the ancient
one, who is the Devil and Satan, and bound him for a thousand
years, 3 and cast him into the abyss and shut and sealed it
upon him, that he might not any more deceive the nations till
the thousand years have been completed. Thereafter he must
be let loose a little time. 4 Then I saw thrones, and they sat
on them and judgment was given to them[2]—the souls of those
beheaded for the witness of Jesus and the word of God, and
whosoever had not worshipped the beast nor his image and
had not received the mark on their foreheads and on their
hands. They lived and reigned with Christ a thousand years.
5 The rest of the dead did not live until the thousand years
were ended. This is the first resurrection. 6 Blessed and holy
is he who has part in this first resurrection. Over them the
second death has not power, but they shall be priests of God
and of Christ, and shall reign with Him the thousand years.
7 But when the thousand years are ended, Satan shall be loosed
from his prison, 8 and shall come forth to deceive the nations
which are in the four corners of the earth, Gog and Magog,
to gather them to battle, their number being as the sand of
the sea[3]. 9 They came up over the breadth of the earth and
encircled the encampment of the saints, even the beloved
city. But fire came down from heaven and consumed them[4].
10 And the Devil who deceived them was cast into the lake of
fire and brimstone, where is the beast and the false prophet;

[1] Lk. xii. 39, 40. If the master of the house had known in what hour the thief was coming, he would have watched....Be ye also ready, for in an hour that ye think not the Son of Man cometh. [2] Dan. vii. 22. And judgment was given to the saints of the Most High. [3] Ez. xxxviii. 2. Son of Man set thy face toward Gog of the land of Magog. *vv.* 15, 16. And thou shalt come from thy place out of the uttermost parts of the north, thou and many peoples with thee, all of them riding upon horses, a great company and a mighty army: and thou shalt come up against my people Israel, as a cloud to cover the land. [4] Ez. xxxviii. 22. And I will rain upon him and upon his hordes...great hailstones, fire and brimstone.

§ XX

Ch. xx. 10, iv. 1—v. 2

βασανισθήσονται ἡμέρας καὶ νυκτὸς[1] *εἰς τοὺς αἰῶνας τῶν αἰώνων.*
1 Μετὰ ταῦτα ἴδον, καὶ ἰδοὺ θύρα ἠνεῳγμένη ἐν τῷ οὐρανῷ,
καὶ ἡ φωνὴ ἡ πρώτη ἣν ἤκουσα ὡς σάλπιγγος λαλούσης μετ'
ἐμοῦ, λέγων· ἀνάβα ὧδε, καὶ δείξω σοι ἃ δεῖ γενέσθαι μετὰ
ταῦτα. 2 εὐθέως ἐγενόμην ἐν πνεύματι· καὶ ἰδοὺ θρόνος ἔκειτο
ἐν τῷ οὐρανῷ, καὶ ἐπὶ τὸν θρόνον καθήμενος, 3 καὶ ὁ καθήμενος
ὅμοιος ὁράσει λίθῳ ἰάσπιδι καὶ σαρδίῳ, καὶ ἶρις κυκλόθεν τοῦ
θρόνου ὅμοιος ὁράσει σμαραγδίνῳ. 4 καὶ κυκλόθεν τοῦ θρόνου
θρόνους εἴκοσι τέσσαρας, καὶ ἐπὶ τοὺς θρόνους εἴκοσι τέσσαρας
πρεσβυτέρους καθημένους περιβεβλημένους ἐν ἱματίοις λευκοῖς,
καὶ ἐπὶ τὰς κεφαλὰς αὐτῶν στεφάνους χρυσοῦς. 5 καὶ ἐκ τοῦ
θρόνου ἐκπορεύονται ἀστραπαὶ καὶ φωναὶ καὶ βρονταί· καὶ ἑπτὰ
λαμπάδες πυρὸς καιόμεναι ἐνώπιον τοῦ θρόνου, ἅ εἰσιν τὰ ἑπτὰ
πνεύματα τοῦ θεοῦ· 6 καὶ ἐνώπιον τοῦ θρόνου ὡς θάλασσα ὑαλίνη
ὁμοία κρυστάλλῳ· καὶ ἐν μέσῳ τοῦ θρόνου καὶ κύκλῳ τοῦ θρόνου
τέσσερα ζῶα γέμοντα ὀφθαλμῶν ἔμπροσθεν καὶ ὄπισθεν. 7 καὶ
τὸ ζῶον τὸ πρῶτον ὅμοιον λέοντι, καὶ τὸ δεύτερον ζῶον ὅμοιον
μόσχῳ, καὶ τὸ τρίτον ζῶον ἔχων τὸ πρόσωπον ὡς ἀνθρώπου, καὶ
τὸ τέταρτον ζῶον ὅμοιον ἀετῷ πετομένῳ. 8 καὶ τὰ τέσσερα ζῶα,
ἓν καθ' ἓν αὐτῶν ἔχων ἀνὰ πτέρυγας ἕξ, κυκλόθεν καὶ ἔσωθεν
γέμουσιν ὀφθαλμῶν, καὶ ἀνάπαυσιν οὐκ ἔχουσιν ἡμέρας καὶ
νυκτὸς λέγοντες· ἅγιος ἅγιος ἅγιος κύριος ὁ θεὸς ὁ παντοκράτωρ
ὁ ἦν καὶ ὁ ὢν καὶ ὁ ἐρχόμενος. 9 καὶ ὅταν δώσουσιν τὰ ζῶα
δόξαν καὶ τιμὴν καὶ εὐχαριστίαν τῷ καθημένῳ ἐπὶ τῷ θρόνῳ
τῷ ζῶντι εἰς τοὺς αἰῶνας τῶν αἰώνων, 10 πεσοῦνται οἱ εἴκοσι
τέσσαρες πρεσβύτεροι ἐνώπιον τοῦ καθημένου ἐπὶ τοῦ θρόνου,
καὶ προσκυνήσουσιν τῷ ζῶντι εἰς τοὺς αἰῶνας τῶν αἰώνων, καὶ
βαλοῦσιν τοὺς στεφάνους αὐτῶν ἐνώπιον τοῦ θρόνου, λέγοντες·
11 ἄξιος εἶ, ὁ κύριος καὶ ὁ θεὸς ἡμῶν, λαβεῖν τὴν δόξαν καὶ
τὴν τιμὴν καὶ τὴν δύναμιν, ὅτι σὺ ἔκτισας τὰ πάντα, καὶ διὰ
τὸ θέλημά σου ἦσαν καὶ ἐκτίσθησαν. v. 1 καὶ εἶδον ἐπὶ τὴν
δεξιὰν τοῦ καθημένου ἐπὶ τοῦ θρόνου βιβλίον γεγραμμένον ἔσωθεν καὶ ὄπισθεν, κατεσφραγισμένον σφραγῖσιν ἑπτά. 2 καὶ εἶδον

[1] 'Day and night' probably a gloss (note, p. 144).

§ XX

THE LAST THINGS

XX. 10 and they shall be tested to the ages of ages. IV. 1 Thereafter I saw and lo a door opened in heaven, and the first voice
which I heard as a trumpet speaking with me is saying: Come
up hither, and I will show thee what must come to pass after
these things. 2 Straightway I was in the spirit, and lo a throne
was set in heaven and sitting on the throne 3 was one like in
appearance to a jasper stone and a sardius, and the rainbow
round about the throne was like in appearance to an emerald[1].
4 Around the throne were twenty-four thrones, and on the
thrones twenty-four elders sitting clothed in white garments,
and on their heads golden crowns. 5 From the throne were
going forth lightnings and voices and thunders, and before
the throne were burning seven torches of fire, which are the
seven spirits of God[2]. 6 Also before the throne as it were a
glassy sea like crystal[3]. In the midst of the throne and round
about the throne were four living creatures, full of eyes before
and behind—7 the first living creature being like a lion, the
second like an ox, the third having its face like a man's, and
the fourth being like a flying eagle. 8 Each of the four living
creatures had six wings, round about and on the inner side
full of eyes[4]. Without ceasing day and night they say: Holy,
holy, holy Lord, the all-sovereign God, who was, who is, and
is to be[5]. 9 And whensoever the living creatures will give
glory and honour and thanks to Him who sits on the throne
—the living one to ages of ages—10 the twenty-four elders
will fall down before Him who sits on the throne and worship
Him who is the living one to ages of ages and cast their crowns
before His throne saying: 11 Worthy art Thou, Lord and our
God, to receive the glory and the honour and the power,
because Thou has created all things, and by Thy will they
were, even were created. V. 1 Then I saw on the right hand of
Him who was sitting on the throne, a roll written within and
without, sealed with seven seals. 2 And I saw

[1] Ez. i. 26 ff. And above the firmament that was over their heads, was the likeness of a throne as the appearance of a sapphire stone...a likeness as the appearance of a man upon it above. And I saw as the colour of amber as the appearance of fire...and there was brightness round about him. As the appearance of the bow that is in the cloud....This was the appearance of the likeness of the glory of the Lord. [2] Dan. x. 6. His eyes as lamps of fire. Is. iii. 8. The eyes of his glory. [3] 1 K. vii. 23. He made a molten sea. Ez. i. 22. A firmament like the colour of the terrible crystal. [4] Ez. i. 10. They had the face of a man; and the four had the face of a lion on the right side; and the four had the face of an ox on the left side; the four had also the face of an eagle. *v.* 18. And they four had their rings full of eyes round about. [5] Is. vi. 1. The Lord sitting upon a throne high and lifted up...seraphim: each one had six wings and said Holy, holy, holy is the Lord of hosts: the whole earth is full of his glory.

§ XXI

Ch. v. 2—vi. 1.

ἄγγελον ἰσχυρὸν κηρύσσοντα ἐν φωνῇ μεγάλῃ· τίς ἄξιος ἀνοῖξαι
τὸ βιβλίον καὶ λῦσαι τὰς σφραγῖδας αὐτοῦ; 3 καὶ οὐδεὶς ἐδύνατο
ἐν τῷ οὐρανῷ οὔτε ἐπὶ τῆς γῆς οὔτε ὑποκάτω τῆς γῆς ἀνοῖξαι τὸ
βιβλίον οὔτε βλέπειν αὐτό. 4 καὶ ἔκλαιον πολύ, ὅτι οὐδεὶς ἄξιος
εὑρέθη ἀνοῖξαι τὸ βιβλίον οὔτε βλέπειν αὐτό. 5 καὶ εἷς ἐκ τῶν
πρεσβυτέρων λέγει μοι· μὴ κλαῖε· ἰδοὺ ἐνίκησεν ὁ λέων ὁ ἐκ τῆς
φυλῆς Ἰούδα, ἡ ῥίζα Δαυείδ, ἀνοῖξαι τὸ βιβλίον καὶ τὰς ἑπτὰ
σφραγῖδας αὐτοῦ. 6 Καὶ εἶδον ἐν μέσῳ τοῦ θρόνου καὶ τῶν
τεσσάρων ζώων καὶ ἐν μέσῳ τῶν πρεσβυτέρων ἀρνίον ἑστηκὼς
ὡς ἐσφαγμένον, ἔχων κέρατα ἑπτὰ καὶ ὀφθαλμοὺς ἑπτά, οἵ εἰσιν
τὰ ἑπτὰ πνεύματα τοῦ θεοῦ ἀπεσταλμένα εἰς πᾶσαν τὴν γῆν.
7 καὶ ἦλθεν καὶ εἴληφεν ἐκ τῆς δεξιᾶς τοῦ καθημένου ἐπὶ τοῦ
θρόνου. 8 καὶ ὅτε ἔλαβεν τὸ βιβλίον, τὰ τέσσερα ζῷα καὶ οἱ
εἴκοσι τέσσαρες πρεσβύτεροι ἔπεσαν ἐνώπιον τοῦ ἀρνίου, ἔχοντες
ἕκαστος κιθάραν καὶ φιάλας χρυσᾶς γεμούσας θυμιαμάτων, αἵ
εἰσιν αἱ προσευχαὶ τῶν ἁγίων. 9 καὶ ᾄδουσιν ᾠδὴν καινὴν λέ-
γοντες· ἄξιος εἶ λαβεῖν τὸ βιβλίον καὶ ἀνοῖξαι τὰς σφραγῖδας
αὐτοῦ, ὅτι ἐσφάγης καὶ ἠγόρασας τῷ θεῷ ἐν τῷ αἵματί σου ἐκ
πάσης φυλῆς καὶ γλώσσης καὶ λαοῦ καὶ ἔθνους, 10 καὶ ἐποίησας
αὐτοὺς τῷ θεῷ ἡμῶν βασιλείαν καὶ ἱερεῖς, καὶ βασιλεύσουσιν ἐπὶ
τῆς γῆς. 11 καὶ εἶδον, καὶ ἤκουσα ὡς φωνὴν ἀγγέλων πολλῶν
κύκλῳ τοῦ θρόνου καὶ τῶν ζώων καὶ τῶν πρεσβυτέρων, καὶ ἦν ὁ
ἀριθμὸς αὐτῶν μυριάδες μυριάδων καὶ χιλιάδες χιλιάδων, 12 λέ-
γοντες φωνῇ μεγάλῃ· ἄξιός ἐστιν τὸ ἀρνίον τὸ ἐσφαγμένον λαβεῖν
τὴν δύναμιν καὶ πλοῦτον καὶ σοφίαν καὶ ἰσχὺν καὶ τιμὴν καὶ
δόξαν καὶ εὐλογίαν. 13 καὶ πᾶν κτίσμα ὃ ἐν τῷ οὐρανῷ καὶ ἐπὶ
τῆς γῆς καὶ ὑποκάτω τῆς γῆς καὶ ἐπὶ τῆς θαλάσσης καὶ τὰ ἐν
αὐτοῖς πάντα καὶ ἤκουσα λέγοντας· τῷ καθημένῳ ἐπὶ τῷ θρόνῳ
καὶ τῷ ἀρνίῳ ἡ εὐλογία καὶ ἡ τιμὴ καὶ ἡ δόξα καὶ τὸ κράτος εἰς
τοὺς αἰῶνας τῶν αἰώνων. 14 καὶ τὰ τέσσερα ζῷα ἔλεγον· ἀμήν,
καὶ οἱ πρεσβύτεροι ἔπεσαν καὶ προσεκύνησαν. 1 Καὶ ἴδον ὅτε
ἤνοιξεν τὸ ἀρνίον μίαν ἐκ τῶν ἑπτὰ σφραγίδων, καὶ ἤκουσα ἑνὸς ἐκ
τῶν τεσσάρων ζώων λέγοντος ὡς φωνὴ βροντῆς· ἔρχου καὶ βλέπε[1].

[1] Omitted in Geb.

§ XXI

THE LAST THINGS

v. 2 a strong angel proclaiming with a great voice: Who is
able to open the roll and undo the seals of it? 3 But no one
in heaven or on earth or under the earth was able to open the
book or see into it. 4 Then I wept sore that no one was found
worthy to open the roll or see into it[1]. 5 But one of the elders
says to me: Do not weep. Lo the lion who is of the tribe of
Judah[2], the root of David[3], has prevailed to open the book,
even its seven seals. 6 Then I saw in the midst of the throne
and of the four living creatures, and in the midst of the elders,
a lamb standing. It was as though he had been slain[4]; and
he had seven horns and seven eyes which are the seven spirits
of God sent forth unto all the earth[5]. 7 He came and took
from the right hand of Him who is sitting on the throne.
8 And when He had taken the roll, the four living creatures
and the twenty-four elders fell before the throne, each having
a harp and golden vials full of incense, which is the prayers
of the saints[6]. 9 And they sing a new song saying: Worthy
art Thou to receive the roll and to open its seals, because
Thou wast slain and hast purchased to God with Thy
blood some from every tribe, language, people and nation,
10 and made them to our God a kingdom and priests, and
they shall reign on the earth[7]. 11 Then I saw and heard like
a voice of many angels round about the throne and the living
creatures and the elders, and their number was myriads of
myriads and thousands of thousands, 12 saying with a great
voice: Worthy is the Lamb, he who was slain, to receive the
might and riches and wisdom and strength and honour and
glory and praise. 13 And every creature that is in heaven and
in the earth and under the earth and in the sea, and all that
in them is I heard saying: To Him that sitteth on the throne
and to the Lamb be the praise and the honour and the glory
and the power to ages of ages. 14 And the four living creatures
said: Amen, and the elders fell down and worshipped.
VI. 1 And lo, when the Lamb had opened one of the seven
seals, I heard one of the living creatures saying like a voice of
thunder: Come and see[8].

[1] Dan. xii. 1. At that time thy people shall be delivered, every one that shall be found written in the book. [2] Gen. xlix. 9, 10. Judah is a lion's whelp...until Shiloh come; and unto him shall the obedience of the people be. [3] Is. xi. 10. The root of Jesse, which standeth for an ensign of the peoples. [4] Is. liii. 7. As a lamb that is led to the slaughter. [5] Dan. x. 6. His eyes like lamps of fire. Cf. Rev. iv. 5 (§ xx) and 2 Chron. xvi. 9. For the eyes of the Lord run to and fro throughout the whole earth. [6] Ps. cxli. 2. Let my prayer be set forth as incense before thee. [7] Dan. vii. 10. Thousand thousands ministered unto him and ten thousand times ten thousand stood before him. *v.* 14. There was given him dominion and glory and a kingdom. 1 Pet. ii. 9. A royal priesthood. [8] Rom. viii. 19. For the earnest expectation of the creation waiteth for the revealing of the sons of God.

§ XXII

Ch. vii. 1–17

1 Καὶ μετὰ τοῦτο ἴδον τέσσαρας ἀγγέλους ἑστῶτας ἐπὶ τὰς
τέσσαρας γωνίας τῆς γῆς, κρατοῦντας τοὺς τέσσαρας ἀνέμους τῆς
γῆς, ἵνα μὴ πνέῃ ἄνεμος ἐπὶ τῆς γῆς μήτε ἐπὶ τῆς θαλάσσης
μήτε ἐπὶ πᾶν δένδρον. 2 καὶ ἴδον ἄλλον ἄγγελον ἀναβαίνοντα
ἀπὸ ἀνατολῆς ἡλίου, ἔχοντα σφραγῖδα θεοῦ ζῶντος, καὶ ἔκραξεν
φωνῇ μεγάλῃ τοῖς τέσσαρσιν ἀγγέλοις, * 3 λέγων· μὴ ἀδικήσητε
τὴν γῆν μήτε τὴν θάλασσαν μήτε τὰ δένδρα, ἄχρι σφραγίσωμεν
τοὺς δούλους τοῦ θεοῦ ἡμῶν ἐπὶ τῶν μετώπων αὐτῶν. 4 καὶ
ἤκουσα τὸν ἀριθμὸν τῶν ἐσφραγισμένων, ἑκατὸν τεσσεράκοντα
τέσσαρες χιλιάδες ἐσφραγισμένοι ἐκ πάσης φυλῆς υἱῶν Ἰσραήλ.*
9 Μετὰ ταῦτα ἴδον, καὶ ἰδοὺ ὄχλος πολύς, ὃν ἀριθμῆσαι αὐτὸν
οὐδεὶς ἐδύνατο, ἐκ παντὸς ἔθνους καὶ φυλῶν καὶ λαῶν καὶ γλωσσῶν, ἑστῶτες ἐνώπιον τοῦ θρόνου καὶ ἐνώπιον τοῦ ἀρνίου, περιβεβλημένους στολὰς λευκάς, καὶ φοίνικας ἐν ταῖς χερσὶν αὐτῶν·
10 καὶ κράζουσιν φωνῇ μεγάλῃ λέγοντες· ἡ σωτηρία τῷ θεῷ
ἡμῶν τῷ καθημένῳ ἐπὶ τῷ θρόνῳ καὶ τῷ ἀρνίῳ. 11 καὶ πάντες οἱ
ἄγγελοι εἱστήκεισαν κύκλῳ τοῦ θρόνου καὶ τῶν πρεσβυτέρων
καὶ τῶν τεσσάρων ζώων, καὶ ἔπεσαν ἐνώπιον τοῦ θρόνου ἐπὶ τὰ
πρόσωπα αὐτῶν καὶ προσεκύνησαν τῷ θεῷ, 12 λέγοντες· ἀμήν,
ἡ εὐλογία καὶ ἡ δόξα καὶ ἡ σοφία καὶ ἡ εὐχαριστία καὶ ἡ τιμὴ
καὶ ἡ δύναμις καὶ ἡ ἰσχὺς τῷ θεῷ ἡμῶν εἰς τοὺς αἰῶνας τῶν
αἰώνων, ἀμήν. 13 καὶ ἀπεκρίθη εἷς ἐκ τῶν πρεσβυτέρων λέγων
μοι· οὗτοι οἱ περιβεβλημένοι τὰς στολὰς τὰς λευκὰς τίνες εἰσὶν
καὶ πόθεν ἦλθον; 14 καὶ εἴρηκα αὐτῷ· κύριέ μου, σὺ οἶδας. καὶ
εἶπέν μοι· οὗτοί εἰσιν οἱ ἐρχόμενοι ἐκ τῆς θλίψεως τῆς μεγάλης,
καὶ ἔπλυναν τὰς στολὰς αὐτῶν καὶ ἐλεύκαναν αὐτὰς ἐν τῷ αἵματι
τοῦ ἀρνίου. 15 διὰ τοῦτό εἰσιν ἐνώπιον τοῦ θρόνου τοῦ θεοῦ, καὶ
λατρεύουσιν αὐτῷ ἡμέρας καὶ νυκτὸς ἐν τῷ ναῷ αὐτοῦ, καὶ ὁ
καθήμενος ἐπὶ τοῦ θρόνου σκηνώσει ἐπ' αὐτούς. 16 οὐ πεινά-
σουσιν ἔτι οὐδὲ διψήσουσιν ἔτι, οὐδὲ μὴ πέσῃ ἐπ' αὐτοὺς ὁ ἥλιος
οὐδὲ πᾶν καῦμα, 17 ὅτι τὸ ἀρνίον τὸ ἀνὰ μέσον τοῦ θρόνου
ποιμανεῖ αὐτοὺς καὶ ὁδηγήσει αὐτοὺς ἐπὶ ζωῆς πηγὰς ὑδάτων,
καὶ ἐξαλείψει ὁ θεὸς πᾶν δάκρυον ἐκ τῶν ὀφθαλμῶν αὐτῶν.

§ XXII

The Last Things

VII. 1 Thereafter I saw four angels standing on the four corners of the earth[1], holding the four winds of the earth, that the wind might not blow on the earth or on the sea or on any tree[2]. 2 Then I saw another angel coming up from the rising of the sun, having the seal of the living God, and he cried with a great voice to the four angels, 3 saying: Hurt not the earth, nor the sea, nor the trees, till we have sealed the servants of God in their foreheads[3]. 4 And I heard the number of the sealed, a hundred and forty-four thousand, the sealed of every tribe of the sons of Israel. 9 Thereafter I saw and lo a great multitude which no one could number, from every nation and tribe and people and language, standing before the throne and before the Lamb, clothed in white robes and palms in their hands. 10 And they shout with a great voice saying: The salvation is our God's, who sits on the throne, and the Lamb's! 11 And all the angels were standing round about the throne and the elders and the four living creatures, and they fell before the throne on their faces and worshipped God, 12 saying: Amen, the praise and the glory and the wisdom and the thanksgiving and the honour and the power and the strength is our God's unto ages of ages, Amen. 13 Then one of the elders answered, saying to me: These that are clothed in white robes, who are they and whence have they come? 14 When I had said to him: Sir, thou knowest, he said to me: These are those coming out of great tribulation and they have washed their robes and made them white in the blood of the Lamb. 15 Therefore they are before the throne of God, and serve Him day and night in His temple; and He who is sitting on the throne will be a tent over them. 16 No more shall they ever hunger or thirst, neither shall the sun smite on them nor any heat[4]; 17 because the Lamb, He who is in the midst of the throne, shall rule them and lead them to fountains of waters of life; and God shall wipe away every tear from their eyes[5].

[1] Zech. vi. 5. These are the four spirits (R.V. winds) of heaven, which go forth from standing before the Lord of all the earth. [2] Dan. vii. 2. And behold the four winds of the heaven brake forth upon the great sea. xi. 4. His kingdom...shall be divided toward the four winds of heaven. [3] Eph. iv. 30. Sealed unto the day of redemption. [4] Is. xlix. 10. They shall not hunger nor thirst; neither shall the heat nor sun smite them: for he that hath mercy on them shall lead them, even by springs of water shall he guide them. [5] Is. xxv. 8. The Lord God will wipe away tears from off all faces.

§ XXIII

Ch. VIII. 1—IX. 7

1 Καὶ ὅταν ἤνοιξεν τὴν σφραγῖδα τὴν ἑβδόμην, ἐγένετο σιγὴ
ἐν τῷ οὐρανῷ ὡς ἡμίωρον. 2 καὶ ἴδον τοὺς ἑπτὰ ἀγγέλους οἳ
ἐνώπιον τοῦ θεοῦ ἑστήκασιν, καὶ ἐδόθησαν αὐτοῖς τρέις[1] σάλπιγγες.
3 καὶ ἄλλος ἄγγελος ἦλθεν καὶ ἐστάθη ἐπὶ τοῦ θυσιαστηρίου ἔχων
λιβανωτὸν χρυσοῦν, καὶ ἐδόθη αὐτῷ θυμιάματα πολλά, ἵνα δώσει
ταῖς προσευχαῖς τῶν ἁγίων πάντων ἐπὶ τὸ θυσιαστήριον τὸ χρυσοῦν τὸ ἐνώπιον τοῦ θρόνου. 4 καὶ ἀνέβη ὁ καπνὸς τῶν θυμιαμάτων ταῖς προσευχαῖς τῶν ἁγίων ἐκ χειρὸς τοῦ ἀγγέλου ἐνώπιον
τοῦ θεοῦ. 5 καὶ εἴληφεν ὁ ἄγγελος τὸν λιβανωτόν, καὶ ἐγέμισεν
αὐτὸν ἐκ τοῦ πυρὸς τοῦ θυσιαστηρίου καὶ ἔβαλεν εἰς τὴν γῆν· καὶ
ἐγένοντο βρονταὶ καὶ φωναὶ καὶ ἀστραπαὶ καὶ σεισμός. 6 Καὶ οἱ
* ἄγγελοι οἱ ἔχοντες τὰς * σάλπιγγας ἡτοίμασαν αὐτοὺς ἵνα σαλπί-
σωσιν. * 13 καὶ ἴδον, καὶ ἤκουσα ἑνὸς ἀετοῦ πετομένου ἐν μεσου-
ρανήματι λέγοντος φωνῇ μεγάλῃ· οὐαὶ οὐαὶ οὐαὶ τοὺς κατοικοῦντας
ἐπὶ τῆς γῆς ἐκ τῶν φωνῶν τῆς σάλπιγγος τῶν τριῶν ἀγγέλων
τῶν μελλόντων σαλπίζειν. 1 Καὶ ὁ πέμπτος ἄγγελος ἐσάλπισεν·
καὶ ἴδον ἀστέρα ἐκ τοῦ οὐρανοῦ πεπτωκότα εἰς τὴν γῆν, καὶ ἐδόθη
αὐτῷ ἡ κλεὶς τοῦ φρέατος τῆς ἀβύσσου. 2 καὶ ἤνοιξεν τὸ φρέαρ
τῆς ἀβύσσου· καὶ ἀνέβη καπνὸς ἐκ τοῦ φρέατος ὡς καπνὸς καμίνου
μεγάλης, καὶ ἐσκοτώθη ὁ ἥλιος καὶ ὁ ἀὴρ ἐκ τοῦ καπνοῦ τοῦ
φρέατος. 3 καὶ ἐκ τοῦ καπνοῦ ἐξῆλθον ἀκρίδες εἰς τὴν γῆν, καὶ
ἐδόθη αὐτοῖς ἐξουσία ὡς ἔχουσιν ἐξουσίαν οἱ σκορπίοι τῆς γῆς.
4 καὶ ἐρρέθη αὐτοῖς ἵνα μὴ ἀδικήσουσιν τὸν χόρτον τῆς γῆς οὐδὲ
πᾶν χλωρὸν οὐδὲ πᾶν δένδρον, εἰ μὴ τοὺς ἀνθρώπους οἵτινες
οὐκ ἔχουσιν τὴν σφραγῖδα τοῦ θεοῦ ἐπὶ τῶν μετώπων. 5 καὶ
ἐδόθη αὐτοῖς ἵνα μὴ ἀποκτείνωσιν αὐτούς, ἀλλ' ἵνα βασανισθήσονται μῆνας πέντε· καὶ ὁ βασανισμὸς αὐτῶν ὡς βασανισμὸς
σκορπίου, ὅταν παίσῃ ἄνθρωπον. 6 καὶ ἐν ταῖς ἡμέραις ἐκείναις
ζητήσουσιν οἱ ἄνθρωποι τὸν θάνατον καὶ οὐ μὴ εὑρήσουσιν
αὐτόν, καὶ ἐπιθυμήσουσιν ἀποθανεῖν καὶ φεύγει ὁ θάνατος ἀπ'
αὐτῶν. 7 καὶ τὰ ὁμοιώματα τῶν ἀκρίδων ὅμοιοι ἵπποις ἡτοι-
μασμένοις εἰς πόλεμον, καὶ ἐπὶ τὰς κεφαλὰς αὐτῶν ὡς στέφανοι
ὅμοιοι χρυσῷ, καὶ τὰ πρόσωπα αὐτῶν ὡς πρόσωπα ἀνθρώπων,

[1] Geb. ἑπτά.

§ XXIII

The Last Things

VIII. 1 And when he had opened the seventh seal, silence
was in heaven as it were half an hour. 2 Then I saw the seven
angels who stand before God, and three trumpets were given
them. 3 Another angel then came and took his stand by the
altar. He had a golden censer, and much incense was given
him, that he might offer with the prayers of all the saints on
the golden altar, that which is before the throne. 4 Then from
the angel's hand the smoke of the incense with the prayers of the
saints went up before God. 5 Then the angel took the censer
and filled it from the fire of the altar and cast it on to the
earth. Then were there thunders, voices and lightnings and
earthquake. 6 When the angels having the trumpets had
made themselves ready to blow, 13 I saw and heard an eagle
flying in mid-air saying with a great voice: Woe, woe to those
who dwell on the earth from the voices of the trumpet of the
three angels which are about to sound[1]! IX. 1 Then the fifth
angel sounded, and I saw a star fallen from the heavens to the
earth; and to him was given the key of the pit of the abyss.
2 He opened the pit of the abyss; and smoke rose from the
pit like the smoke of a great furnace, till the sun and the air
were made dark from the smoke of the pit[2]. 3 And from the
smoke came forth locusts on to the earth, and such power
was given them as have earthly scorpions. 4 Yet it was told
them not to hurt the pasture of the earth, nor aught green,
nor any tree—nothing save the men who have not the seal of
God on their foreheads. 5 Even these it was charged them
not to kill, but they were to be tried five months[3], their anguish
as the anguish of a scorpion when it strikes a man. 6 In those
days shall men seek death and in no way find it. They shall
desire to die, while death flees from them. 7 The appearances
of the locusts were like horses made ready for battle[5], and on
their heads as it were crowns resembling gold, and their faces
as human faces,

[1] Hos. viii. 1. Set the trumpet to thy mouth. As an eagle he cometh against the house of the Lord: because they have transgressed my covenant and trespassed against my law. [2] Joel ii. 2. A day of darkness and gloominess, a day of clouds and thick darkness. *v.* 10. The sun and the moon are darkened, and the stars withdraw their shining. [3] Gen. vii. 24. And the waters prevailed upon the earth an hundred and fifty days. [4] Job iii. 21. Which long for death, but it cometh not, and dig for it more than for hid treasures. [5] Joel ii. 4. The appearance of them is as the appearance of horses; and as horsemen do they run.

§ XXIV

Ch. ix. 8–21

8 καὶ εἶχαν τρίχας ὡς τρίχας γυναικῶν, καὶ οἱ ὀδόντες αὐτῶν ὡς
λεόντων ἦσαν, 9 καὶ εἶχον θώρακας ὡς θώρακας σιδηροῦς, καὶ ἡ
φωνὴ τῶν πτερύγων αὐτῶν ὡς φωνὴ ἁρμάτων ἵππων πολλῶν
τρεχόντων εἰς πόλεμον. 10 καὶ ἔχουσιν οὐρὰς ὁμοίας σκορπίοις
καὶ κέντρα, καὶ ἐν ταῖς οὐραῖς αὐτῶν ἡ ἐξουσία αὐτῶν ἀδικῆσαι
τοὺς ἀνθρώπους μῆνας πέντε· 11 ἔχουσιν ἐπ' αὐτῶν βασιλέα τὸν
ἄγγελον τῆς ἀβύσσου, ᾧ ὄνομα αὐτῷ Ἑβραϊστὶ Ἀβαδδών, καὶ
ἐν τῇ Ἑλληνικῇ ὄνομα ἔχει Ἀπολλύων. 12 Ἡ οὐαὶ ἡ μία
ἀπῆλθεν· ἰδοὺ ἔρχεται ἔτι δύο οὐαὶ μετὰ ταῦτα. 13 Καὶ ὁ ἕκτος
ἄγγελος ἐσάλπισεν· καὶ ἤκουσα φωνὴν μίαν ἐκ τῶν τεσσάρων
κεράτων τοῦ θυσιαστηρίου τοῦ χρυσοῦ τοῦ ἐνώπιον τοῦ θεοῦ,
14 λέγων τῷ πρώτῳ[1] ἀγγέλῳ ὁ ἔχων τὴν σάλπιγγα· λῦσον τοὺς
τέσσαρας ἀγγέλους τοὺς δεδεμένους ἐπὶ τῷ ποταμῷ τῷ μεγάλῳ
Εὐφράτῃ. 15 καὶ ἐλύθησαν οἱ τέσσαρες ἄγγελοι οἱ ἡτοιμασμένοι
εἰς τὴν ὥραν καὶ ἡμέραν καὶ μῆνα καὶ ἐνιαυτόν, ἵνα ἀποκτείνωσιν
τὸ τρίτον τῶν ἀνθρώπων. 16 καὶ ὁ ἀριθμὸς τῶν στρατευμάτων
τοῦ ἱππικοῦ δισμυριάδες μυριάδων· ἤκουσα τὸν ἀριθμὸν αὐτῶν.
17 καὶ οὕτως ἴδον τοὺς ἵππους ἐν τῇ ὁράσει καὶ τοὺς καθημένους
ἐπ' αὐτῶν, ἔχοντας θώρακας πυρίνους καὶ ὑακινθίνους καὶ θειώδεις·
καὶ αἱ κεφαλαὶ τῶν ἵππων ὡς κεφαλαὶ λεόντων, καὶ ἐκ τῶν
στομάτων αὐτῶν ἐκπορεύεται πῦρ καὶ καπνὸς καὶ θεῖον. 18 ἀπὸ
τῶν τριῶν πληγῶν τούτων ἀπεκτάνθησαν τὸ τρίτον τῶν ἀνθρώπων,
ἐκ τοῦ πυρὸς καὶ τοῦ καπνοῦ καὶ τοῦ θείου τοῦ ἐκπορευομένου ἐκ
τῶν στομάτων αὐτῶν. 19 ἡ γὰρ ἐξουσία τῶν ἵππων ἐν τῷ
στόματι αὐτῶν ἐστὶν καὶ ἐν ταῖς οὐραῖς αὐτῶν· αἱ γὰρ οὐραὶ
αὐτῶν ὅμοιαι ὄφεσιν, ἔχουσαι κεφαλάς, καὶ ἐν αὐταῖς ἀδικοῦσιν.
20 καὶ οἱ λοιποὶ τῶν ἀνθρώπων, οἳ οὐκ ἀπεκτάνθησαν ἐν ταῖς
πληγαῖς ταύταις, οὐδὲ μετενόησαν ἐκ τῶν ἔργων τῶν χειρῶν
αὐτῶν, ἵνα μὴ προσκυνήσουσιν τὰ δαιμόνια καὶ τὰ εἴδωλα τὰ
χρυσᾶ καὶ τὰ ἀργυρᾶ καὶ τὰ χαλκᾶ καὶ τὰ λίθινα καὶ τὰ ξύλινα,
ἃ οὔτε βλέπειν δύνανται οὔτε ἀκούειν οὔτε περιπατεῖν, 21 καὶ οὐ
μετενόησαν ἐκ τῶν φόνων αὐτῶν οὔτε ἐκ τῶν φαρμακιῶν αὐτῶν
οὔτε ἐκ τῆς πορνείας αὐτῶν οὔτε ἐκ τῶν κλεμμάτων αὐτῶν.

[1] Geb. λέγοντα τῷ ἕκτῳ.

§ XXIV

THE LAST THINGS

IX. 8 and they had hair as women's hair, and their teeth
were as those of lions. 9 Breastplates they had like iron breastplates, and the noise of their wings was as the noise of many
horse-chariots racing into battle[1]. 10 They have tails like
scorpions and stings. In their tails is their power to hurt men
five months[2]. 11 Over them they have as king the angel of
the abyss, whose name in Hebrew is Abaddon and in the
Greek he has the name Apollyon. 12 The first woe is past.
Lo, there come yet two woes after. 13 Then the sixth angel
sounded; and I heard a blast from the four horns of the altar
of gold[3] that is before God, 14 while he who had the trumpet
was saying to the first angel: Let loose the four messengers
which are bound at the great river Euphrates. 15 Then were
loosed the four messengers which had been made ready for
this hour and month and year, that they might kill one third
of men. 16 The number of the armies of cavalry was twice a
myriad myriad. I heard their number, 17 and I saw how the
horses and those sitting on them were in appearance. Breastplates fiery and dark-red and sulphurous they have, and the
heads of their horses as lions' heads, and from their mouths
go out fire, smoke and brimstone. 18 By these three plagues
were killed the third of mankind, even from the fire, the
smoke, the brimstone which go forth from their mouths.
19 For the power of the horses is in their mouths and in their
tails; for their tails are like serpents, having heads, and with
them they injure[4]. 20 Yet the rest of the men, those who were
not slain by these plagues, repented not of the works of their
hands, that they should not worship the demons and the idols
of gold, silver, brass, stone or wood, which cannot see or hear
or walk. 21 Nor did they repent of their murders or of their
sorceries or of their fornication or of their thefts.

[1] Joel ii. 5. Like the noise of chariots on the tops of the mountains. [2] Is. xxx. 6. Through the land of trouble and anguish, from whence come the lioness and the lion, the viper and fiery flying serpent. [3] Ex. xxvii. 2. The horns of it upon the four corners thereof. [4] Prov. xxiii. 32. Read as: the end biteth like a serpent and stingeth like an adder.

§ XXV

CH. XI. 14–19, XIV. 6–11

14 Ἡ οὐαὶ ἡ δευτέρα ἀπῆλθεν· ἰδοὺ ἡ οὐαὶ ἡ τρίτη ἔρχεται ταχύ.
15 Καὶ ὁ ἕβδομος ἄγγελος ἐσάλπισεν· καὶ ἐγένοντο φωναὶ με-
γάλαι ἐν τῷ οὐρανῷ, λέγοντες· ἐγένετο ἡ βασιλεία τοῦ κόσμου
τοῦ κυρίου ἡμῶν καὶ τοῦ Χριστοῦ αὐτοῦ, καὶ βασιλεύσει εἰς τοὺς
αἰῶνας τῶν αἰώνων. 16 καὶ οἱ εἴκοσι τέσσαρες πρεσβύτεροι οἱ
ἐνώπιον τοῦ θεοῦ, οἱ κάθηνται ἐπὶ τοὺς θρόνους αὐτῶν, ἔπεσαν
ἐπὶ τὰ πρόσωπα αὐτῶν καὶ προσεκύνησαν τῷ θεῷ, 17 λέγοντες·
εὐχαριστοῦμέν σοι, κύριε ὁ θεὸς ὁ παντοκράτωρ, ὁ ὢν καὶ ὁ ἦν,
καὶ ὅτι εἴληφας τὴν δύναμίν σου τὴν μεγάλην καὶ ἐβασίλευσας,
18 καὶ τὰ ἔθνη ὠργίσθησαν, καὶ ἦλθεν ἡ ὀργή σου καὶ ὁ καιρὸς
τῶν νεκρῶν κριθῆναι καὶ δοῦναι τὸν μισθὸν τοῖς δούλοις σου τοῖς
προφήταις καὶ τοῖς ἁγίοις καὶ τοῖς φοβουμένοις τὸ ὄνομά σου,
τοῖς μικροῖς καὶ τοῖς μεγάλοις, καὶ διαφθεῖραι τοὺς διαφθείροντας
τὴν γῆν. 19 καὶ ἠνοίγη ὁ ναὸς τοῦ θεοῦ ὁ ἐν τῷ οὐρανῷ, καὶ
ὤφθη ἡ κιβωτὸς τῆς διαθήκης αὐτοῦ ἐν τῷ ναῷ αὐτοῦ, καὶ ἐγένοντο ἀστραπαὶ καὶ φωναὶ καὶ βρονταὶ καὶ σεισμὸς καὶ χάλαζα
μεγάλη. 6 Καὶ εἶδον ἄλλον ἄγγελον πετόμενον ἐν μεσουρανή-
ματι, ἔχοντα εὐαγγέλιον αἰώνιον εὐαγγελίσαι ἐπὶ τοὺς καθημένους
ἐπὶ τῆς γῆς καὶ ἐπὶ πᾶν ἔθνος καὶ φυλὴν καὶ γλῶσσαν καὶ λαόν,
7 λέγων ἐν φωνῇ μεγάλῃ· φοβήθητε τὸν θεὸν καὶ δότε αὐτῷ
δόξαν, ὅτι ἦλθεν ἡ ὥρα τῆς κρίσεως αὐτοῦ, καὶ προσκυνήσατε
τῷ ποιήσαντι τὸν οὐρανὸν καὶ τὴν γῆν καὶ τὴν θάλασσαν καὶ
πηγὰς ὑδάτων. 8 Καὶ ἄλλος ἄγγελος δεύτερος ἠκολούθησεν
λέγων· ἔπεσεν ἔπεσεν Βαβυλὼν ἡ μεγάλη, ἣ ἐκ τοῦ οἴνου τοῦ
θυμοῦ τῆς πορνείας αὐτῆς πεπότικεν πάντα τὰ ἔθνη. 9 Καὶ ἄλλος
ἄγγελος τρίτος ἠκολούθησεν αὐτοῖς λέγων ἐν φωνῇ μεγάλῃ·
εἴ τις προσκυνεῖ τὸ θηρίον καὶ τὴν εἰκόνα αὐτοῦ, καὶ λαμβάνει
χάραγμα ἐπὶ τοῦ μετώπου αὐτοῦ ἢ ἐπὶ τὴν χεῖρα αὐτοῦ, 10 καὶ
αὐτὸς πίεται ἐκ τοῦ οἴνου τοῦ θυμοῦ τοῦ θεοῦ τοῦ κεκερασμένου
ἀκράτου ἐν τῷ ποτηρίῳ τῆς ὀργῆς αὐτοῦ, καὶ βασανισθήσεται
ἐν πυρὶ καὶ θείῳ ἐνώπιον ἀγγέλων ἁγίων καὶ ἐνώπιον τοῦ ἀρνίου.
11 καὶ ὁ καπνὸς τοῦ βασανισμοῦ αὐτῶν εἰς αἰῶνας αἰώνων ἀναβαίνει, καὶ οὐκ ἔχουσιν ἀνάπαυσιν ἡμέρας καὶ νυκτὸς οἱ

§ XXV

The Last Things

XI. 14 The second woe has passed. Lo the third woe comes
quickly. 15 Then the seventh angel sounded; and there were
great voices in heaven saying: The kingdom of the world has
become our Lord's and His Christ's, and He shall reign unto
ages of ages. 16 Then the twenty-four elders, who are before
God, who were seated on their thrones, fell on their faces and
made obeisance to God, 17 saying: We render thanks to
Thee, O Lord the All-sovereign God, who art and who wast,
because Thou hast taken Thy great power and reigned.
18 The nations raged, but Thy wrath has come, and it is the
time for the dead to be judged and to give the reward to Thy
servants the prophets and to the saints and to those that fear
Thy name, to small and to great, and to destroy those who
destroy the earth[1]. 19 Then the temple of God which is in
heaven was opened, and the ark of His covenant was seen in
His temple[2], and there were lightnings and voices, thunders
and earthquake and great hail. XIV. 6 Then I saw another
angel flying in mid-heaven, one having a gospel for every age,
to give good news to the inhabitants of the earth, even every
nation, tribe, language, people. 7 With a great voice he is
saying: Fear God and give Him glory, for the hour of His
judgment has come. Worship the maker of the heaven and
the earth and the sea and fountains of waters. 8 And another,
a second angel, followed saying: Fallen, fallen is Babylon the
Great! which from the wine of her fornication intoxicated all
nations. 9 And another, a third angel, followed them saying
with a great voice: If anyone worship the beast and his image
and receive a mark on his forehead or on his hand, 10 he also
shall drink of the wine of God's anger, mixed unwatered in
the cup of His wrath[3], and he will be tried in fire and brimstone before the holy angels and before the Lamb, 11 and the
smoke of his testing goes up for ages of ages[4]. Nor have they
rest day and night who

[1] Dan. ix. 27. Until the determined consummation is poured out on the desolator.
[2] 1 K. viii. 21. The ark, wherein is the covenant of the Lord. [3] Is. li. 17. Which hast drunk at the hand of the Lord the cup of his fury. [4] Is. xxxiv. 10. It shall not be quenched night nor day; the smoke thereof shall go up for ever: from generation to generation it shall lie waste.

§ XXVI

Ch. xiv. 11–19, xv. 1–4

προσκυνοῦντες τὸ θηρίον καὶ τὴν εἰκόνα αὐτοῦ, καὶ εἴ τις λαμβάνει τὸ χάραγμα τοῦ ὀνόματος αὐτοῦ. 12 ὧδε ἡ ὑπομονὴ τῶν
ἁγίων ἐστίν, οἱ τηροῦντες τὰς ἐντολὰς τοῦ θεοῦ καὶ τὴν πίστιν
Ἰησοῦ. 13 καὶ ἤκουσα φωνῆς ἐκ τοῦ οὐρανοῦ λεγούσης· γράψον·
μακάριοι οἱ νεκροὶ οἱ ἐν κυρίῳ ἀποθνήσκοντες ἀπάρτι. ναί, λέγει
τὸ πνεῦμα, ἵνα ἀναπαήσονται ἐκ τῶν κόπων αὐτῶν· τὰ γὰρ ἔργα
αὐτῶν ἀκολουθεῖ μετ' αὐτῶν. 14 Καὶ ἴδον, καὶ ἰδοὺ νεφέλη
λευκή, καὶ ἐπὶ τὴν νεφέλην καθήμενον *ὅμοιον υἱὸν ἀνθρώπου*, ἔχων
ἐπὶ τῆς κεφαλῆς αὐτοῦ στέφανον χρυσοῦν καὶ ἐν τῇ χειρὶ αὐτοῦ
δρέπανον ὀξύ. 15 καὶ ἄλλος ἄγγελος ἐξῆλθεν ἐκ τοῦ ναοῦ, κράζων
ἐν φωνῇ μεγάλῃ τῷ καθημένῳ ἐπὶ τῆς νεφέλης· πέμψον τὸ δρέ-
πανόν σου καὶ θέρισον, ὅτι ἦλθεν ἡ ὥρα θερίσαι, ὅτι ἐξηράνθη ὁ
θερισμὸς τῆς γῆς. 16 καὶ ἔβαλεν ὁ καθήμενος ἐπὶ τῆς νεφέλης
τὸ δρέπανον αὐτοῦ ἐπὶ τὴν γῆν, καὶ ἐθερίσθη ἡ γῆ. 17 καὶ
ἄλλος ἄγγελος ἐξῆλθεν ἐκ τοῦ ναοῦ τοῦ ἐν τῷ οὐρανῷ, ἔχων
καὶ αὐτὸς δρέπανον ὀξύ· 18 καὶ ἄλλος ἄγγελος ἐξῆλθεν ἐκ τοῦ
θυσιαστηρίου, ἔχων ἐξουσίαν ἐπὶ τοῦ πυρός, καὶ ἐφώνησεν φωνῇ
μεγάλῃ τῷ ἔχοντι τὸ δρέπανον τὸ ὀξὺ λέγων· πέμψον σου τὸ
δρέπανον τὸ ὀξὺ καὶ τρύγησον τοὺς βότρυας τῆς ἀμπέλου τῆς
γῆς, ὅτι ἤκμασαν αἱ σταφυλαὶ αὐτῆς. 19 καὶ ἔβαλεν ὁ ἄγγελος
τὸ δρέπανον αὐτοῦ εἰς τὴν γῆν, καὶ ἐτρύγησεν τὴν ἄμπελον τῆς
γῆς. * 1 Καὶ ἴδον ἄλλο σημεῖον ἐν τῷ οὐρανῷ μέγα καὶ θαυμαστόν,
ἀγγέλους ἑπτὰ ἔχοντας πληγὰς ἑπτὰ τὰς ἐσχάτας, ὅτι ἐν αὐταῖς
ἐτελέσθη ὁ θυμὸς τοῦ θεοῦ. 2 καὶ ἴδον ὡς θάλασσαν ὑαλίνην
μεμιγμένην πυρί, καὶ τοὺς νικῶντας ἐκ τοῦ θηρίου καὶ ἐκ τῆς
εἰκόνος αὐτοῦ καὶ ἐκ τοῦ ἀριθμοῦ τοῦ ὀνόματος αὐτοῦ ἑστῶτας
ἐπὶ τὴν θάλασσαν τὴν ὑαλίνην, ἔχοντας κιθάρας τοῦ θεοῦ. 3 καὶ
ᾄδουσιν τὴν ᾠδὴν Μωϋσέως τοῦ δούλου τοῦ θεοῦ καὶ τὴν ᾠδὴν
τοῦ ἀρνίου, λέγοντες· *μεγάλα καὶ θαυμαστὰ τὰ ἔργα σου, κύριε
ὁ θεὸς ὁ παντοκράτωρ· δίκαιαι καὶ ἀληθιναὶ αἱ ὁδοί σου, ὁ
βασιλεὺς τῶν ἐθνῶν·* 4 *τίς οὐ μὴ φοβηθῇ*, κύριε, καὶ *δοξάσει τὸ
ὄνομά σου;* ὅτι μόνος *ὅσιος*, ὅτι *πάντα τὰ ἔθνη ἥξουσιν καὶ προσκυνήσουσιν ἐνώπιόν σου*, ὅτι τὰ δικαιώματά σου ἐφανερώθησαν.

§ XXVI

The Last Things

XIV. 11 worship the beast and his image, yea, if anyone receive the mark of his name. 12 Herein is the patience of the
saints who hold fast the commandments of God and the faith
of Jesus. 13 Then I heard a voice from heaven saying: Write,
Blessed are the dead who die in the Lord from henceforth. Yea,
says the Spirit, seeing they shall rest from their labours[1]. For
their works follow with them. 14 Then I saw, and lo a white
cloud, and sitting on the cloud was one like a son of man[2], having
on his head a golden coronet and in his hand a sharp sickle.
15 Then another angel came out from the temple crying with
a great voice to him sitting on the cloud: Put forth thy sickle
and reap, for the hour has come to reap, for the harvest of the
world is over-ripe[3]. 16 Then he who sat on the cloud put his
sickle to the earth, and the earth was reaped. 17 Then another
angel came out from the temple which is in heaven, he too
having a sharp sickle. 18 And another angel came out from
the altar—the one having the charge of the fire. With a great
voice he called to him having the sharp sickle, saying: Put
forth thy sharp sickle and gather the clusters of the vine of
the earth, for its grapes are just ripe. 19 Then the angel put
his sickle to the earth and gathered the vine of the earth.
XV. 1 Then I saw another sign in heaven, great and wonderful,
seven angels having seven plagues, the last, for by them is
brought to completion the anger of God. 2 And I saw, as it
were a glassy sea mingled with fire, and those who had come
victorious from the beast and his image and the number of
his name, standing by the glassy sea, having harps of God.
3 They sing the song of Moses, the servant of God, and the
song of the Lamb, saying: Great and wonderful are Thy
works, O Lord, All-sovereign God. Righteous and true are
Thy ways, O king of the nations. 4 Who would not fear Thee,
O Lord, and glorify Thy name? Because Thou only art holy,
for all the nations shall come and worship before Thee, for
Thy righteous doings have been made manifest.

[1] Many O.T. passages. Heb. iv. 9. There remaineth therefore a Sabbath rest for the people of God. [2] Lk. xxi. 27. See the Son of Man coming in a cloud with power and great glory. [3] Mk iv. 29. But when the fruit is ripe, straightway he putteth forth the sickle, because the harvest is come.

§ XXVII

Ch. xx. 11—xxi. 8

11 Καὶ εἶδον θρόνον μέγαν λευκὸν καὶ τὸν καθήμενον ἐπ' αὐτόν, οὗ ἀπὸ τοῦ προσώπου ἔφυγεν ἡ γῆ καὶ ὁ οὐρανός, καὶ τόπος οὐχ εὑρέθη αὐτοῖς. 12 καὶ εἶδον τοὺς νεκροὺς τοὺς μεγάλους καὶ τοὺς μικροὺς ἑστῶτας ἐνώπιον τοῦ θρόνου, καὶ βιβλία ἠνοίχθησαν· καὶ ἄλλο βιβλίον ἠνοίχθη, ὅ ἐστιν τῆς ζωῆς· καὶ ἐκρίθησαν οἱ νεκροὶ ἐκ τῶν γεγραμμένων ἐν τοῖς βιβλίοις κατὰ τὰ ἔργα αὐτῶν.
13 καὶ ἔδωκεν ἡ θάλασσα τοὺς νεκροὺς τοὺς ἐπ' αὐτήν[1], καὶ ὁ θάνατος καὶ ὁ ᾅδης ἔδωκαν τοὺς νεκροὺς τοὺς ἐν αὐτοῖς, καὶ ἐκρίθησαν ἕκαστος κατὰ τὰ ἔργα αὐτῶν.
14 καὶ ὁ θάνατος καὶ ὁ ᾅδης ἐβλήθησαν εἰς τὴν λίμνην τοῦ πυρός. οὗτος ὁ θάνατος ὁ δεύτερός ἐστιν, *
15 καὶ εἴ τις οὐχ εὑρέθη ἐν τῇ βίβλῳ τῆς ζωῆς γεγραμμένος, ἐβλήθη εἰς τὴν λίμνην τοῦ πυρός.
1 Καὶ εἶδον οὐρανὸν καινὸν καὶ γῆν καινήν· ὁ γὰρ πρῶτος οὐρανὸς καὶ ἡ πρώτη γῆ ἀπῆλθαν, καὶ ἡ θάλασσα οὐκ ἔστιν ἔτι.
2 καὶ τὴν πόλιν τὴν ἁγίαν Ἱερουσαλὴμ καινὴν εἶδον καταβαίνουσαν ἐκ τοῦ οὐρανοῦ ἀπὸ τοῦ θεοῦ, ἡτοιμασμένην ὡς νύμφην κεκοσμημένην τῷ ἀνδρὶ αὐτῆς.
3 καὶ ἤκουσα φωνῆς μεγάλης ἐκ τοῦ θρόνου λεγούσης· ἰδοὺ ἡ σκηνὴ τοῦ θεοῦ μετὰ τῶν ἀνθρώπων, καὶ σκηνώσει μετ' αὐτῶν, καὶ αὐτοὶ λαοὶ αὐτοῦ ἔσονται, καὶ αὐτὸς ὁ θεὸς ἔσται μετ' αὐτῶν,
4 καὶ ἐξαλείψει πᾶν δάκρυον ἐκ τῶν ὀφθαλμῶν αὐτῶν, καὶ θάνατος οὐκ ἔσται ἔτι, οὔτε πένθος οὔτε κραυγὴ οὔτε πόνος οὐκ ἔσται ἔτι· ὅτι τὰ πρῶτα ἀπῆλθαν.
5 καὶ εἶπεν ὁ καθήμενος ἐπὶ τῷ θρόνῳ· ἰδοὺ καινὰ ποιῶ πάντα. καὶ λέγει· γράψον, ὅτι οὗτοι οἱ λόγοι πιστοὶ καὶ ἀληθινοί εἰσιν.
6 καὶ εἶπέν μοι· γέγοναν. ἐγὼ τὸ ἄλφα καὶ τὸ ω, ἡ ἀρχὴ καὶ τὸ τέλος. ἐγὼ τῷ διψῶντι δώσω αὐτῷ ἐκ τῆς πηγῆς τοῦ ὕδατος τῆς ζωῆς δωρεάν.
7 ὁ νικῶν κληρονομήσει ταῦτα, καὶ ἔσομαι αὐτῷ θεὸς καὶ αὐτὸς ἔσται μοι υἱός.
8 τοῖς δὲ δειλοῖς καὶ ἀπίστοις καὶ ἐβδελυγμένοις καὶ φονεῦσιν καὶ πόρνοις καὶ φαρμακοῖς καὶ εἰδωλολάτραις καὶ πᾶσιν τοῖς ψευδέσιν τὸ μέρος αὐτῶν ἐν τῇ λίμνῃ τῇ καιομένῃ πυρὶ καὶ θείῳ, ὅ ἐστιν ὁ θάνατος ὁ δεύτερος.

[1] Geb. ἐν αὐτῇ

§ XXVII

The Last Things

xx. 11 Then I saw a great white throne and Him sitting on
it, from whose face the earth and the heavens fled, and place
was not found for them. 12 I saw the dead, great and small,
standing before the throne and rolls were opened[1]. Also
another roll was opened, that of life. From what was written
in the rolls the dead were judged according to their works.
13 The sea gave up the dead that were by it, and death and
hades gave up the dead that were in them, and each was
judged according to his works. 14 Then death and hades
were cast into the lake of fire[2]. This is the second death 15 that
if anyone was not found written in the roll of life, he was cast
into the lake of fire[3]. xxi. 1 Then I saw a new kind of heavens
and a new kind of earth; for the former heavens and the
former earth had passed away, and the sea is not any more.
2 Then I saw the city, the new kind of holy Jerusalem, coming
down out of heaven from God, prepared as a bride adorned
for her husband, 3 and I heard a great voice from the throne
saying: Lo the dwelling-place of God is with men, and He
will dwell with them and they shall be His people and God
Himself shall be with them. 4 And He shall wipe away every
tear from their eyes. Death shall no more be[2]. Nor shall
grief, nor wailing, nor distress any more be[4], for the former
things have passed away. 5 He who sits on the throne says:
Lo I make all things new. And He says to me: Write that these
are the faithful and true words. 6 Then He said to me: They
have come to pass. I am the alpha and the omega, the beginning and the end. I will give to him that thirsts of the fountain
of the water of life freely. 7 He who overcomes shall inherit
these things; and I shall be to him God, and he will be to me
son. 8 But to the fearing and unbelieving, and those taking
part in abominations, and murderers and fornicators and
sorcerers and those serving idols, and all liars, their portion
is in the lake which burns with fire and brimstone, which is
the second death.

[1] Dan. vii. 9. I beheld till thrones were placed and one that was ancient of days did sit...the judgment was set and the books were opened. [2] Is. xxv. 8. He hath swallowed up death for ever and the Lord God shall wipe away tears from off all faces. [3] Is. lxix. 28. Let them be blotted out of the book of life, and not be written with the righteous. [4] Is. xxxv. 10. And everlasting joy shall be upon their heads: they shall obtain gladness and joy, and sorrow and sighing shall flee away.

Editor's Introduction

I. 1 Ἀποκάλυψις Ἰησοῦ Χριστοῦ, ἣν ἔδωκεν αὐτῷ ὁ θεός, δεῖξαι
τοῖς δούλοις αὐτοῦ ἃ δεῖ γενέσθαι ἐν τάχει, καὶ ἐσήμανεν ἀπο-
στείλας διὰ τοῦ ἀγγέλου αὐτοῦ τῷ δούλῳ αὐτοῦ Ἰωάννῃ, 2 ὃς
ἐμαρτύρησεν τὸν λόγον τοῦ θεοῦ καὶ τὴν μαρτυρίαν Ἰησοῦ
Χριστοῦ, ὅσα ἴδεν. 3 μακάριος ὁ ἀναγινώσκων καὶ οἱ ἀκούοντες
τὸν λόγον τῆς προφητείας καὶ τηροῦντες τὰ ἐν αὐτῇ γεγραμμένα·
ὁ γὰρ καιρὸς ἐγγύς. 4 Ἰωάννης ταῖς ἑπτὰ ἐκκλησίαις ταῖς ἐν τῇ
Ἀσίᾳ· χάρις ὑμῖν καὶ εἰρήνη ἀπὸ ὁ ὢν καὶ ὁ ἦν καὶ ὁ ἐρχόμενος,
καὶ ἀπὸ τῶν ἑπτὰ πνευμάτων ἃ ἐνώπιον τοῦ θρόνου αὐτοῦ, 5 καὶ
ἀπὸ Ἰησοῦ Χριστοῦ, ὁ μάρτυς ὁ πιστός, ὁ πρωτότοκος τῶν νεκρῶν
καὶ ὁ ἄρχων τῶν βασιλέων τῆς γῆς. τῷ ἀγαπῶντι ἡμᾶς καὶ
λύσαντι ἡμᾶς ἐκ τῶν ἁμαρτιῶν ἡμῶν ἐν τῷ αἵματι αὐτοῦ, 6 καὶ
ἐποίησεν ἡμᾶς βασιλείαν, ἱερεῖς τῷ θεῷ καὶ πατρὶ αὐτοῦ, αὐτῷ ἡ
δόξα καὶ τὸ κράτος εἰς τοὺς αἰῶνας τῶν αἰώνων· ἀμήν. 7 Ἰδοὺ
ἔρχεται μετὰ τῶν νεφελῶν, καὶ ὄψεται αὐτὸν πᾶς ὀφθαλμὸς καὶ
οἵτινες αὐτὸν ἐξεκέντησαν, καὶ κόψονται ἐπ' αὐτὸν πᾶσαι αἱ φυλαὶ
τῆς γῆς. ναί, ἀμήν. 8 ἐγώ εἰμι τὸ ἄλφα καὶ τὸ ω, λέγει κύριος
ὁ θεός, ὁ ὢν καὶ ὁ ἦν καὶ ὁ ἐρχόμενος, ὁ παντοκράτωρ.

Editor's Epilogue

XXII. 18 Μαρτυρῶ ἐγὼ παντὶ τῷ ἀκούοντι τοὺς λόγους τῆς
προφητείας τοῦ βιβλίου τούτου. ἐάν τις ἐπιθῇ ἐπ' αὐτά, ἐπιθήσει
ἐπ' αὐτὸν ὁ θεὸς τὰς πληγὰς τὰς γεγραμμένας ἐν τῷ βιβλίῳ τούτῳ·
19 καὶ ἐάν τις ἀφέλῃ ἀπὸ τῶν λόγων τοῦ βιβλίου τῆς προφητείας
ταύτης, ἀφελεῖ ὁ θεὸς τὸ μέρος αὐτοῦ ἀπὸ τοῦ ξύλου τῆς ζωῆς καὶ
ἐκ τῆς πόλεως τῆς ἁγίας, τῶν γεγραμμένων ἐν τῷ βιβλίῳ τούτῳ.
20 Λέγει ὁ μαρτυρῶν ταῦτα· ναί, ἔρχομαι ταχύ. Ἀμήν, ἔρχου
κύριε Ἰησοῦ. 21 Ἡ χάρις τοῦ κυρίου Ἰησοῦ μετὰ πάντων.

Editor's Glosses

§ I. I. 20 οἱ ἑπτὰ ἀστέρες ἄγγελοι τῶν ἑπτὰ ἐκκλησιῶν εἰσίν, καὶ αἱ λυχνίαι αἱ ἑπτὰ ἑπτὰ ἐκκλησίαι εἰσίν.

§ II. II. 11 and 17 and § III. II. 29 and III. 6 and § IV. III. 13: ὁ ἔχων οὖς ἀκουσάτω τί τὸ πνεῦμα λέγει ταῖς ἐκκλησίαις.

§ VI. XI. 13 καὶ ἔδωκαν δόξαν τῷ θεῷ τοῦ οὐρανοῦ.

§ IX. XIV. 4 παρθένοι γάρ εἰσιν.

§ X. XV. 8 καὶ οὐδεὶς ἐδύνατο εἰσελθεῖν εἰς τὸν ναὸν ἄχρι
τελεσθῶσιν αἱ ἑπτὰ πληγαὶ τῶν ἑπτὰ ἀγγέλων. XVI. 2 τοὺς
ἔχοντας τὸ χάραγμα τοῦ θηρίου καὶ τοὺς προσκυνοῦντας τῇ εἰκόνι

Editor's Introduction

I. 1 An apocalypse of Jesus Christ, which God gave him to show to His servants what must come to pass shortly. And he showed, having sent by His angel to His servant John 2 who witnessed the word of God and the witness of Jesus Christ, those things he saw. 3 Blessed is he who reads and those who hear the word of the prophecy and hold fast the things written in it. For the time is near. 4 John to the seven churches which are in Asia. Grace to you and peace from the one who is, who was and is to come, and from the seven spirits that are before His throne, 5 and from Jesus Christ, the faithful witness, the first born of the dead and the ruler of the kings of the earth. To Him who loves us and has loosed us from our sins by His blood, 6 and made us a kingdom, priests to God, even our Father, to Him be the glory and the power to ages of ages. Amen. 7 Lo He comes with the clouds, and every eye shall see Him, especially those who pierced Him; and all the tribes of the earth shall wail because of Him. Verily, Amen. 8 I am the alpha and the omega, says the Lord God, the one who is, who was and who is to come, the All-sovereign.

Editor's Epilogue

XXII. 18 I witness to all who hear the words of the prophecy of this book. If anyone add to them God will add to him the plagues written in this book; 19 and if anyone take away from the words of the book of this prophecy, God will take away his part from the tree of life and from the holy city—the things written about in this book. 20 He who witnesses these things says: Verily I come quickly. Amen. Come Lord Jesus! 21 The grace of the Lord Jesus be with all.

Editor's Glosses

§ I. I. 20 The seven stars are the angels of the seven churches, and the seven lights are the seven churches.

§ II. II. 11 and 17 and § III. II. 29 and III. 6 and § IV. III. 13: He who has an ear, let him hear what the Spirit says to the churches.

§ VI. XI. 13 And gave glory to the God of Heaven.

§ IX. XIV. 4 For they are virgins.

§ X. XV. 8 And no one was able to enter the temple till the seven plagues of the seven angels were finished. XVI. 2 those having the mark of the beast and those worshipping his image.

αὐτοῦ. 3 αἷμα...καὶ πᾶσα ψυχὴ ζωῆς ἀπέθανεν, τὰ ἐν τῇ θαλάσσῃ. 4 καὶ ἐγένετο αἷμα. 6 καὶ αἷμα αὐτοῖς ἔδωκας πιεῖν. 9 καὶ ἐκαυματίσθησαν οἱ ἄνθρωποι καῦμα μέγα, καὶ ἐβλασφήμησαν τὸ ὄνομα τοῦ θεοῦ τοῦ ἔχοντος τὴν ἐξουσίαν ἐπὶ τὰς πληγὰς ταύτας, καὶ οὐ μετενόησαν δοῦναι αὐτῷ δόξαν. 11 καὶ ἐβλασφήμησαν τὸν θεὸν τοῦ οὐρανοῦ ἐκ τῶν πόνων αὐτῶν καὶ ἐκ τῶν ἑλκῶν αὐτῶν, καὶ οὐ μετενόησαν ἐκ τῶν ἔργων αὐτῶν. 12 τὸν μέγαν.

§ XII. VI. 3 καὶ ὅτε ἤνοιξεν τὴν σφραγῖδα τὴν δευτέραν, ἤκουσα τοῦ δευτέρου ζώου λέγοντος· ἔρχου. 5 καὶ ὅτε ἤνοιξεν τὴν σφραγῖδα τὴν τρίτην, ἤκουσα τοῦ τρίτου ζώου λέγοντος· ἔρχου. 7 καὶ ὅτε ἤνοιξεν τὴν σφραγῖδα τὴν τετάρτην, ἤκουσα φωνὴν τοῦ τετάρτου ζώου λέγοντος· ἔρχου. 9 ὅτε ἤνοιξεν τὴν πέμπτην σφραγῖδα. 12 καὶ ὅτε ἤνοιξεν τὴν σφραγῖδα τὴν ἕκτην.

§ XIII. XVI. 18 καὶ ἐγένοντο ἀστραπαὶ καὶ φωναὶ καὶ βρονταί. 21 καὶ ἐβλασφήμησαν οἱ ἄνθρωποι τὸν θεὸν ἐκ τῆς πληγῆς τῆς χαλάζης, ὅτι μεγάλη ἐστὶν ἡ πληγὴ αὐτῆς σφόδρα.

§ XIV. XVII. 14 ὅτι κύριος κυρίων ἐστὶν καὶ βασιλεὺς βασιλέων.

§ XVI. XVIII. 21 καὶ οὐ μὴ εὑρεθῇ ἔτι.

§ XVII. XXI. 9 τῶν ἐσχάτων. 16 καὶ τὸ ὕψος.

§ XXII. VII. 2 οἷς ἐδόθη αὐτοῖς ἀδικῆσαι τὴν γῆν καὶ τὴν θάλασσαν. 5 ἐκ φυλῆς Ἰούδα δώδεκα χιλιάδες ἐσφραγισμένοι, ἐκ φυλῆς Ῥουβὴν δώδεκα χιλιάδες, ἐκ φυλῆς Γὰδ δώδεκα χιλιάδες, 6 ἐκ φυλῆς Ἀσὴρ δώδεκα χιλιάδες, ἐκ φυλῆς Νεφθαλεὶμ δώδεκα χιλιάδες, ἐκ φυλῆς Μανασσῆ δώδεκα χιλιάδες, 7 ἐκ φυλῆς Συμεὼν δώδεκα χιλιάδες, ἐκ φυλῆς Λευεὶ δώδεκα χιλιάδες, ἐκ φυλῆς Ἰσσάχαρ δώδεκα χιλιάδες, 8 ἐκ φυλῆς Ζαβουλὼν δώδεκα χιλιάδες, ἐκ φυλῆς Ἰωσὴφ δώδεκα χιλιάδες, ἐκ φυλῆς Βενιαμεὶν δώδεκα χιλιάδες ἐσφραγισμένοι.

§ XXIII. VIII. 6 ἑπτὰ...ἑπτὰ. 7 Καὶ ὁ πρῶτος ἐσάλπισεν· καὶ ἐγένετο χάλαζα καὶ πῦρ μεμιγμένον ἐν αἵματι καὶ ἐβλήθη εἰς τὴν γῆν· καὶ τὸ τρίτον τῆς γῆς κατεκάη, καὶ τὸ τρίτον τῶν δένδρων κατεκάη, καὶ πᾶς χόρτος χλωρὸς κατεκάη. 8 Καὶ ὁ δεύτερος ἄγγελος ἐσάλπισεν· καὶ ὡς ὄρος μέγα πυρὶ καιόμενον ἐβλήθη εἰς τὴν θάλασσαν· καὶ ἐγένετο τὸ τρίτον τῆς θαλάσσης αἷμα, 9 καὶ ἀπέθανεν τὸ τρίτον τῶν κτισμάτων τῶν ἐν τῇ θαλάσσῃ, τὰ ἔχοντα ψυχάς, καὶ τὸ τρίτον τῶν πλοίων διεφθάρησαν. 10 Καὶ ὁ τρίτος ἄγγελος ἐσάλπισεν· καὶ ἔπεσεν ἐκ τοῦ οὐρανοῦ ἀστὴρ μέγας καιόμενος ὡς λαμπάς, καὶ ἔπεσεν ἐπὶ τὸ τρίτον τῶν ποταμῶν καὶ ἐπὶ τὰς πηγὰς τῶν ὑδάτων.

3 blood...and every soul of life died that was in the sea. 4 and it became blood. 6 and thou hast given them blood to drink. 9 And men were scorched a great scorching, and they blasphemed the God who had power over these plagues, and did not repent to give glory to Him. 11 And they blasphemed the God of Heaven for their distress and their sores, and did not repent of their deeds. 12 the great.

§ XII. vi. 3 And when he had opened the second seal, I heard the second living creature saying, Come. 5 And when he had opened the third seal, I heard the third living creature saying, Come. 7 And when he had opened the fourth seal, I heard the voice of the fourth living creature say, Come. 9 when he had opened the fifth seal. 12 when he had opened the sixth seal.

§ XIII. xvi. 18 Then were lightnings and voices and thunders. 21 And men blasphemed God because of the plague of the hail, because the plague of it was great exceedingly.

§ XIV. xvii. 14 because he is lord of lords and king of kings.

§ XVI. xviii. 21 and it was not found any more.

§ XVII. xxi. 9 the last. 16 and the height.

§ XXII. vii. 2 to whom it was given to hurt the land and the sea. 5–8 Of the tribe of Judah were sealed twelve thousand, of the tribe of Reuben twelve thousand, of the tribe of Gad twelve thousand, of the tribe of Asher twelve thousand, of the tribe of Naphtali twelve thousand, of the tribe of Manasseh twelve thousand, of the tribe of Simeon twelve thousand, of the tribe of Levi twelve thousand, of the tribe of Issachar twelve thousand, of the tribe of Zebulon twelve thousand, of the tribe of Joseph twelve thousand, of the tribe of Benjamin twelve thousand were sealed.

§ XXIII. viii. 6 seven...seven. 7–12 And the first sounded. And there was hail and fire mingled with blood and it was cast on the earth. And the third of the earth was burned, and the third of the trees was burned and all green grass was burned. And the second angel sounded. And as it were a great mountain burning with fire was cast into the sea: and the third of the sea became blood, and the third of the creatures that were in the sea, those having life, died, and the third of the ships were destroyed. And the third angel sounded. And a great star, blazing like a torch, fell from heaven, and fell on a third of the rivers and on the fountains of the waters.

11 καὶ τὸ ὄνομα τοῦ ἀστέρος λέγεται ὁ ἄψινθος. καὶ ἐγένετο τὸ
τρίτον τῶν ὑδάτων εἰς ἄψινθον, καὶ πολλοὶ τῶν ἀνθρώπων ἀπέθανον
ἐκ τῶν ὑδάτων ὅτι ἐπικράνθησαν. 12 Καὶ ὁ τέταρτος ἄγγελος
ἐσάλπισεν· καὶ ἐπλήγη τὸ τρίτον τοῦ ἡλίου καὶ τὸ τρίτον τῆς
σελήνης καὶ τὸ τρίτον τῶν ἀστέρων, ἵνα σκοτισθῇ τὸ τρίτον
αὐτῶν καὶ ἡ ἡμέρα μὴ φάνῃ τὸ τρίτον αὐτῆς, καὶ ἡ νὺξ ὁμοίως.
13 λοιπῶν.

§ XXVII. xx. 14 ἡ λίμνη τοῦ πυρός.

xxii. 8 καὶ ὅτε ἤκουσα καὶ ἔβλεψα, ἔπεσα προσκυνῆσαι ἔμπροσθεν τῶν ποδῶν τοῦ ἀγγέλου τοῦ δεικνύντος μοι ταῦτα. 9 καὶ
λέγει μοι· ὅρα μή· σύνδουλός σου εἰμὶ καὶ τῶν ἀδελφῶν σου τῶν
προφητῶν καὶ τῶν τηρούντων τοὺς λόγους τοῦ βιβλίου τούτου·
τῷ θεῷ προσκύνησον.

And the name of the star is called Wormwood: and a third of the waters became wormwood; and many men died of the waters because they were embittered. And the fourth angel sounded. And a third of the sun was smitten and a third of the moon and a third of the stars, in order that the third of them should be darkened, and the day, the third of it, might not show, and the night similarly. 13 rest.

§ XXVII. xx. 14 the lake of fire.

Ch. XXII. 8, 9, doublet of XIX. 10 And when I saw and heard I fell down to worship at the feet of the angel who showed me these things. But he says to me: See thou do it not. I am a fellow servant of thee and of thy brethren the prophets and of those who keep the words of this book. Worship God.

PART III
COMMENTARY
I
THE PROPHETIC CALL
§§ I–V
(*a*) *The Situation in the Church*

THE Christians had apparently long suffered from calumny, social ostracism, material loss and the general hostility of the authorities, but systematic suppression by the government, if it had begun at all, seems to have been of recent date, and the special mention of the faithful martyr Antipas looks as though hitherto he alone had been put to death. John himself, who must have been a very prominent leader among the Christians, was only banished. Banishment to an isolated convict settlement, possibly with slave labour, was a severe enough punishment, but it may show that the authorities still hoped to suppress Christianity merely by removing the leaders and exercising a pressure which was mainly economic (xiii. 17).

Yet the slighter the persecution, the more ominous were two things which had happened.

1. Many had failed through weakness and more had shown that they had not their old fervour.

2. False teachers had arisen who taught compromise on principle.

Ephesus had so far stood firm, but had lost her first love (ii. 4), and Philadelphia had held fast Christ's word and had not denied His name, yet she had only a little strength (iii. 8). And without fervour and strength how was a severer persecution to be met?

This persecution John saw impending. It was to be universal, systematic, relentless, and, in one case at least, to endure for ten unbroken years. The world-power was to be drunk with the blood of the martyrs, and a chaos was to follow in which all visible manifestation of true religion would be suppressed.

We have to conceive our author regarding this impending trial as the greatest crisis in the history of humanity and brooding on it in his lonely exile, day by day. This brooding was guided by much meditation on the prophets: for, was not this the closing event of the 1260 years of the World-rule, under which they too had suffered and the end of which they had foretold, and was not the significance of the present its relation to this age-long conflict? Like the prophets, every man who was faithful unto death to his witness died to the world, though, as it was for an eternal cause, even if it meant actual death, in the truest sense he could not die. But those who failed could not justify themselves by the excuse that their compromise with idolatry was only a temporary accommodation, while in their hearts they remained uncontaminated, for this compromise was merely the old unchanging worldly religion which, in God's name, denied God and served the World.

The Rule of God has two standing enemies upon earth. They are the World-empire and the worldly religious teaching: and the former could have little power to hurt in anything of eternal import, but for the support of the latter. Thus the theme of all the Messages is the danger of a compromise, which follows worldly motives, but justifies itself by degrading to its use spiritual reasons.

In the Church there was a party of this kind numerous enough and prominent enough to have a name. They were called Nicolaitans, after their leader; and John nicknames them Balaamites, because of the resemblance of their doctrine to the false prophet who taught the civil power to put a stumbling-block before the children of Israel, to eat things sacrificed to idols and to commit fornication, and probably from some resemblance in the meaning of the names. 'So in like manner' (ii. 15) means that as Balaam did of old, Nicolas does now. As this compromise is the essence of all false prophecy, later on it is summed up as the False Prophet, Balaam being its 'pneumatic' or allegorical name. Like Balaam, this sect knew in their hearts the better way, and probably did not profess that they chose the worse for any higher reason than fear and the desire to avoid worldly loss. But in one church a woman had arisen, who declared that she had received by inspiration a commission to teach that the Christians could take part in the idolatrous worship, and even share in the pagan festivals, without contamination. She is nicknamed Jezebel, after the pagan woman who served Baal and tried to corrupt Israel from its allegiance to Jehovah[1].

The fornication to which Balaam tempted Israel was the actual sin. Therefore, it might be supposed that we have to do here with the licentious forms of pagan worship. But a church, which is accused of giving too lenient an ear to this false teaching, is otherwise faithful. That such a church could tolerate the idea that an actually immoral woman was a prophetess is very improbable. Nor is there any proof, apart from this reference, that there ever was an antinomianism of this type in the Church. Fornication is elsewhere used in the book for compromising with the pagan worship; and the whole drift of the Messages seems to show that the author is dealing with this evil, and this evil alone. Had he

[1] There is no evidence here of a sect of Gnostics called Balaamites. There was a sect of persons who conformed on some kind of religious excuse, nicknamed Balaamites. But that this name was given them by John himself appears from his not giving it to them on the first mention of them, but on the second, as if it only occurred to him on second thoughts. 2 Peter ii. 15, Jude *v.* 11 and especially Josephus, *Antiquities*, IV, vi. 6, are evidence of the important place this story had come to occupy in Jewish tradition; and for Balaam as the typical false prophet there is considerable evidence in later Jewish literature. I am indebted to Mr Manson for references to *Mishnah*, *Pirke Aboth*, v, 28, 29, in Taylor's *Sayings of the Jewish Fathers*, pp. 94 f., and for a reference to Jesus as Balaam in Herford's *Christianity in Talmud and Midrash*, pp. 63 ff. The identification of the woman with Jezebel appears to be John's alone, but it came naturally after Balaam. Probably John thought he had also philological grounds for these identifications. Scientific etymology has nothing to do with the matter. The question is not what the names mean, but what they were taken to mean. In *Talmud*, *Sanhedrim*, 105ª, Balaam is derived from בלע עם, 'devourer of the people'; and, if John took Nicolas to mean 'Conqueror of the people,' with his view of conquerors, the meanings were not far apart. The woman's name cannot have been anything like Jezebel, else it would have been mentioned, but, if the claim is to maintain a pure heart amid outward conformity to idolatry, John may have related this to Jezebel by ascribing to the name the same meaning as Gesenius does, 'The chaste or pure one.'

had actual immorality to consider, he must have spoken of it as something different from false prophecy. The end of such concession would be the immoral rites and the old pagan licentiousness, but, if this stage were already reached, and the woman had had disciples who followed her example, and the church at Thyatira had not condemned it, nothing could have been held fast. The only phrase which might seem contrary to this view is about knowing the depths of Satan, because it might mean that men could go through any vileness of action, yet remain pure in heart. But it is much more likely to mean the depths of his subtilty. The Christians were to learn, as it were, to overreach him. He had brought this engine of persecution against them, and they were to make all the concessions required of them, while they defeated him in his purpose by remaining loyal and pure in heart. The real depths of Satan is this self-deception, and those who have not known it are those not misled by this error.

Thus we may sum up the chief thoughts which were working in John's mind, in two points:

1. The present persecution being only another phase of the long struggle between the Rule of God and the Rule of the World, in essentials the present conflict does not differ from the past. The forms change but the principles are the more manifested to be the same.

2. Compromise with paganism is not a mere accommodation which might be expected to be temporary in its outward aspect and to have no inward aspect in one who believes that an idol 'is not anything,' and that what matters alone is the heart's real allegiance. On the contrary, it is a transference of loyalty from the kingdom of light to the kingdom of darkness, which is at once a denial of one's calling to worship and serve God and Him only and a certain relapse into conditions in which the inward light will become darkness.

If we would understand, not this part alone, but the book as a whole, we must think of John pondering on this situation and asking himself what, in view of God's word to his own heart and what was written in His word to the prophets, was his own call regarding it.

(*b*) *The Unity of these Sections and the Purpose of the Book*

As there is no break in §§ I–IV, the only question is whether § V belongs to the same experience.

The chief reason for thinking that it does is that several things in § V become plain when we read it in close connexion with §§ I–IV, and that the situation in §§ I–IV is clearer, when we regard § V as belonging to it.

1. John introduces these visions by saying that he was in the Spirit on the Lord's Day; and he closes them with the declaration that it was he who was seeing and hearing these things, and that the rest he wrote at the call and under the direction of what he saw and heard. We shall see reason later for regarding this as a claim that the experience was different in quality from the other visions in the book; and in that case, the claim being both at the beginning and the end, must include the whole. Moreover, § V is not the call to write the book, but an instruction to carry out the call in § I in a particular way.

2. The connexion may not, at first sight, be obvious, but, when it is seen, it explains expressions otherwise incomprehensible.

The natural reading of § V, x. 1 is, 'Then I saw another angel, a strong one.' As there is no other angel in the old connexion, it has been rendered: 'I saw another, a strong angel.' Grammatically this is possible, but a Greek reader would naturally have read it 'another angel.' In the new connexion, the other angel is the angel with a great voice like a trumpet (§ I, i. 10), who is again introduced in § V, x. 8. This explains the sequence. John is in Patmos and this angel summons him to behold a vision. This vision within a vision is elsewhere, but John and this angel remain in Patmos. The second angel is also in Patmos, because he stands on sea and land, and this follows without explanation, because, in John's sense of place, this has been the scene all the time. Then we understand why one is loud and the other strong, for the former is the angel of God's warnings and the latter the angel of His deeds.

Thereupon, we have the explanation of the still more perplexing passage about the voices of the seven thunders and the sealing up of what they uttered (§ V, x. 3–4). It means that the trumpet voices of warning deepen into the thunder voices of judgment. This was the way of the prophets, and especially of Amos, from whom the angel which roars like a lion comes. But John is told to seal up these judgments until the days of the seventh angel, which is a way of saying, 'Leave them to the final judgment of God.'

This also explains why the Messages end so abruptly. We should expect some emphatic closing word, vibrating with earnest warning and appeal. John hears this word, but he learns that his real warning must be a much larger task of showing his contemporaries their whole position in an age-long conflict. The rest of the book being an exhortation on this large scale, he breaks off abruptly here with mere warning.

3. Reading the whole as one experience, we see that John's call is based on the four great prophetic calls of the O.T.; and this explains where the vision of one like to a Son of Man is seen, and what is its purport, while the place establishes a connexion for the measuring of the Temple which immediately follows.

The strong angel who roars like a lion depends upon the call of Amos (iii. 8), who prophesies when God speaks with the same overwhelming necessity as a man fears when he hears the lion roar. The roll depends on the call of Ezekiel (iii. 1–3). Here, as in Ezekiel, it is eaten and is sweet in the mouth. John adds that it was bitter in the belly, and Ezekiel says he went in the bitterness of his spirit. The summing up as reliable and true words is probably suggested by the assurance in Jeremiah's call that God is watching over his word to perform it (i. 12).

As Isaiah's call is the most impressive and memorable of all the O.T. calls, its omission would be strange, all the more that the part of the book which immediately follows is largely dependent on his prophecies.

The explanation would seem to be that the vision of One like to a Son of Man is just a Christianised form of Isaiah's vision. That it is in the Temple, or the sanctuary of it, appears from John's passing directly to the measuring of it, without any explanation of how, being in Patmos, he was in a position to carry out the command. This also explains the essential purpose of the symbolism. Isaiah too sees the Rule of God, but only in the vaguely majestic form of His skirts filling the Temple. John, probably with conscious reflexion on the significance of the fuller Christian revelation, sees it in One who, being in the likeness of man, is the express image of God's person. Yet he goes back not merely to the Son of Man in the Gospels, but to Daniel and the symbolism there of the Ancient of Days, and, behind that, to God making man in His own image (Gen. i. 27), on which the whole conception of the Divine Rule as the truly human rests. The details of the appearance are thus symbols of the essential qualities of the Divine Rule: and forthwith we understand how John identifies the Christ-rule with the Rule of God, yet distinguishes sharply between Jesus and God[1].

Though this experience rests on the four great prophetic calls, it is, for John, a vivid personal experience, and is one call; and this explains, not only how he came to write his book, but the purpose for which it was written and how he came to enlarge its scope to so vast a scheme.

At the beginning and at the end it is declared to be his call. When he has seen the vision of Jesus walking amid the earthly lights, holding the heavenly, he is to write the mystery or inner meaning of it, and thereby to explain the present and declare the future. This is a true and adequate account of his book, which is not, as the preface says, mere prediction about the approaching apocalyptic end, but it deals with the principles upon which God governs the present and determines the future.

The section ends with John's own reflexion on what he had seen and heard. 'They say to me,' he tells us, 'Thou must prophesy again regarding many peoples, nations,

[1] We have here a definite step towards the conception of the *Logos*; and the relation to Isaiah is a clear help in understanding it. Yet 'The Word' in the Apocalypse still means just God's prophetic word. Dr Burney's theory that John wrote the Fourth Gospel before Revelation is little probable in any case, and this fact alone is fatal to it.

tongues and kingdoms[1].' 'Again' seems to mean 'as the prophets did of old.' The Messages are an integral part of the book, setting forth the situation to which it all applies and uttering the warnings it all reinforces. All the prophets had added judgment to warning. The call of Amos is followed by a series of woes; Isaiah is to prophesy till the land become utterly waste; Ezekiel's face is to be as adamant when he deals with the wicked; Jeremiah sees an evil break forth upon all the inhabitants of the land. But the purpose of the strong angel is to show John that God has other ways than immediate judgment and another appeal than mere fear, and that he must expand his prophecy into an account of the age-long, world-wide conflict between the Rule of God and the Rule of the World, so that every humble Christian, as he refuses to worship the imperial image, may realise the great warfare in which he is a soldier.

(c) *The Nature of the Experience*

As John introduces this experience by saying that he was in the Spirit on the Lord's Day and closes it with the declaration that it was he who was hearing and seeing these things, it would seem as though he regarded it as different in quality from the rest, which he wrote at the call and under the direction of it.

The meaning might merely be that he had a specially intense experience of being rapt away from time and sense, but the natural interpretation would be that, in some measure at least, he saw in ecstatic vision.

Against this view there are reasons which, at first sight at least, appear to our minds convincing.

1. The long train of reflexion upon the situation.

We might suppose that this was added after, but the vision of the strong angel depends, not on the previous vision of One like a Son of Man, but on the Messages based on it.

This does not require us to assume more in the original experience than some general guidance to the author's thought; but vision in ecstasy is so foreign to our experience that we do not know what measure of consistent thinking

[1] See note, p. 135.

it could embody. A dreamer can at times carry through remarkable trains of thought; and we may suppose that the spirit of the prophet was more subject to the prophet than the spirit of the dreamer to the dreamer. Moreover, John's state was one of absorption in intense, continuous brooding on the situation, and the experience was only illumination and guidance on a problem already the subject of much reflexion.

2. The detailed and complicated nature of the picture.

The vision of One like a Son of Man seems to be a vision within a vision. The seer is in Patmos; the vision is elsewhere: yet he continues in Patmos and there sees another vision, after a series of messages on which the new vision depends. This makes the whole longer, more complicated and more elaborate than anything in the O.T. which could be regarded as ecstatic vision.

But scenes within scenes and a sense of being in two places at the same time are not unknown even in dreams; and, when the connexion is sought, it is usually found in a complicated, though rapid, train of subconscious thought, which by later reflexion can be made explicit.

3. It depends on O.T. calls and O.T. symbolism.

In addition to the four prophetic calls, already considered, all the details of the descriptions are drawn from the O.T. Moreover, they are there as symbol and not as picture: and the application is so elaborate as to seem to our minds at times artificial, with the result of suggesting that the whole is deliberate mosaic. The symbols of the central figure are all derived from Daniel. They reappear *seriatim* in the Messages; and are manifestly thought to be specially appropriate to the defect rebuked and the type of victory promised over it.

In three cases the description is repeated in the same words, and the agreement of the symbol with the message is, in each case, plain. Smyrna: 'The first and the last who was dead and came to life,' goes with faithfulness unto death and receiving a crown of life. Pergamum: 'He who has the sharp two-edged sword,' goes with a situation which needs a sharp judgment and a victory marked by the white stone of acquittal. Ephesus: 'He who holds the seven stars and walks amid the seven lampstands,' agrees with testing the false, maintaining love by truth, removing the lampstand and possibly with the paradise of God as the seat of the heavenly light.

Where the description varies, the identity can usually be traced in the O.T. The Son of Man (i. 13) is the Son of God (ii. 18). Both were titles of the Messiah, and the identification depends on God making man in His own image (Gen. i. 27). 'He who has the keys of death and Hades' (i. 18) has become 'He who has the key of David' (iii. 7); and this is explained by Is. xxii. 22, that it opens and none shuts and shuts and none opens[1]. In the message to Laodicea 'the Amen, the faithful and true witness, the beginning or principle of the creation of God' all say the same thing with rising emphasis: and that it must at least have some relation to 'clothed to his feet,' 'girt about the breast with a golden girdle,' 'hair white as wool,' and 'a countenance as the sun,' appears from the blessings which are 'raiment to the naked,' 'gold to the poor,' 'sitting down on his throne' as the Ancient of Days, and 'eye-salve to the blind.'

Only 'His voice as the voice of many waters' (ii. 15) seems to be omitted. The corresponding phrase in iii. 1 is 'He who has the seven spirits of God,' and the evils in this church are having a name to live and being dead, and defiled garments. Both are easy to connect with waters through the water of life and cleansing. But the difficulty is to see the connexion with the seven spirits, unless it be through the idea of them as torches of fire (iv. 5), and with some such meaning as the saying of John the Baptist 'I indeed baptize you with water...he shall baptize you with the Holy Ghost and with fire' (Luke iii. 16).

This elaborate use of symbolism suggests the studied,

[1] There is a similar combination in Mt. xvi. 18, 19 of the gates of Hades and the key that opens and no one shuts. In the earlier writings of the N.T. Jesus, not Peter, is the foundation, and, a little later, it is He who bursts the gates of Hades. It would, therefore, appear that the key of David, the key of the Kingdom of Heaven, and the key of Hades were combined and given to Jesus; and only later were transferred to Peter. This might indicate that Revelation is earlier than Matthew, which would determine for it a fairly early date.

even the artificial. But the symbolism of dreams is often strangely elaborate. The present systematising of it seems to go beyond probability, precisely because it is hard to discover any basis for it. But here we have the ground to our hand in the O.T. and the symbolism especially of its later books, which possibly was systematised vision symbolism from the first.

Nor is the result a mere mosaic of Scripture passages. All parts of it have an individual message, and combine to serve one purpose. If vision is a state of mind in which the subject receives in pure passivity external impressions, this is clearly not vision. But what little we do know of such states concerns the surprising activity, rapidity and subtlety of the subconscious working of the mind. Moreover, vision, even ecstatic vision, may be an uncertain description, as there may be all shades of the intensity of it, even as there are all varieties of depths in the subconscious.

But even should we regard this experience as purely ecstatic, there would be no reason for thinking the rest of the book to have the same character, any more than we should suppose that, because Isaiah had one vision, he never wrote of things he had seen in the common light of day. John, indeed, seems to say quite plainly that he wrote the rest deliberately, in response to the call of this very special experience, as a prophetic testimony to his time. Therefore, vision in the rest of the book would seem to be little more than the accepted literary prophetic form. Whatever may have been the case with the earlier prophets, long before this time vision had come to be as much the recognised form of prophecy as dialogue of philosophy, both doubtless traditions from a time when prophecy was ecstasy and philosophy public discussion. Had it been otherwise with John, he would have given the assurance about seeing and hearing at the end and not here; and, moreover, while he could receive a commission to write a book in which he might expect Divine guidance, he could not receive a commission to see a series of visions. This does not preclude the possibility of some influence from the intensity of the first experience upon the rest, or of the effect of his solitary state in Patmos, when the pageantry of his inward eye may have seemed far more real than the world which spoke to him through his senses. Yet visions in what is written in obedience to a call and according to a plan must be in essence literary form, not ecstasy.

II

THE FORCES IN CONFLICT DURING THE WORLD-ERA

§§ VI–IX

THE seer has been called to prophesy like the prophets of old: and, from this point onwards, we have the book of his prophecy in fulfilment of this task.

It consists of two almost equal parts: I. §§ VI–XVI, The Rule of the World and its Fall; II. §§ XVII–XXVII, The Rule of Christ and the Final Order. These subdivide into:

I. (1) §§ VI–IX. The Forces in Conflict.
(2) §§ X–XVI. The Fall of the World-empires and of the World-rule.

II. (1) §§ XVII–XIX. The Millennial Kingdom.
(2) §§ XX–XXVII. The Last Things.

Under these four heads the rest of the book will be discussed.

In accord with Daniel the World-era, or more probably only the era of the World-empire, is to last 1260 days or 42 months or a time and times and half a time, meaning three years and a half. This John regards as a definite prediction: and he seems to reckon days as years. His references to Moses and Egypt may show that he begins with the first empire which oppressed Israel. This period, he thought, was nearing its close, yet the end was still far enough away for much to happen in the interval.

§ VI. He is given a reed as a measuring rod, and is instructed to measure the sanctuary and the altar. This is after the pattern of Ezek. xl. 5. He is to leave out the outer court, because it is to be given over to the Gentiles, by whom the Holy City itself is to be trodden under foot during all this period. As 'the Holy City' is later the description of the Millennial Rule, we have to do, not with the actual Jerusalem, but with the earthly manifestation of the Rule or Kingdom of God. This Rule is afterwards personified as a woman, who, though a heavenly sign, is also a city in the world. Measuring only the sanctuary and the altar of this city seems to follow the thought in the Messages that uncompromising religion alone will count in the great struggle which is before the Church. Yet the fact that the treading down is to cease with the end of the World-rule means that, even for the weak, there is hope in a new order.

During all this period God's two witnesses continue to prophesy in sackcloth. Two olive trees and two lights do not mean four witnesses, but two who are lights fed with an unfailing supply of oil. They are the prophets and the law, represented by Elijah and Moses, as is shown by their being able to shut up the heavens that they do not rain, like Elijah, and turn the waters into blood and smite the earth with every curse, like Moses. While their task lasts, they are unassailable, but, when it is ended, they will be conquered and slain.

Their corpse lies exposed for all to see on the streets of the Great City. This is not a real city, but one allegorically called Sodom and Egypt, and afterwards Babylon the Great. We shall see later reasons for taking it to be the World-rule incarnate in the worldly civilisation. As this is sustained by the world-empires, it could be called after any of them. Elsewhere in the N.T. Babylon is used thus allegorically. This, and not the mere local Jerusalem, is the real city in which our Lord was crucified, the city which is drunk with the blood of the saints and in which all the martyrs of all ages have suffered.

For three days and a half the corpse of God's representatives lies exposed; and, at the sight, the peoples rejoice that such troublesome, or possibly testing, witnesses have been silenced. This is the half of the week from Daniel; and again we are probably to understand years for days. At the end of this time they come to life and ascend to heaven, and, in that very hour, there is a great earthquake by which a tenth of the city falls, 7000 are slain and the rest are terror-struck.

This is how it seems to read, for 'names of men' sometimes means in Hebrew little more than a number of people. Yet it must mean more here, and 7000 is a number of perfection and suggests the blotting out of a class. The explanation, as usual, is found in Daniel. The three days and a half are the half of the week during which the sacrifice and the oblation cease (Dan. ix. 27). This shows that the dead body of law and prophecy means that all the offices of religion will be suppressed. But Dan. ix. 27 is an exposition by Gabriel of viii. 24. There we read that the evil power is to 'destroy the mighty ones and the people of the saints.' The death of the two witnesses is the destruction of 'the people of the saints.' Therefore, the names of men must be the 'mighty ones,' and must mean something like 'men of name.' Then we should read 'the tenth' in accord with Rev. xvii. 12 as equivalent to the province, and 'fell,' in accord with a Hebrew usage, as 'fell away or revolted.' The meaning is that these troubling witnesses were the real bond of society and, when they are removed, revolution at once begins, the ruling class is massacred, and panic falls on mankind. Thus, in accord with his usual method, John brings down his story to the point at which the era ends, which, in this case, is a state of sheer anarchy[1].

§ VII. The story now goes back again to the beginning of this period of the World-empire. That it is not the beginning of time, but only of this period, appears from Satan, immediately after his fall, calling up the World-empire from the sea, and from the woman being nourished in the wilderness for the 1260 days.

John does not enter upon the question of the state of the world before this period. Yet he does not seem to have regarded it as a state of primitive innocence, as though, up to this point, the demonic powers of the air had exercised justly their duty of supervising and reporting, and man had lived in accord with God's mind under them. The victory of Michael and the heavenly hosts over them, while it is the beginning of a long struggle on earth between the Christ-rule and the World-rule, is, from the first, a guarantee that the victory of the saints is sure. If, therefore, John did

[1] See note, p. 136.

not regard the previous state as one of submission to those doubtful, though as yet divinely appointed, rulers, he must have had some such idea as Paul's, of the previous state as one of law in which these powers were man's accusers, and which he could not obey, and of the new state, with all its difficulties, as the hope of the Gospel.

After this question of date comes the question of the place of the conflict. It is generally assumed to be heaven, as though Satan followed the male-child to God's throne, and there engaged in conflict with the heavenly hosts. Apart from John's idea of heaven and the unquestioned power there of the Almighty, we have the fact that the sign is seen from earth, from which it would appear that, Satan having abused his power, Michael comes down to dethrone him, and that the conflict takes place in the lower heaven of the stars, which to us is merely the heavens. The victory would then mean that Satan is deposed from his old position as the prince of the powers of the air, and with it is broken the religious dominion of the demonic powers, so that, from the beginning of the conflict, they are, for the saints at least, mere incarnations of earthly violence. Thus the very rage of persecution is a proof for the saints of the lost dominion of their chief enemies, because it was a mere counsel of despair.

It may be that some accepted form of Jewish mythology lay behind this symbolism. But nothing really parallel is found in any Jewish writing. It is, therefore, at least possible that we have merely our author's own development of Daniel and Job, working with the Christian idea of casting down the principalities and powers of the heavenly spheres which hinder free access to high heaven. That this sense of deliverance from the fear of demons had a large place in the faith and peace of the early Christians many ancient writings testify.

The birth of the male-child is interpreted as a prehistoric, probably mythological, possibly astrological account of the birth of the Messiah. Nothing we know of in Judaism or in Christianity or in our author's own conception of the Messiah gives support to this idea. All this part of his book is so steeped in the influence of Daniel that we ought first to seek the explanation there. We have a prophecy about the Holy City (Dan. ix. 24) and the time being decreed to bring in everlasting righteousness. This, being the true rule of the Holy City, goes with her anointing as a most holy place. In that case, the child with which the woman is in labour is her true righteous rule. The other passage which may have influenced the author is Mic. iv. 7–10. Again it is God's righteous reign in Mount Zion, described as 'the former dominion, the rule of the daughter of Zion.' She is in travail with this rule, or at least John might read it so. But she is to go forth and dwell in the field, which may have given the suggestion for her fleeing into the wilderness. Here again we have Zion's divine righteous rule. The child, in Revelation, is caught up to the throne of God, which seems to say that God's own rule is at present the only guarantee that it ever will exist on earth. But this guarantees its destiny to rule the nations with a rod of iron. This quotation from Ps. ii. is also used in Rev. ii. 27, where the victorious saints share in this rule, and in xix. 15, where it is exercised by the Word of God, which there is just God's prophetic word, in preparation for the Holy Jerusalem. Later it seems to be this same rule which descends upon it from God out of heaven, and by which the promise of the saints to share in it is fulfilled. As the two women are parallel conceptions, we would seem to have a rule related to the Rule of God in the same way as the World-empire is related to the Rule of the World, being the kind of *real-politik* which ought to be in the earth, but the place of which is usurped by brutal, idolatrous imperialism. It is the woman's own child, because it is the natural product of her spirit; whereas the imperial rule is Satan's usurpation of its place. Yet she has given it birth and, in spite of all usurpation, it is secure, and God is working for it and has made His victory certain by beginning at once with the casting down of the demonic powers of the air. The woman is the God- or Christ-rule, as the woman who sits in state in the wilderness is the World-rule, and just as the World-empire is related to the Rule of the World, as the corporate state which expresses in visible form the whole spirit of the corrupt worldly civilisation, so this is related to the Rule of

God or Christ as the actual just government of the peoples which is to embody its spirit.

This method of describing an invisible conflict behind the earthly manifestation is copied from Daniel, where all conflicts have this twofold aspect. The woman, being the Rule of God, is clothed with the sun, stands on the moon, and has on her head a crown of twelve stars, which may, in the connexion of heavenly lights, mean, as has been suggested, the stars of the Zodiac, though, as they are constellations, this is doubtful. However we interpret these details—and perhaps they were never meant to be interpreted—the general meaning is that she possesses all the heavenly lights, which must mean, as in the general symbolism of the book, the higher truth which should guide humanity. A similar idea appears in the dragon sweeping down a third of the stars with his tail. Out of light should come order. The Divine order is removed meantime to heaven to await God's time, but the conflict which remains on earth is to end in its perfect rule.

Like all similar representations in the book, the picture is a reflexion of principles. The main elements are drawn from Daniel. In Dan. xii. 1, Michael is already the great prince who stands for God's people. In x. 21, there is a suggestion that what happens upon earth is a mere reflexion of the warfare of unseen powers, in which Michael is the leader of God's hosts. In later Judaism he becomes the guardian angel of the saints of Israel (1 Enoch xx. 5). But what is even more relevant is that, later still, he has to do with the righteousness of all nations. Thus he comes to be the champion of righteousness against evil[1].

It has been suggested that in this heavenly sign we have the influence of pagan astrology as well as of pagan mythology—the sign of the woman and the dragon being the constellations of Virgo and Draco. It would not be difficult to conceive our author thinking that these constellations appeared long ago as a sign after some great spiritual event, as the rainbow appeared after the flood. But, just as this sign in heaven introduces the conflict of the Christ-rule and the World-rule, so the only other sign in heaven men-

[1] For fuller details see Charles, *Revelation*, I. 323.

tioned in the book—the seven angels with the last plagues which are to make an end of the whole World-era (xv. 1)—closes it: and it would be difficult to find in this an astrological meaning.

The dragon as the enemy of God's people depends on Is. xxvii. 1 and li. 9. Possibly by our author's time this may have been a familiar name for the devil. Yet it may have been he who first gave it currency. Satan is still, as in Job, the accuser of his brethren, but we know that in Jewish thought, before this time, he was a fallen angel and the organiser of evil. As the thought of no people is in a water-tight compartment, influences outside of Judaism may have contributed to this development. Yet common elements in the beliefs of different peoples may arise from a common experience. What we do find at this period is a widespread, deep perplexity about a power so disintegrating as evil being able to organise itself mightily against the good, with the problem intensified for a Jew by the religious nature of his country's struggle and its political weakness. This agrees with the idea of Satan in Revelation, because, as evil continues after he is shut up in the Abyss, he cannot be the source of individual temptation. But, as the powers of evil cannot organise themselves without his presence, he is the organiser of evil.

The great voice speaking from heaven (*v.* 10) is an aside to John's contemporaries, which assures them that there can be no dubiety about victory, though the conquest has to be won, as Christ and the martyrs had won it, by not loving their lives even to death. The purified heavens can already rejoice, for God's salvation and the authority of Christ are secure; and if the earthly conflict is terrible, it is only for a little time.

Why the woman comes down to earth to be persecuted John does not explain. But she has now the succour of the purified heavens. The wings of the great eagle, which carry her to safety in the wilderness, must be a reference to the fourth living creature which is like an eagle. If the living creatures, as is probable, represent the four elements of nature—earth, fire, water, air—this is the air, now purified by the fall from it of the powers of evil.

In the Old Testament the wilderness is the place to which true religion has to betake itself (Amos v. 25; Hos. ii. 14; Is. vii. 23–25, and in particular Ezek. xxxiv. 25, 'and they shall dwell securely in the wilderness'). The meaning seems to be that the Christ-rule on earth sought refuge in simplicity and poverty and humility, and left the stirring, wealthy, bustling ways to the World-rule.

§ VIII. The Christ-rule itself Satan could not destroy, but he cast floods of water, possibly calumny, after her. This flood the earth, which, as opposed to the sea, is the fruitful, religious element, swallows up, which may mean that the calumny, or whatever the assault may be, is turned to blessing.

Having failed to destroy the Christ-rule herself, the devil sets himself to persecute her seed, the faithful in all generations. For this purpose he calls up from the sea the World-empire. This is from Daniel, but the sea is also for our author the barren, restless pagan element. As Satan is now the prince of this world, he gives to the World-empire his seven heads and ten horns, as the symbol of universal dominion. That the beast is not Rome in particular, but World-empire in general, appears later in the use made of it. Here it appears also in the fact that the four beasts in Daniel are combined into one picture. Of the four beasts in Daniel one has four heads, which, with the other three, make seven; in Rev. the beast has seven heads. In Dan. one has ten horns; in Rev. the beast has ten horns. In Dan. one is like a lion, one like a bear, and one like a leopard; in Rev. it is like a leopard with feet as a bear's and a mouth as a lion's. In Dan. only one has 'a mouth speaking great things'; in Rev. this belongs to the general picture. The heads are afterwards explained to be rivers and also peoples, and this seems to mean seats of empire, and so to be equivalent to the various empires in which this World-power has been manifested.

Then comes the verse which reads literally, 'And one of his heads as smitten to death, and the stroke of his death was healed' (xiii. 3). This is usually explained by an illness of Caligula, whose recovery gave a vast stimulus to the imperial cult. That this may have suggested the idea is possible, though barely probable, but, if so, our author gave it his own application, because, for several reasons, the explanation cannot be a particular emperor. First, heads are not emperors, but seats of empire, or at least of monarchies. Second, John is not dealing with particular events, but is explaining the inwardness of the World-rule. Again, as it is something which increases the power of the World-empire for the whole forty and two months, which means the whole 1260 years of its continuance, it must describe, not one event, but a general characteristic. Finally, it is a stroke of the sword, and not an illness, and it is the beast which recovers, not the head[1].

The application to the whole era also excludes another possible explanation, which is that, as heads are regions of the world, this might have some reference to the late troubles in Judea, which to a Jew might seem to have threatened the security of the whole Empire; and John might have generalised by thinking of other occasions, such as the revolt of the Maccabees, which had shaken the World-empire at other times.

But the context requires an even more general meaning, and this is found more simply by regarding 'one' as indefinite and construing according to an ordinary Hebrew construction[2], 'when one of his heads was as smitten to death, then the stroke of his death was healed.' The meaning is that a head might receive a mortal blow, but the beast itself does not die. Interpreted by the symbolism of the book, it means that when, at any time, its seat of power, or the particular empire which ruled at the moment falls, World-empire does not pass, but is presently as strong as ever in another form. This power of recuperation causes all save the elect to follow it in abject awe, and worship the Evil One who gives it authority and makes it magnify itself as though it were God. God will suffer it to act during all this period, and those written from the world's foundation in the book of the Lamb, the supreme example of not fearing them that

[1] *αὐτοῦ*, xiii. 3. The head would be *αὐτῆς*.

[2] The ו conversive. For the indefinite use of אחד, on which *μίαν* is based, cf. Deut. xxviii. 55, 2 Sam. ii. 1 (trans. 'any one' in R.V.) and, if the M.T. be right, 2 Sam. vii. 23.

kill the body, alone among men, refuse it worship. Yet to go into captivity is to make captive, and to slay is the true loss of one's life[1]. And herein is the faith and patience of the saints.

§ IX. This beast rose out of the sea. John now sees another beast coming up out of the land. The sea is from Daniel, but this origin from the land seems to have no O.T. parallel. In any case, John would give this his own meaning, but, if it is his own, a symbolic significance is the more certain. The sea seems to be the troubled political element, and the land the religious element, which ought to be quiet and fruitful. In any case this second beast is from religion, for it is afterwards called the False Prophet, the personification of false religious teaching. Hitherto this has been false Christian teaching, but here John seems to be thinking specially of pagan religious leaders, and probably, in particular, of the priesthood of the pagan worship, for they alone could exercise all the authority of the Imperial Power before it. Now would any kind of Christian urge the penalty of death for refusing to take part in the imperial cult.

The only thing which might seem to call this in question is the beast's symbol. Though it speaks like a dragon, which is to say, in the service of the devil, it has, not ten horns like the Imperial Power, but two like a lamb, which might be the symbol of Christ. This might mean that the Christians who taught concession were the worst cause of persecution, or it might mean that they had drawn so near the pagan teachers that the empire was ready to recognise and use them. In a figurative sense, too, they might have given life to the image; and as John is speaking of the False Prophet of all time, he may not be referring to particular doings in his own time. In Deut. xiii. 1 if any prophet says, 'Let us go after other gods,' and confirms what he says by a wonder which comes to pass, it is only to prove men, to know whether they love the Lord their God with all their heart and soul. And Jesus spoke of the Jews as an evil generation which seeks after a sign. Yet these wonders have a prominence here, and once again have a prominence later on,

[1] This is the only possible translation of the text as it stands. It does not make the clauses parallel, but it makes a contrast and relates it closely to John's own experience.

which suggests personal experience. Further, these wonders, especially making the image actually speak, are known to have been practised by the pagan priests, while it is very unlikely that any kind of Christian would take part in such doings. The likeness to a lamb might mean that persecution was proclaimed as the way to peace, like the English writer who affirmed that toleration would require the maintenance of a standing army to keep order.

Here we seem to have an important piece of contemporary history. Though it has not yet succeeded, the pagan priesthood is working to make refusal to worship the imperial image a capital offence, and it will succeed in time. Already it has managed to impose a device which exercises an effective economic pressure. The 'mark' was the technical name of the stamp or seal necessary for making business documents legal. A circular stamp-plate has been preserved with 'In the 35th year of Caesar' engraved round it. It is in Greek and the numbers are in Greek letters. As business could not be done without sealed documents, the device seems to have been hit upon of making the wearing of this stamp on the forehead or the right hand the licence to buy or sell; and, from the connexion, it must have been given only to those who had observed the imperial rites[1].

The only perplexing question is the number of the name (*vv.* 17–18). We have seen that the mark had a name and a number: and the meaning must be that the name is itself a number and does not need another, which is typical apocalyptic interpretation. The name on the seal-plate is simply 'Caesar.' On a seal of Domitian it is 'Emperor Caesar Domitian.' As the seal was proof of due rites being paid to the Imperial Power, it might, in any reign, only have had on it 'Caesar.' But as John is generalising the imperial cult, he would have fixed on the title and not the personal

[1] Deissmann, *Bible Studies* (Eng. trans.), p. 242. The general interpretation of the number and the name I had wrought out before, but till Mr Manson drew my attention to this important information from the papyri, I assumed that the mark was only a metaphorical expression for having worshipped the imperial image. But this seems to make it certain that the description should be taken literally: and it is a remarkable confirmation of the view here taken of the number.

name in any case. The name, therefore, we have to work with is 'Caesar.' The 'number of a man' suggests 'with the pen of a man' (Is. viii. 1) which is supposed to mean the present phonetic Hebrew characters. Therefore, we are probably to interpret by Hebrew numerals. It is a number any person of penetration can understand, which would seem to mean that the key to it has already been given. But the only characteristic number hitherto found is the 1260 years of the World-empires. Finally, this is the number in the passage in Daniel (xii. 7–10) from which the saying about 'He that has understanding let him reckon' is taken, being there in the form of 'time and times and half a time.' 'Caesar' in Hebrew was written sometimes with three letters and sometimes with four. If we suppose either that the first letter (if there were only three) was raised by the same mark as was used in Greek to multiply by ten or (if there were four) was multiplied by the second, the value of which is ten, its value is 1000. The value of the second (or third, if there were four) is 60 and of the last 200. And 1000 + 60 + 200 is the number required. The Greek letters of the text are usually read straight on and are taken to mean 666. A later tradition gives 616, but this, being influenced by a desire to work in a reference to Titus, is improbable. Yet it shows that there was an early doubt about the letters. The number 666 runs so smoothly that a change in the last might easily come by a transcriber's error, especially as the only correction needed is from the ordinary sigma to the digamma, which is very like it. That the whole is an inscription is important, because in inscriptions the first letter does not signify 600, but 1000. Then by giving each letter its value and adding them together, as in the former case, we have again 1000 + 60 + 200[1].

The meaning which the wise are to understand is, then, that the imperial cult is merely a form of the age-long idolatry of the whole era of the World-empire, which is a repetition

[1] קיסר or קסר. χξσ for χξϛ. χ the first letter of χίλιος. It seems probable that the Greek usage of letters for numerals was borrowed from the Phoenicians, from whom the Hebrews took their alphabet. It is possible, therefore, that the ʹ by which the Greeks multiplied by 10 is a relic of the Semitic Yod.

of the idea in the Messages, and that compromise with it is not a mere temporary concession, but is a passing over from the Rule of God to the Rule of the World.

This number has the still further confirmation that it forms the transition to the next passage, which otherwise is entirely abrupt. The years of the World-rule are long, but they draw to a close: and John sees, and would have others who, like him, are faithful unto death, see the Rule of God waiting to take its place. In accord with his usual method, he brings down his narrative to the great event which closes the period; and here it is the Rule of Christ in the Holy Jerusalem. Also he hears the heavenly song, all pervading as the voice of many waters and loud as great thunder, yet melodious as a chorus of harps, making melody amid all this discord. As many more than the 144,000 learn this new heavenly song before the end, he is obviously speaking of a present experience. None can see this vision of hope, none can learn this melody at less cost than being redeemed from earthly things, especially fear of earthly powers. But those who keep free from all contamination, especially of idolatry, and follow the Lamb whithersoever he goes, even if it be to Calvary, and have no lie in their mouths, especially the lie of professing to be pagans, when they were Christians, have their triumph in it and are already the firstfruits to God and to the Lamb, the promise, that is, of the multitude of the redeemed from all nations, which no man can number[1].

[1] The passage is largely dependent on Isaiah. There is the Zion which is inviolable, the holy remnant, which is the chief source of the 144,000, the servant of the Lord, which John applies both to Christ and to the faithful, and the figure of the Lamb. And this dependence on Isaiah is carried over into the next part, especially with Is. xiv. 20, 'The Lord has founded Zion, and in her shall the afflicted of his people take refuge.'

III

THE FALL OF THE MONARCHIES AND THE END OF THE WORLD-RULE

§§ X–XVI

THE last part closed with a vision of the Rule of Christ in the Holy Jerusalem, and John now proceeds to describe the events in time by which this is to be realised.

§ X. He begins, as before, with the Temple and the prophetic witness. But last time it was a temple on earth exposed to earthly enemies, and the prophets prophesied in sackcloth and finally succumbed to their foes; now, it is its heavenly and inviolable counterpart, the temple of the tent of witness in heaven, where the prophetic word is treasured and from which the power to fulfil it now comes forth.

This combination of the expectation of the ideal Zion with the necessity of desolating judgments on earth to prepare its way has many parallels in the O.T., but it probably depends specially on Is. xi. 1–9, where with the breath of His lips God will slay the wicked, to the end that there may be no hurting or destruction in all His Holy Mountain, and the earth be full of the knowledge of the Lord as the waters cover the sea.

That the angels who carry out the judgments come forth from the temple of the tent of witness means that they come to fulfil prophecy; and the opening of its temple means that this is now to take effect in history. That they wear the symbols of Christ means that they have come to prepare the way for His Rule. Finally, that the vials of judgment are put in their hands by one of the living creatures means that these judgments are to take place by what we would call natural causes. The living creatures are the heavenly representatives of the four elements of nature—as appears from the vials being poured out on the earth, the water, the sun as fire, and the air[1].

John is not content to relegate God's working wholly to the future. The new song, the echo of which he hears on

[1] See note, p. 164.

earth, is given later (§ XXVI, xv. 3, 4), and in it we find God called King of the Ages, which would include the World-era, and, while He is to manifest His righteous acts, all His ways are righteous and true. Wherefore, before relating the fuller manifestation which is yet to come, John returns as usual upon his steps, going over the whole era of the World-empires, to show that in His judgments of them God has never left Himself without a witness.

The seven vials effect the fall of the seven ungodly and persecuting World-empires. The Imperial Power seems to be immortal, but God has never left Himself without a witness, for no incarnation of it has ever endured, and what impresses man as eternal has in fact been fleeting and insecure.

The interpretation here given depends on the meaning assigned to 'The five have fallen, the one is, the other has not yet come' (§ XIV, xvii. 10), as 'Five empires have passed, Rome still is, and one is yet to follow[1].' But even in this passage, taken by itself, while there may be some question about the particular empires intended, the general meaning is not doubtful. Nor is there really much question about the empires. Egypt, Sodom and Babylon are mentioned elsewhere. The throne of the beast is the reference to Antiochus in Daniel and must be Greece. The only one not introduced elsewhere in the book is the one interpreted as Persia. Persia has a prominence in Daniel which might ensure its inclusion, but it never really oppressed Israel, and we should, therefore, have expected Assyria. But the explanation probably is that John confines himself to the powers to which, at one time or another, the Jews had been subject. Then the only difficulty is Sodom. In accord with Is. i. 10, it might be imperialistic idolatrous Israel itself, but more probably it depends on Ezekiel, and means the nations round about Judah, which oppressed her in her weakness, the Sodom which was 'haughty and committed abominations before me' (Ezek. xvi. 49, 50).

With this key we can interpret the references. 'A foul and grievous sore' refers to the plagues of Egypt, and 'A sea as of a dead man' to the Dead Sea and so to Sodom. Babylon the Great is elsewhere represented as sitting upon many

[1] See p. 135.

waters; and, while both Babylon and the waters have allegorical meaning, the description is no doubt drawn from the natural features of the actual empire. The pollution of these waters by the blood of the martyrs, so that the angel of them complains of their pollution, and the angel of the altar, under which the spirits of the martyrs are preserved, replies with an assurance of the righteous judgments of God, probably refers to the sufferings of the Exile. Pouring the vial on the sun at least suggests sun-worship and the turning of the god into the destroyer. Long before the Persian Empire there were symbols of this worship even in Jerusalem, but, especially coming after Babylon, the description would naturally apply to the Persian Empire in which sun-worship was a recognised imperial cult. The darkening of the kingdom may refer to the chaos in which the Greek dominion fell, or it may have some reference to the Greek claim to preeminence in the realm of knowledge; and the drying up of their tongues may be a reference to the vast extension of the Greek language.

With the sixth John passes from history to prophecy. That it is Rome and that he expects it to fall by an invasion of the eastern hordes admits of no question, as the Euphrates, the frontier of civilisation in that quarter, is dried up to prepare the way of the kings of the East.

The suggestion for the unclean spirits like frogs was no doubt taken from the lying spirits in the mouth of the false prophets who persuaded Ahab, by the promise of victory, to his fatal venture at Ramoth-Gilead. That they work miracles would seem to show that the defence of the empire is to be proclaimed as a holy war. This may show that excitement and fear had already fallen upon the civilised world; or the example of Ahab may make it only mean that it is to ensure that all the forces of the empire shall be involved in its overthrow. The 'kings' are probably, as in § XIV, xvii. 12, the provincial governors.

There are references to a decisive battle on the mountains of Judah in Ezekiel, Zechariah, Joel, Daniel and Enoch, and the restoration to its place of the passage about the winepress outside the city, which must be Jerusalem, removes any doubt which may have existed that they are the scene of the great battle. The only known reference to a Hill of Magedon in that neighbourhood is in Greek translations of what in the Hebrew text is called Migron[1]. The name Migron is not formed according to any known form of place-names, and Magedon may be the right form, or John may have simply taken it from the LXX. Yet the mention that it is so called in Hebrew shows that the important point is not the place, but the significance of the name. That it may be very unscientific philology is probable, because the later Jewish writers had no scientific fetters upon their phantasy in finding allegorical interpretations.

§ XI. In the old order of the text there is nothing more. This, after such a stupendous staging of the scene, is incredible. But in the new we have a sequel which justifies this setting of the vast armies of the whole civilised world against the countless hordes of barbarism.

Though these hordes are terrible in their own strength, the victory is given to them by a power neither side recognises. This is none other than the Word of God. In the connexion, this must be the promise of deliverance to which all the prophets had testified, from the sanctuary of whose testimony, now open, the judgment comes forth. In short we have once again the idea derived from Daniel of an invisible warfare as the inner reality of visible events.

John sees this Word, as a rider on a white horse, the symbol of victory, coming forth from heaven. He is faithful

[1] This reference to Migron was suggested by Mr Manson. Before it was made, the name seemed to me connected in some way with הַר מוֹעֵד and to be dependent on Is. xiv. 13, 'The Hill of the Assembly,' originally probably the assembly of the gods under the north star, of the Babylonian mythology. But the above is at least possible. The word occurs twice in the M.T. of the O.T., 1 Sam. xiv. 2 and Is. x. 28. In the former the LXX has Μαγών, which the Lucianic recension changes to Μαγεδδώ: in the latter the LXX has Μαγεδώ. John's form would explain all these variations, and it only requires the change of ד into ר to explain the present Hebrew text. The place, moreover, is suitable. It was in the more inaccessible part of the hill-country of Benjamin (1 Sam. xiv. 2) and it is a notable place in the advance of the Assyrians (Is. x. 28). But the meaning is probably more important than the locality. It has some reference to 'multitudes' and it may conceivably have been related to 'judging.'

and true. Prophecy is spoken of as faithful and true words, so this would appear to mean that he comes to fulfil prophecy. And he has eyes to look into the heart, and power over all, which are again symbols of the Christ-rule.

'No one knows his name, except himself' means that no one in these vast armies recognises that their invisible opponent is God's long declared purpose. About his real name there is no doubt. It is The Word of God.

He is followed by the heavenly host, also on white horses of victory and clothed with robes of righteousness, and his work is described, in accordance with Is. lxiii. 3, as treading the wine-press: and upon this passage in Isaiah the whole description is dependent. In particular this is the source of 'clothed in a garment bathed in blood.' Moreover, we have in *v.* 1 of the same chapter the kind of judgment to be exercised, the end it is to serve and God Himself as doing it: 'I that speak in righteousness, mighty to save.'

The victorious heavenly rider sets up the great wine-press of God's wrath and treads it outside the city. This must be Jerusalem, because the blood, which rises to the bridles of the horses, flows out for 1600 stadia, which is the whole length of Palestine from Lebanon to the Red Sea. Possibly this has some reference to the destruction of Jerusalem by the same power there to be overthrown, but it also seems to be a cleansing flood to purify the land from all the idolatries which have been set up in it, which may mean that the Holy Land is to be in some sense the centre of the Holy Jerusalem.

After this there can be no doubt that it is God's Word and not man's will that is King of kings and Lord of lords, for it is written plainly on his garment and on his thigh in the blood of the earthly kings and potentates who have acted as though they were God. This is confirmed by an angel standing in the sun and calling to all the carrion birds to come to God's great feast of His fallen enemies, small and great.

The end is that the beast is mastered and cast alive into the lake of fire which burns with brimstone; and the False Prophet who misled the people into taking part in the imperial cult and the worship of the emperor shares his fate. Though there is still to be one short evanescent empire, it is to be a mere shadow of reality, so that, with the fall of Rome, all real universal empire is at an end, and with it, the temptation for worldly, compromising religion to worship it.

§ XII. The next section describes the completion of this victory. The white horse again represents victory, and, if the rider on him is not still the Word of God, he must be his agent. Now his weapon is a bow, shooting arrows far and wide over the world. The voice from the midst of the living creatures shows that the agents again are the elements of nature. The riders on the horses are just the natural calamities which follow a great military disaster and the fall of government. They are internecine wars, famine and pestilence, with Hades following to gather up the spirits of the dead, while beasts of prey replace men on the earth. The sparing of the oil and the wine may mark another effect not unknown in days of calamity—the false gaiety and excess which hinder men from bethinking themselves about mending their sorrowful estate. Yet, while all these disasters are natural events, once again the real drama is in the unseen.

After this victory of God's Word, the end might seem to have come, and the writer hears the souls from under the altar in heaven[1], who have suffered martyrdom in testifying to it, speak in expectation of their immediate vindication (*v.* 9). But they are given white garments, and told that, as their number is not yet complete, they must still wait for a little time. White garments must have its usual meaning of a robe of righteousness. It has been taken to mean spiritual bodies, but (1) This meaning cannot be carried through the uses of this symbol, and, as has been said, our author uses his symbols with consistency: (2) The white raiment of the bride of Christ is explained as the righteous doings of the saints: (3) These saints in heaven do not return to earth in spiritual bodies, but by a resurrection, which would seem to mean that they return in ordinary human bodies: (4) The

[1] This has been taken to m n that the writer had a definite theory that martyrdom was a ıcrifice to God, but it is more probably meant to be related to the general idea in Rom. xii. 1, 'Present your bodies a living sacrifice, holy, acceptable to God,' and to signify their devotion and not merely the act of dying.

saints on earth are afterwards equipped by the same gift for the task which lies before them in the millennial reign. The meaning would, therefore, seem to be that, as this task is now imminent, the martyrs in heaven are equipped beforehand.

Apparently the number of the martyrs is to be completed in the anarchy which now follows, sometime in which, as we have already seen, the testimony of law and prophecy is to be utterly suppressed. The calamities after the fall of Rome finally culminate in a revolution, so appalling in its effects that John regards it as the Great Day of the Lord of O.T. prophecy, and he draws almost the whole of his description of it from that source.

§ XIII. Here the story of Rome ends, and with it the writer's interest in imperial power. He has still to provide, according to his scheme, for a seventh empire, and this he seems to do by a triple sovereignty. But whether this is the seventh, or it combines again into the seventh, it is merely a shadow of authority, for the old national cities have revolted and speedily even this shadow passes. But that the interest is now directed to the fall of the whole World-rule and the civilisation in which it is embodied appears from his dividing the Great City. Had his mind still been directed to empire, he would have set up three beasts.

The seventh vial is poured out upon the air, and then he hears a voice from the heavenly temple, from the throne, which is probably a reverent way of referring to God Himself, saying, 'It is done.' This seems to mean that it is done already, and that no special calamity needs to be inflicted, as past events have brought anarchy naturally in their train. This would, by itself, show that the earthquake with which this vial begins is the same as that with which the last ends. The last, moreover, was so final, that a greater could not well happen after it, or, if it did, it, and not the previous one, would have been the Great Day of the Lord. The repetition is to explain a new aspect of it. Last time it was the overthrow of Empire, now it is the beginning of the destruction of the whole worldly civilisation. The pouring out of the vial on the air would seem to mean that, without definite happenings, a disease of anarchy spreads like a plague over the whole world. The descriptions no longer belong to natural events, but even if they are, as is probable, only metaphors for the shaking of all stability and order and for deadly fear, they are of a supernatural and apocalyptic magnitude.

This alone would show that we are no longer dealing merely with the fall of empires. For the first time we have the name Babylon the Great. But she is the same Great City as has been mentioned before, and which has already been called Sodom and Egypt, as if she could be named after any of her representatives.

What is intended we see more clearly when we come to the description of her, which now follows.

It has already been said that the idea of the present interpretation of the book began with the view that the woman who was a heavenly sign and was a city and this woman who sits enthroned in the wilderness of an evil world and was also a city were parallel conceptions, and that the former represents the Rule of God or Christ and this the Rule of the World, and that the whole subject of the book is how the Rule of the World becomes the Rule of God.

What this second woman is appears from the seer being carried in the spirit by one of the angels of judgment into the wilderness to look upon her, for this is clearly a reminiscence of Christ's temptation in which He saw the kingdoms of this world and the glory of them.

She is described as the source of all idolatries, which is to say that all idolatry is atheistic materialism. And it is to be noted that she is different from all the kings of the earth. She is seated upon many waters, which are explained afterwards as many peoples, so that it is a way of saying that her dominion is world-wide. That she is not any empire or Empire generally appears from the fact that she is not the beast, but is seated on it, which is to say, she is not the imperial power, but is the World-rule manifested in the worldly civilisation, which is sustained by the imperial power. With this power the beast on which she sits is identified by having seven heads and ten horns. Further, that it is this bloodthirsty persecuting dominion appears from its colour as scarlet.

Our author, as is his method, is again going back upon another aspect of the whole World-era. 'Full of names of blasphemy,' on the interpretation of 'names' of men according to Daniel (§ VI), would signify that the empires were crowded with great ones whose overbearing pride was blasphemy.

The woman herself is clothed in flaunting luxury, has a cup of the unclean things of her adultery in her hand, and is drunk with the blood of the saints of old and of the witnesses of Jesus. On her forehead there is a name written which is a mystery. As there is no secret about her name, 'mystery' cannot mean a secret. Her name Babylon is sufficiently distinguished from Babylon as an empire by being called the Great[1]. In a way parallel to 'no one knew his name,' we might take the mystery to be that her real nature was not discerned, save by those who had never fallen under her blandishments. But 'mystery' is elsewhere in the book the religious meaning of something; and this appears here also in the fact that her name is on her forehead. A name written on the forehead has hitherto been the name of the object of worship of him who bore it—the name of the beast on the false Christians, the name of the Father on the true. As it is her own name which is on her forehead, the mystery would not be her name, but that she is her own religion. In plain language this would mean that the worship of worldly wealth, splendour and renown is the essence of all idolatries.

At God's endurance of such a rival the seer is amazed with a great amazement. That this is the cause, and not perplexity, appears from what follows. The angel explains that her true 'mystery' is her utter destruction, which will turn the seer's dismay at her power into the world's dismay at her fall.

§ XIV. This exposition by an angel is after the pattern of Daniel, as the quotation about having wisdom (xvii. 9) shows; and it is of the same type, being a combination of history and prediction. From Daniel, too, we have the explanation of the 'kings,' because there they are sometimes

[1] This might mean that belief in visible greatness is her sole real faith, but the use of 'great' elsewhere shows that it means 'above the local and visible.'

equivalent either to 'monarchies' or personified kingdoms. Therefore, the five kings who have fallen are, as before explained, Egypt, Sodom, Babylon, Persia and Greece. The sixth which now is, is Rome. A seventh is to follow, but it is only to be a fleeting shadow. This may have been looked for as an empire in the West, but as the eighth beast seems to be the fourth of Daniel, before which three kingdoms are plucked up by the roots, the seventh seems to be the three into which Rome is to divide. The eighth is also the beast; which means also an incarnation of World-empire. But it is this time the beast from the Abyss, a pure satanic rule of anarchy. In accord with Daniel the ten subject kings set up as independent monarchs, which for John probably meant each province was to become a separate kingdom. Their only common mind is to serve the devil, so that they no longer sustain civilisation, but are its deadly foes. The World-rule thus ends in utter destruction, and unwittingly God's purpose of blotting out a morally effete order, to make room for His righteous order, is fulfilled.

The overcoming of these forces of anarchy by Christ and the saints finally closes the period. Thus we have John's usual way of carrying down his narrative in rapid summary and then returning upon his steps to relate the same in detail. As this victory probably depends on the saying in Daniel (viii. 25) about the evil power which is broken 'without hands,' the meaning is not visible warfare, but that this chaos will only disappear before the Rule of the Holy Jerusalem when warfare is no more.

Nothing less than the fall of the whole worldly civilisation will suit the description of the luxury which disappears. The fall of Rome, even if that event were not already past, in no way meets the requirements. (1) The event is the final fulfilment of prophecy. Many prophets had predicted the destruction of the corrupt civilisation of their time. The belief in a spiritual purpose for which this would not be too large a sacrifice was, indeed, the fountain-head of prophecy. But no prophet was concerned with Rome, as so serious a student of the Old Testament as our author must have known. (2) Rome could not be held responsible for all the martyrdoms, and still less for all the murders which had been committed in the world. (3) Rome, as a city, was not a port, much less the only one, so that all the merchants and seamen should be ruined by her fall. Nor could she have had all the luxury at any time. And if we take it to be the Roman empire and not merely the capital, how could all the Christians be exhorted to come out of her? Whither could they betake themselves? The only possible meaning is that, while they must be in the world, they should not be of it, but must be ready to lose the world to gain their souls. Therefore, it must be the world, in the sense in which this word is used in the New Testament—the world, not as God uses it to work together for good to them that love Him and are called according to His purpose, but as it is used by self-love and for the lusts of the flesh and the lusts of the eye and the pride of life. It is this that has had dominion over all the kings of the earth, and it is the wanton arrogance of this whole worldly display by which the merchants of the earth have been made rich.

§§ XV–XVI. If this be the meaning, we see at once why the description of endless pomp and luxury is so elaborated in detail, why the merchants have so large a place as mourners, and why among the sources of her wealth are slavery and the lives of men, reckoned merely with sheep and horses.

Before political and, in its train, social anarchy, the World-rule falls with startling suddenness, though she thought herself the eternal ruler of the world. She is utterly cremated, yet, as a warning, her smoke goes up for ever and ever. This is based on Is. xxxiv. 10, which shows that it is to be understood as a memorial, somewhat after Butler's idea, that conflict with evil, as well as endurance of suffering, may not be necessary to a perfect state, but the experience of having had them may.

The only difference in all this from the prophets is the feeling towards the civilisation of the time. The prophets, as well as John, thought its moral soul was dead and its body must follow soon, and both regarded this dissolution of the Rule of the World as a necessary preparation for setting up the Rule of God. But the prophets saw this desolation as an appalling, if necessary, calamity, and expected the return of the blessings of civilisation when they could be better used; while John, seeing it from among its wrecks in Patmos and with the scent of Christian blood always in his nostrils, has towards it none of their tenderness. The World, in this sense, is to him simply the great harlot whose meretricious splendour had sunk mankind into materialistic idolatry, turned them from their true allegiance, set their hearts against all the blessings of goodness, and made them persecutors of all who witness to God's truth and live for His kingdom of righteousness and peace.

NOTES

I. On Ch. xvii. 7–12 (§ XIV). The explanation given by the angel here is modelled on a similar explanation in Dan. viii. 15 ff., the most valuable commentary on it being *vv.* 21, 22. The rough he-goat is explained as the 'king of Greece.' Yet the first king is merely a great horn between its eyes. Therefore, 'king' must mean 'kingdom' or at least 'monarchy.' Moreover, it is also the 'nation' out of which four 'kingdoms' arise, after the great horn is broken. But here we have another peculiarity. The LXX translates these four מַלְכֻיוֹת by βασιλεῖς. This might, if it stood alone, merely mean a difference of text. But Mr Manson, who has made an investigation for me, has discovered three more LXX translations of מלכות by βασιλεύς in Daniel (xi. 20 and 21) and similar translations of ממלכה in 2 Chronicles, Esther, Zephaniah, Haggai, Jeremiah, Lamentations, and four in Isaiah. The singular thing is that this translation is confined to the Prophets and Hagiographa, while there is no example in the Pentateuch or in what is known as the Former Prophets, which were earlier translated, where it is always βασιλεία. This proves that, both in the later Hebrew and Jewish-Greek usage, John had precedent for calling empires βασιλεῖς. As βασιλεία had come to be a technical term for an invisible rule, either good or bad, we might suppose that there were occasions when it seemed necessary to avoid the use of it for visible sovereignties. But it more probably shows that the personification of the opposing powers in the world-conflict, of which there are so many examples in Revelation, had been a feature of Apocalyptic literature from the time of Daniel. In the use of this particular word probably both influences were at work.

The explanation of kings as Roman emperors would require us to suppose that there were to be seven single emperors and then ten all together. This is possible, but as seven hitherto has always gone with heads, which are seats of empire, and the ten horns belonging to the heads are almost certainly the provinces, it is very improbable. Nor is there any other evidence in the book that our author was interested in the Roman emperors personally.

Explanations from Roman emperors come to grief on the symbolism alone; and there is nothing in the book to support the theory. Probably being far away in Asia Minor, John thought very little about them, except as the object of idolatrous worship; and even the imperial image he rightly thought of as the symbol of empire and not as the representation of special emperors. The beast wears its diadem on its horns, which, as there are ten of them contemporaneously, probably mean the provincial rule: and with it our author was much more closely concerned.

The Nero *redivivus* theory is a mere erudite ingenuity. The Nero myth did not say he had died and would come to life, but that he was still alive and would return to work further disaster. This at least is the type of belief in the only Jewish source known, *The Sibylline Oracles*, and Jewish sources alone were likely to be accessible to our author. Whether Nero was ever regarded as Anti-Christ has no relevancy, because the only Anti-Christ in Revelation is the False Prophet, who represents simply false religious teaching. Moreover, if any emperor were likely to be in our author's mind, it would not be Nero but Caligula, who first claimed divinity and treated refusal to worship his image as disloyalty to the empire, punishable with death. Further, there is no mention here of Rome, as two other passages (Ch. xvii. 1 and 15) show that 'seven hills' (xvii. 9) is merely a transcriber's error for 'seven waters,' though the seven hills of Rome may have been in the transcriber's mind when he made it.

II. On xi. 13 (§ VI), vi. 12 (§ XII), xvi. 18 (§ XIII),

xvii. 12 (§ XIV). As interpreted, the earthquakes in vi. 12 and xvi. 18 refer to the revolution which followed the fall of the Roman Empire, and the earthquake of xi. 13 is the same event as the division into ten of xvii. 12, which ended all World-empire. Thus we have only two revolutions, The Day of the Lord, bringing the Roman Empire to an end in signal disaster, and a Day of Satan ending all rule in sheer anarchy. At first sight it might seem that xi. 13 is the smallest calamity, and, therefore, is the first of three, deriving its importance, not from its extent but from being the forerunner of all that is to follow. Then it would be the persecution of John's own time which was to slay the heavenly witnesses, and the departure of these witnesses would correspond to the disappearance of men's heavenly lights (vi. 12) and the terror to the enormous hail (xvi. 21). But the proper translation of *εἰς ἀπώλειαν ὑπάγει* in Rev. xvii. 8 and 11, when taken with Daniel, makes the identification of xi. 13 with the later calamity a practical certainty. The usual meaning of *ὑπάγειν* is active and of *ἀπώλεια* is destruction, not perdition in another world. In any case, the translation of the A.V. and R.V. 'and go into perdition' would have no point in a narrative, the very purpose of which is to show that this doom is decreed against all the powers, and much less can it explain the emphatic repetition. The explanation is in Dan. viii. 24, 'and he shall destroy to a marvel'; and it is the same power which comes on the wings of abomination and makes desolate in Dan. ix. 27. This power does not work as the former empires by strong government, but by anarchy. Thus we translate 'to bring into destruction,' and the meaning is that the seven empires, in spite of their evil, had some measure of order and stability, but this is the mere chaos which will bring the whole World-rule and the civilisation in which it is embodied to ruin. This accounts for the emphatic repetition, which, moreover, may depend on the repetition in Daniel, and it goes with the use of 'The City' in xi. 13, which is never Rome, but the World-rule. Then 'the tenth' in xi. 13 means either that on that day the first province revolted, or more probably it is quite general, meaning the province revolted, and is identical with the setting up of the ten kings as independent tyrants in xvii. 12.

IV

THE MILLENNIAL RULE

§§ XVII–XIX

WHILE our author is more concerned with the Divine meaning of events than with the events themselves, up to this point we can be reasonably certain of at least the kind of events anticipated. In this account of the Holy Jerusalem we are still dealing with what is to take place upon earth, but, while nowhere does the meaning shine more clearly through the symbolism, it is perhaps impossible to determine the type of historical event in which this is to be embodied. Nor is the only reason the difficulty of interpretation. Our author seems to have written in a period of transition between two ways of thinking of the second advent. From Judaism Christianity had inherited the idea of the Kingdom of God as a catastrophic change. But, possibly from the beginning, interest was transferred from outward circumstances to a new relation to God, whereby any sudden change of the order of the world depended upon a change of heart. For Paul the Kingdom of God was righteousness and peace and joy in the Holy Ghost; and increasing emphasis on this aspect of it in his later writings probably shows that he largely moved away from his earlier apocalyptic expectation. Our author seems to have retained something of both views; and, in his desire to do justice to both, he seeks to combine elements which he was unable to fashion into one harmonious conception.

When the original type of apocalyptic hope ultimately disappeared, the ideas connected with the Kingdom of God were transferred to the Church on the one hand and to eternal life on the other. This involved the very great loss of ceasing to think of Christianity as a new world-order and of concentrating interest on the Church as chiefly the ark of individual salvation.

That John is not touched by this later development seems beyond question. His central interest is still in a new world-order; and his deep concern with the salvation of individuals had its root in the conviction that only the saved can serve it. Even the saints in heaven continue active in its interest, while they are there made ready for returning to earth to serve it more perfectly.

That John expected this new order to come as a sharp and decisive crisis in the world's history, appears from his expectation that Christ was to come quickly and from the vivid contrast of His Rule with the old World-rule. But several elements in the description cannot be harmonised with the view that the second coming is outwardly visible and catastrophic and the Holy City a territory with geographical frontiers.

The descriptions which might be so interpreted seem rather to be the usual symbolisms which are transparencies of principles and not mere pictures of events. As this view differs widely from the usual interpretation, it is necessary to set forth in some detail the reasons for it.

1. The second coming is stripped as much as possible of all spectacular elements. The most remarkable change from earlier expectations is the absence of everything like Christ coming on the clouds of heaven and the saints being caught up to meet Him in the air. That this is not an omission which we are to fill in for ourselves appears from the deliberate transference of this kind of coming to the end of the world (§ XXVI, xiv. 14) which, on this view, would be the only purely catastrophic element in the book.

2. There is a resurrection of the saints for service in this new rule, but nothing is said either about coming down from heaven or rising from the grave. Apparently they return from Hades, because a resurrection would not be a natural description of returning from Heaven[1]. Such a return to earth was probably less difficult for John than it would be for us, so that the saints are simply there in the Holy City

[1] The souls of the martyrs are under the altar in the heavenly temple, but it is a question whether this means the dead themselves or only their heavenly representatives, because the other figures there, such as the elders and the living creatures, are of this type. Christ, having risen, would not be in Hades, but we may have here the source of the belief that He spent the interval between His death and resurrection there.

exercising the Divine Rule. And they come in ordinary human bodies, because, while the second death has no power over them spiritually, they seem to be included in the end among the dead who die in the Lord (§ XXVI, xiv. 13).

3. At the end of the 1000 years, while the Holy Jerusalem is not said either to have fallen or to have been withdrawn from earth, the saints are still scattered so indistinguishably among men that they have to be sealed on their foreheads to be preserved from the final woes; and this cannot be done till they are first made known by the opening of the Book of Life. This would seem to be a quite incontrovertible proof that the Holy Jerusalem is a kind of rule and not a visible geographical territory with its inhabitants marked off definitely from the rest of mankind. The absence of death from this new order was also less remarkable for John than it would be for us, because death was for him a consequence of the Fall. As the city is a return to the Paradise of God, death, as a result of the Fall, naturally ceases. Nor does it cease merely for the righteous, because the wicked afterwards seek death, apparently for 150 years, and cannot find it. Thus there is not even in this respect any visible mark of the righteous. It is true they live by the Tree of Life, but that is for spiritual and not merely material healing.

Satan is shut up during all the thousand years, but only as a security against deceiving the nations, in order that the promise that the fullness of the Gentiles shall come in may be fulfilled. Yet individual evil goes on as before, and has to be overcome as before by a change of heart. The very purpose of the millennial state, indeed, is to be God's supreme mission to mankind. And that it works only with spiritual appeal appears from the fact that it requires a 1000 years for its task, and that even at the end, its success is not universal. Though, like all God's agencies, it is unassailable till its work is done, it is still among the precarious earthly things, with enemies around and its chief foe only in temporary durance. In short we have come to the time when men felt that no earthly state could ever be the final, perfect order.

There is abundant evidence of a Jewish expectation that

the Messiah would be a visible ruler over Israel; and there are indications that this rule was not merely for a purified Jewish state, but also for the conversion of the Gentiles. That our author was familiar with this expectation is beyond question, and that it deeply influenced him is equally certain. But the life of Jesus had done more than transfer this expectation from the first coming to the second. It had also given a conception of a Rule of God which could not be brought in merely by outward conditions, however catastrophically changed from the present. Though this did not do away with the expectation of the new rule as an event, it slowly altered the idea of what the event would be. The sudden change came to depend upon the world being made a new creation by a change of heart, and no longer upon the heart being changed by a new creation. Something of this appears in the prophets, and was probably never quite absent from the expectation[1].

Our author still held an apocalyptic view in some form. That the coming of Christ was in some way a tremendous reality and Christianity a new world-order, as well as the promise of life eternal, was the corner-stone of his faith. But, whether consistently or not, the reality of it was a change of heart, and, in view of this, we must interpret his symbolism, not as history, but, as in the rest of the book, as transparency of the inner spiritual aspect of events, of which the visible might only be a pale reflexion.

We must note, to begin with, the length of the reign. The longest time in any other Jewish writer known to us is in the writings of a contemporary (4 Ezra vii. 28 ff.). There it is 400 years. A thousand years may only be a figure for a very long time. But the woes follow; and the first woe takes five months, which, if we are to interpret in the usual way, means 150 years. Though no figure is given, the second woe is apparently also of considerable duration, because the third is distinguished from it by coming quickly. No length of time may be given for the reason that the reader is expected to know that it is the rest of the period which made the whole era given for man to repent in equal to the World-era of

[1] There is some evidence that the two views existed together even in all Apocalyptics, Jewish and Christian.

1260 years. Or if we suppose the second woe also to be 150, and the last a month or over 30 years, it may depend on 'Blessed is he that waiteth and cometh to the 1335 days' of Dan. xii. 12[1]. During this period the saints, though guarded from its woes, still remain on the earth, which must mean that their work was still being done in it. Moreover, we are told that they only rest from their labours when this time is past. This again must mean that these torments are God's final appeal to men to repent of their idolatries. During these woes a third of mankind are released by death. These seem to be the persons with whom the discipline of their sufferings and the ministry of the saints have succeeded, because they are specially excepted from the number of those who remain hardened (§ XXIV, ix. 20). For the rest John certainly argues no happy destiny, but the fact that the period of the Christ-rule, first and longest in every blessing of grace and peace, and then in a full manifestation to men of the calamity of their rejection of God's goodness and of the appalling nature and consequences of sin, is to continue as long as the World-rule had lasted, seems to show his conviction that nothing will be lacking on God's part for working their deliverance.

Only one phrase in the book, which, however, is repeated more than once, seems to contradict this interpretation and to make all salvation of individuals depend upon God's foreordination. It is the account of those whom idolatry never touches, who, not only make no outward concession to it, but never bow down to it in their hearts, whether it be the power of the world-state or the magnificence of the world's possessions, as having 'their names written in the book of life from the foundation of the world' (§ VIII, xiii. 8).

But plainly those who are ever thus ready to witness for true religion in face both of the menace and the attraction of worldly power, not counting their lives dear unto them, are not alone the whole company of the redeemed. They are

[1] 'Blessed are the dead who die in the Lord' may also depend on this: and 'Blessed are they who are called to the marriage supper of the Lamb' may be the same, and may mean that after the 1260 years of the empires we have 75 years of anarchy.

the 144,000 who are only the firstfruits to God. The thought is the same as Paul's conviction of being dedicated to his ministry from his mother's womb: and is not the mere idea of foreordination to personal salvation, which might carry with it the foreordination of others to damnation. Of that kind of foreordination we have no hint in the whole book, but the whole course of God's action is designed to lead men to repentance, a course which would not be necessary, could God determine it all by the mere fiat of His power. The only hindrance to His mercy is that men will not turn from idols to worship and serve Him. The explanation is to be found in the fuller expression, 'having their names written from the foundation of the world in the Lamb's book of life.' That is to say, they have been appointed with Christ, to be, after His manner of fulfilling all righteousness, witnesses of God to men, that the chastisement of men's peace should be upon them and with their stripes men should be healed. The ground of this assurance was our author's humble sense that, in his own trials, he had stood in some other strength than his own, and his conviction, as he considered the solitary unwavering witness of the prophets and beheld the steadfastness of plain Christian people, that they lived in a sphere different from the uncertainties of human fears and weaknesses.

The whole of this part of the book is influenced by later Jewish apocalyptic views, yet it is doubtful whether we have to go beyond the Old Testament here, any more than elsewhere, for the symbolism.

§ XVII. The only close parallel in any known later writing is 2 Enoch lxv. 10, 'And there shall be to them a great wall that cannot be broken down.' But as the author of Enoch was a contemporary, it is exceedingly improbable that his writings ever came into the hands of our author. The frequent mention of the wall of Jerusalem in the Old Testament might be sufficient, and we have a parallel idea in Jeremiah (xv. 20): 'And I will make thee unto this people a fenced brazen wall; and they shall fight against thee; but they shall not prevail against thee: for I am with thee to save thee and deliver thee, saith the Lord.' As the wall in Revelation is of jasper, which we learn from Ch. iv. 3 is the symbol of the glory of God, it signifies a similar kind of protection to Jeremiah's[1].

We have also the idea in the Jewish apocalyptic writings of the seat of paradise as a mountain. But the site of the Holy Jerusalem is not a mountain, except as Mount Zion is the centre of it. It is, on the contrary, a large part of the earth, if not the whole of what was understood by the world at that time[2]. As the seer is merely carried in spirit to a great and high mountain to see its descent, we must rather think of Christ's temptations, when He was taken to an exceeding high mountain to see the World-rule, which was the opposite of this.

That other kingdom was for John not an actual city but a principle of rule, and, therefore, it is probable that this city is the same. This would also mean that she comes down from heaven in the same sense as the World-empire came up out of the sea. As this other rule belonged to the restless, selfish political element of life, so this belonged to the peaceful, blessed Divine element.

In later Rabbinical writings we have the gate of Jerusalem being one pearl. But it is at least possible that the suggestion came from the parable of the merchantman seeking goodly pearls, which may have suggested the change from Is. liv. 12, 'thy gates of carbuncles.' As the gates are always open, the figure can only mean that they have every attraction to him who would enter. The twelve stones are the stones of the high-priest's breastplate. It is not certain what all the stones are, and much less what they mean. They have been connected with the signs of the Zodiac, and this may have been their origin, but to introduce the explanation here is probably like interpreting words by etymology not usage. The names of the Apostles on them, instead of the tribes, seems to be a claim for Christianity as the true Israel. Yet, with this fact

[1] The only part of the description which looks like a visible city of a supernatural nature is 'for night is not there,' § XVIII, xxi. 25. But that has a suspicious resemblance to the editor's typical gloss, and probably the original was 'day and night' as in Is. lx. 11, which the editor took to be inconsistent with Rev. xxii. 5,—which is a quotation from Is. lx. 19 and must have its typical significance—and transferred it to ch. xx. 10 (cf. p. 78), where it conveys a wrong impression.

[2] Possibly everything except its 'corners.'

we must take the other that it is not their names, but the names of the tribes which are on the gates. For this there may be some recondite reason, but the suggestion that our author is thereby opposing two claims—both the claim of the Jews to be the only true Israel and the equally exclusive claim of the Christians to possess the only way into the Kingdom—has at least the advantage of simplicity.

The city which the seer first measured was this same Holy City. But it was then within his power to measure, even if his task had not been further limited to the temple. The significance of the fall of the World-rule is that the treading down by the Gentiles is at an end. All true religion of every kind can now be manifest and effective, the order of righteous, humble, sacrificing witness to the mind of God having at last no organised opponent in its task of fashioning a new world. The Lamb in the midst of the throne does not signify endowment with material might, but means that Christ's way of serving man is the heart of God's rule.

The description of this new world begins with the preparation of the Holy Jerusalem which has always been upon earth, because, while John hears the heavenly host rejoicing over it, he is on earth, and only sees what takes place there. This preparation is to clothe her in white and bright raiment, the usual symbol for righteousness. This raiment is the righteous doings of the saints, which would seem to mean that she now really enters into the heritage of her whole past.

She is now fitted to be the bride of Christ, one with Him in mind and heart. Though of heavenly origin from the beginning, her new rule comes as a new descent from heaven, with a joy which is described as the marriage supper of the Lamb. Yet the principles of the new order are continuous with the old, and only those who have observed the old requirements share in the blessing. The changes we can sum up as (1) her own perfect equipment for her task, (2) the conditions of an altered world in which she has no organised opponent, and (3) the presence of her true leader with His well-approved helpers.

Now she is so large that the seer can measure her no more, and an angel has to measure her, though he uses human measurements[1]. She lies four square, which seems to have been the ancient idea of a perfect figure. As each side is 1500 miles, it seems to mean the whole sphere of the old World-empire, possibly extended on the north and the south, in accordance with Is. xi. 9: 'For the earth shall be full of the knowledge of the Lord, as the waters cover the sea.' The unclean things, therefore, which are without, cannot depend on a geographical distribution, but can only mean, outside of power to do her harm or pollute her. She herself remains a city of pure gold, all of her a temple of God, all her common life, figured as a street of gold, pure as transparent glass, all of it a Divine worship.

This view of how she is to extend may explain the peculiar order in which her gates are given—east, north, south, west. The author's own world lay east and west, and he begins with east and ends with west, and simply puts north and south between[2]. Whether she begins with this extent or merely attains it, our author probably does not ask, because there was by this time a very extended Christian witness, so that even at an earlier time Paul could speak of the faith of the Roman church being proclaimed throughout the whole world. Besides our author's mind was upon prophecy and not geographical conditions.

§ XVIII. Really to enter into her is to put away all idolatries, to be written in the Lamb's book of life, drink of the waters of life, and be healed by her tree of life. And this tree heals nations, which must mean, orders all public life on new principles. But the heart of the matter is that her true inhabitants are the pure in heart who really see God, and have His name on their foreheads, which is the usual figure for worshipping and serving Him only.

The scene closes with the usual interruption of the prophetic narrative by a warning and encouragement to the seer's contemporaries. Yet this time it is not the usual

[1] If the second clause is genuine, it seems to say that angels use the same measure as we do. This would seem to suggest that they are of human stature. But the clause may be a gloss.

[2] Mr Manson notes that E. was the main point of the compass to the Hebrews, and the E., N., S., W. only seems peculiar to us because our fixed point is N.

angelic interpreter but Jesus Himself who speaks. In view of the nearness of this coming John is not, like Daniel (vii. 28), to keep his prophecy secret, but Jesus instructs him to publish it forthwith. Because the time is at hand the faithful are to suffer those who do injustice from corrupt hearts to be unjust and corrupt still, while those who are just out of pure hearts are to be just and pure still[1]. But all are invited freely to take of the water of life. Then when He comes suddenly, they will not be ashamed in their nakedness.

To put together the two descriptions of Jesus here may be impossible, but the union of them shows more clearly than anything else in the book the leading idea of our author, an idea which was of the utmost importance for the development of the Church's doctrine of Christ. In one aspect He is the alpha and the omega, the first and the last, the root and offspring of David, the bright and morning-star; in the other He is only the seer's fellow-servant, and of His brethren who hold the witness of the prophets. In this aspect He forbids men to worship Him and tells them to worship God alone, which testimony is declared to be the spirit of prophecy.

In most New Testament interpretation, at least of more recent date, the former view is regarded as later, based on the latter, but replacing it. Here we clearly have them together. Further, this combination is explained by John's view of an invisible, as well as a visible aspect of all earthly happenings, and in the similar view that a person like Moses or a state like Rome can be the incarnation of an unchanging principle. But the principle which Jesus embodies is not, as with Moses, a passing dispensation, or, as with Rome, a rule limited to the World-era, but is the mind and rule of the Eternal. In this aspect He is the first and the last—the beginning and the end of all right earthly rule, and the morning-star heralding the sun of God's own perfect rule. Yet, as

[1] That this is a declaration that the state of both parties is now fixed for ever is inconsistent with the context. It is only for the interval of waiting, and seems to be a Hebrew way of saying, injustice must be endured and righteousness must be done till the end come.

a man, and in His own individual aspect, He is just God's most faithful witness entrusted with the highest task in God's kingdom.

§ XIX. For a thousand years the Holy City continues its gracious mission to mankind, because Satan is bound, and the martyrs, who have never bowed before any evil power, dispense only righteous judgment. This is our author's version of Is. ii. 3: 'Out of Zion shall go forth the law, and the word of the Lord from Jerusalem,' and lx. 17: 'I will also make thy officers peace and thy task-masters righteousness.'

Thereafter Satan is let loose to rally the forces of Gog and Magog against the beloved city. As they are merely burned up by fire from heaven and the devil who has deceived them cast into the lake of fire and brimstone, in marked contrast to the long and detailed description in Ez. xxxviii–xxxix, from which the conception is drawn, it might seem to be introduced merely that so prominent an element in prophecy should not be omitted. But in no other case does our author resort to such a helpless device. On the contrary, while he draws his figures from the Old Testament, he employs them with great freedom for his own purpose. We might take it to mean that the forces which destroyed the Roman power are now to meet their own judgment. But, in this case, he would have made it plain by calling them again the Kings of the East. Nor is it likely that he thus easily disposed of everything outside of the civilised world, because civilisation had not this value for him. Names like Gog and Magog, moreover, were much more likely to be used at this date for abstract, chaotic evil forces than for peoples.

It would appear that, geographically, John conceived the whole world within the sphere of influence of the millennial rule as a square within a square, round which, possibly materially, possibly only invisibly, the Great Euphrates ran, dividing this inner square from the corners of the earth, which were the habitation of demonic powers.

When we read on, we discover what is meant. The invasion of Gog and Magog is the usual kind of rapid summary of what is to be related more fully later on. This fuller story is told in the second woe (§ XXIV, Ch. ix. 14). The woes begin with the giving of the key of the abyss to a star that fell from heaven to earth, who is plainly stated to be the devil. This is his loosing from the Abyss, but if the story of Gog and Magog were different from this and previous to it, he would already be in the lake of fire, and we should have to assume that our author had forgotten this fact, which would be an inconsistency not found elsewhere in the whole book, and is the less likely in parts of it so close together. Or we should have to assume that Satan is taken out of the lake of fire for this new purpose. This again would be inconsistent with the lake of fire as a final destiny, which it seems to mean elsewhere. Further, we are not told there what happens ultimately to the evil forces of the woes: and, only if we had already been told that they are consumed by fire from heaven, would such information be unnecessary.

But, if this identification be right, the Holy City continues through the woes, because these forces of evil are around its frontiers. Though its reign of peace over the world ends with the thousand years, it apparently continues in some form to the close of the present world, when it alone is left on the earth. This is further confirmed by the declaration that the saints are to reign for ages of ages, which at least means to the end of the present world-order.

V

THE LAST THINGS

§§ XX–XXVII

IF the invasion of Gog and Magog closes the history of the present world, we have in the description which follows another and final example of repeating in greater detail the history of the same period under another aspect. 'After these things' would thus not mean after, in the chronological order, but after I had seen what was to take place, I saw the manner of it.

The general subject of this last part is the preparation for the Final State, but there are four definite stages in the process: (*a*) The manifestation of the children of God; (*b*) The separation of the saints from evil men and their protection from evil things; (*c*) Sin when it is full-grown; (*d*) The departure of the saints and the harvesting of their works.

(*a*) *The Manifestation of the Children of God*

§ XX. This is the first scene in heaven, and the interpretation of it depends on the meaning of the roll in the hand of God. The removal of the glosses about opening the seals rids us entirely of the idea that it is a book of mysteries; and when we interpret by Dan. xii. 1, especially 'thy people shall be delivered, every one that shall be found written in the book,' there can be little doubt that it is the Book of Life. This is confirmed by the whole setting of the scene before and the sealing of the saints after its opening.

The book written within and without probably means a roll written on both sides, showing that it approaches completion. The purpose of the august assembly is to learn the names written in it, or, in Paul's words, it awaits the revealing or manifesting of the sons of God. On this purpose all the elements in the scene bear—God who alone knows the secrets of men's hearts, the thunders of His power, the burning spirits probably of His omniscience, the sea which marks the separation of His holiness, and more particularly the living creatures, representing the earnest expectation of the creation waiting for the manifestation of God's sons, and the elders the Church which has waited in hope for the full adoption of her members. The distress of the seer because no one in heaven or on earth or under the earth, no power angelic, human or demonic, was able to open the book, is not because he is ignorant of what it is, but because he knows what it is, and regards the unfolding of its secrets as the consummation of his hope.

One of the elders reassures him, probably meaning that the Church has never been ignorant of where its hope lay. 'The Lion of the tribe of Judah' and 'a lamb standing as it had been slain,' are probably combined, with the intention of showing that, though the weapons of the divine warfare are not carnal, they are effectual. The Lamb in the midst of the throne and of the living creatures and of the elders is a description which can only be pure symbolism. But it is a symbolism of the utmost importance for understanding the mind of our author. Humble submission to God's will and the violence of men, the fulfilling of all righteousness unto death, and so the dying to sin once for all, stands in the midst of God's rule, God's world and God's people, as the true victorious principle in them all.

§ XXI. The symbols of the Lamb show His authority to be just and right and good, being seven the perfect number, not, like Satan's, ten. This is the power which, as it has redeemed men of all races and made them, not slaves to its dominion, but kings and priests to God, is worthy to receive what has been wrongly given to mere might—power and riches and wisdom and strength and honour and glory and renown. And John hears every created thing in the universe ascribing them first to God as the source of all good, and then to the Lamb, through whom His purpose has been manifested and realised.

The Lamb alone is found worthy to open the book, manifestly because the judgment is not on mere outward acts, which even men, who can only look on the outward appearance, might in some way judge. It concerns the things of the heart, therefore His standard alone can be the measure of true judgment. There may further be the thought, as in John xvii. 3, that life eternal is not in mere acts at all, but is in the knowledge of God through Christ; while the later description of the saved as washed in the blood of the Lamb, which, from the general teaching of the book, cannot mean an outward lustration, but must mean sharing in his warfare, would be the real test of the faith that saves.

(*b*) *The Separation and Protection of the Saints*

When the Lamb had opened one of the seals, one of the living creatures calls like a peal of thunder: 'Come and see.' This, as has been said, like Rom. viii. 19, means that all creation waits for the revealing of the sons of God.

§ XXII. That this is the right interpretation appears from what John immediately sees. He sees four angels standing at the four corners of the earth, holding the four winds of the earth that no harm may befall in it till the servants of God are sealed on their foreheads. As the four corners are at the four points of the compass and Gog and Magog have already been described as the nations which are in the four corners of the earth (§ XIX, xx. 8), they must be the same as the four winds.

Thereupon follows the manifesting or revealing. Until now apparently the sons of God are not distinguishable from other people. But now we have what we may describe as the roll-call of the saints.

The part of the book first opened seems to contain only the names of those who were written in the Lamb's book of life from the foundation of the world, elect, not to privilege, but to the task of redeeming the world by denying utterly its idolatries, and who have suffered martyrdom in this service (§ XX, xiv. 1 and § XIX, xx. 4). The distinction between the sons of Israel from every tribe and the great multitude from all the Gentiles would at first appear to show that this body of the elect all belonged to the older dispensation. But 144,000 martyrs from it would be a very large number. This large number apparently John expects from the persecutions which were to follow the time at which he wrote. Moreover, he elsewhere claims that true Christianity is the true Israel[1]. The distinction would, therefore, not appear to be racial, but to rest on the idea of an Israel which is to be a light to lighten the Gentiles. Thus the sons of Israel are the people who, by being in some sense martyrs, shed God's light in the world, while the multitudes of the Gentiles are those who have merely received it. Thus the gloss about the different tribes is a misunderstanding as well as an intrusion.

The rest of the roll apparently contains the names of the Gentiles, in this spiritual sense of those redeemed by sacrificial service of the true Israel. They are from every nation, from all tribes and peoples and languages; and, as the sealing proceeds, their assembly swells till there is at the end a multitude no one can number.

Yet what happens to them? Seeing that they stand before

[1] This explains all that has been taken to be of Jewish origin in the book.

the throne of God, we might conceive that they are at once removed to heaven. But why, then, are they sealed on the forehead? Removal to heaven ought to have been a sufficient distinction and protection by itself. Sealing naturally would be for distinguishing them in the earth and for their protection from its ills: and in ix. 4 we find they are still in the midst of the woes and saved by the seal. Nor can there be day and night in the temple above, nor sun nor heat from which they must have shade. Moreover, the fountains of living waters belong to the Holy Jerusalem on earth, and not to the things of heaven, while, not till the end, are they the blessed dead whose labours are ended and whose works follow them (§ XXVI, xiv. 13). Only then have we a description of them by the heavenly sea, which, if their first state of being before the throne of God were heaven, would be mere repetition. Finally, the angels who stand before God are also on earth (§ XXIII, viii. 2).

It would, therefore, appear that the saints continue their labours to the end of time, which agrees with the view, for which other reasons have already been given, that the Holy City is removed only at the end by the departure of the saints and the reaping of the harvest of their labours. After the 1000 years, therefore, it still continues, and the saints are only more perfectly in it by visible separation from evil, and by being before the throne of God in the sense (1) of an unclouded vision of His rule, (2) of being perfectly clothed with righteousness, and (3) of protection from distress and anguish. As a people thus separated unto God, they abide on earth to aid in God's last appeal to men by the manifesting of true righteousness, while He manifests the real nature of sin, when it no longer borrows light from goodness, and its real consequences, when no longer restrained by holier influences.

(*c*) *Sin when Full-grown*

§ XXIII. Two reasons for interpreting the woes, as in essence a vision of the misery of unrelieved sin and the calamity of its unrestrained consequences, appear from the scene which introduces them. (1) They follow, after an interval of solemn silence in heaven, the opening of the last seal. That is to say they are the direct result of the revealing of the servants of God and the separation of them and their works, which isolates wicked men and evil things and leaves them free to show their own true nature and operation. (2) Before the angels who stand before God blow the trumpets which introduce the woes, another angel offers the prayers of the saints before God and then fills a censer with the fire of the altar upon which they had been offered and casts it to earth. The fire of an altar on which prayers are the incense must be symbolism, and the casting down of it must have some such meaning as that the worst sorrow of evil is the rejection of the good.

The first[1] woe is the giving of the key of the pit of the Abyss to the devil, who lets out all its horrors upon earth in the form of a smoke which blots out the sun and darkens the air, while out of it comes the devil's army of demonic locusts. They are in might as unconquerable war-horses, with men's faces and women's hair, but with teeth like lions, breasts clothed in iron, voices like many chariots racing in battle, and their torment like the sting of scorpions, till men seek deliverance by death, which flees from them. Yet they assail sinners only and spare the fruits of the earth.

This description depends mainly on Joel and we may not overlook the purpose there given of the visitation: 'Rend your hearts and not your garments, and turn unto the Lord your God' (ii. 13).

In view of John's usual method, the meaning of the first woe is reasonably certain. It is the usual invisible conflict which, after the pattern of Daniel, accompanies all visible earthly disasters. It is for him a real transaction in the invisible world, yet, as it can only be described from the earthly reflexion, which in this case is sin in its true nature and unredeemed by good, it is just a vision of sin. What else could come forth from the pit, be wholly the servant of the devil, torment men and spare nature, appear human and have woman's softness, yet tear with its mouth and sting with its tail, blot out man's lights and darken his world[2]?

[1] See note, p. 167.

[2] The whole description is so much drawn from the O.T. that we naturally look for some original for the women's hair and the crowns, as it were of gold. The most probable source is Ez. xxiii.

Yet the earthly experience is never for John more than struggling shadows cast upon earth by the storm-rent clouds above. Evil spirits were for him no mere poetical decoration to earthly happenings, but demonic forces were a tremendous reality. That sin exposed men to their assaults was a certain and terrible fact. The Abyss was as much an actual place for him as Rome or Jerusalem, and the devil and his hordes ascend from it in the same actual way that the Eastern barbarian crosses the Euphrates to destroy Rome. Yet in all previous accounts the conflict is invisible, and there is no reason to suppose this to be different. The visible effects are just the darkness and the distress of unrelieved iniquity.

§ XXIV. If this interpretation of the first woe be correct, the second, which follows, would, in accord with John's usual method, be a visible transaction. Yet it might be something more like the diffused anarchy of the seventh plague than the actual warfare of the sixth. This view is confirmed by these woes being announced by an eagle flying in the firmament, because in the seventh plague the vial is poured out upon the air. The agents in the second woe would be the four unsocial vices, mentioned in the woe, of which men do not repent—murder, sorcery, fornication, theft—the calamitous offspring of sin (*v.* 21). Then we should have to conceive the hordes from the four corners as demonic agencies working in a world in which every social bond was broken and men held nothing sacred in their mutual relations.

The blast from the four corners of the altar shows that these hordes are summoned from the four corners of the earth, and if the suggested correction to the 'first' angel, as the receiver of the order to set them free, be correct, this is confirmed. Then we have to identify them both with Gog and Magog (§ XIX) who are in the four corners of the earth and with the winds restrained also in the four corners of the earth (§ XXII).

36 ff., the lewd women who mingle religion and vice, the worship of Jahveh and the abomination of Moloch. Drunkards from the wilderness put beautiful crowns upon their heads. Thus we have sin as licentiousness, murder, intemperance, extravagance, with the root of all in false religion, which is John's conception of sin throughout.

The only alternative to demonic hordes is barbarians. Nations which are deceived by Satan have hitherto in Revelation been actual nations. It might, therefore, be that John ascribes this final destruction to the same forces as overthrew the Roman Empire, only now extended to all barbarians.

But against this view there are the following considerations:

1. It is unlikely that the same force which was able to overthrow an empire, would be thought equal to obliterating the world of time. Nor is there any other case in the book of the same earthly force being used twice. Moreover, the barbarians would on this occasion themselves belong to the world that was to be destroyed.

2. The winds which brake forth upon the Great Sea in Daniel cannot be nations of men. Gog of Magog in Ezekiel may have had some reference to the Scythians, but the whole description suggests the supernatural. That this suggestion was developed by later Judaism appears from the mistranslation of Amos vii. 1 in the LXX: 'And behold a breed of locusts coming from the east, and lo one wingless locust, Gog the king.' John may not have known this translation, and it can be explained as a misreading of the Hebrew, but it is such a misreading as could not have been made unless these locusts had been interpreted supernaturally and Gog had become a well-known mythological figure. The fact that John speaks of Gog and Magog, and not, as in Ezekiel, of Gog of Magog, further confirms the idea that he had no interest in these hordes as peoples, but that they were for him mere vague names for uncanny forces.

3. The corners of the earth were not, for John, mere places inhabited by human beings, but more probably belonged to the strange demonic world in which he believed. As in the O.T. we have places inhabited by the satyr, the howling creature and the night-monster, the inhabitants of the corners might be earth-demons: and as they were different from Satan's air-demons, they might have to be specially stirred up by him to mischief.

4. If they are really called 'angels' in the text, this would confirm the idea that they were demonic. This reading may be right, and four might mean the four hordes of them in

the four corners. But, as 'winds' are used before and are more appropriate to hordes than 'angels,' possibly we ought to read 'winds.' Yet 'winds' also, with John's way of thinking, would more probably signify demons than men.

5. While the saints, as they are now separate, might have a camp to be surrounded, the whole account of the Holy Jerusalem rather suggests a spiritual state, exposed only to spirit foes, than a geographical territory. Moreover, we might suppose that the saints themselves could defeat earthly foes, while these need to be burned up by fire from heaven.

In either case the Great Euphrates, if it run between the world and its corners, cannot be the river in the East, but must be the ancient Oceanus, a boundary round the whole habitable world. If it is a frontier against demonic foes, as is most probable, it may not have been a visible stream, yet it would not, with John's sense of the reality of the invisible, be any less because of that something actually existing[1].

With this idea of spirit forces to which men have exposed themselves by their iniquities and which are also the moral consequences of sin, the descriptions of them agree.

The iron breastplates of the locusts may either speak of the hardening effect of sin or of the fact that it cannot be killed once it is committed, or both, but that the breastplates of its progeny are fiery, dark-red, sulphurous, probably signifies the appalling nature of its unrestrained consequences, and the description 'tails as serpents' is from the consequences of drunkenness in Proverbs.

From these woes evil men cannot escape even by death. Those who do die seem to be the penitent, escape and not service being apparently the only possibility for those who

[1] This would be in accord with the uniform meaning of 'great' throughout the rest of the book, which is always 'above the natural,' and generally something in a realm of abstract powers, not unlike Plato's ideas. Thus, although Daniel calls his beasts 'great,' John, whose beast is a far vaster conception, does not call it 'great,' because, being World-empire, it is still a visible earthly magnitude. In this case the Great Euphrates (§ X, xvi. 12) would also not be the actual river, unless 'great' there is a gloss from this passage, which, as it dries up for earthly kings to pass, is the more probable hypothesis.

continue so long in sin. Yet they are only a third; and for the rest even this manifestation of sin when it is full-grown does not avail.

(*d*) *The Departure of the Saints and the Harvesting of their Works*

§ XXV. The third woe is heralded by great voices from heaven, which must be the voices of the seven thunders which John heard at the beginning (§ V, x. 3), and which he was to seal up till the days of the third angel. These days have now come and the voices announce in judgment that the kingdoms of the world have become the kingdom of our Lord and of His Christ, thus summing up the whole story of the book. Voices of thunder mean that it is the work of judgment. What could not be done before, is now to be done perfectly and finally, by the utter blotting out of the rage of evil powers, and by the judging of the dead, with the giving of their reward to God's servants and the destroying of those who destroyed the earth. The praise for this is naturally given by the Church, in its representatives the twenty-four elders, who fall on their faces before God and worship Him.

Then the temple of God is opened and the ark of His covenant in it appears, which is the same kind of idea as the opening of the shrine in the tent of witness, to show that the testimony of prophecy was to come into operation in history (§ X, xv. 5). The covenant is evidently the everlasting covenant of the Old Testament, the covenant of life and peace. There is an ark of it in the heavenly temple as there was in the earthly, described (1 Kgs. viii. 21) as the ark wherein is the covenant of the Lord. The opening of its heavenly ark, therefore, means that this covenant is now to be fulfilled.

The passage, xiv. 6–12, is the usual aside to John's contemporaries. The gospel for all the ages, announced by the angel flying in the firmament and the two angels which follow, sums up the whole purpose of the book. It glances backward over the prophetic story to show that it warns and encourages the Christians to be steadfast in the faith through all the persecution which is to come upon them, to worship only the Maker of the things other men worship, and who is the Judge of the earth, to consider the fleeting nature of all worldly glory, to shun idolatry as eternal loss, and, in contrast with the troubled time, to cherish both the present quiet of heart and the eternal rest of the saints.

If 'rest' is to be interpreted by Isaiah, especially xxviii. 12, 'This is the rest, give ye rest to him that is weary...this is the refreshing,' having no rest does not mean ceaseless torment, but it is a present experience of the want of peace and hope in view of the certain annihilation of all that evil men worship.

§ XXVI. The transition, then, to 'Herein is the faith and patience of the saints' is through their having the solid grounds for confidence which the idolaters lack, because, having failed to enter into God's rest because of unbelief (Heb. iv. 6), night and day fears and uncertainties shadow them.

In *v.* 13 the prophetic narrative is resumed. With the end of evil on the earth, the task of the patience of the saints is over. They depart from earth, apparently by the ordinary way of leaving their mortal bodies, because John hears a voice from heaven saying, 'Blessed are the dead who die in the Lord,' and because the final judgment is concerned wholly with discarnate souls.

Hitherto, whether on earth or in heaven, the specially elect at least have been in labour for the salvation of the earth. Now, not only are their toils ended, but their works follow them, for their use apparently in their new state; and the description which follows is just the harvesting of these works. It is based on the saying of Christ, 'But when the fruit is ripe, straightway he putteth forth the sickle, because the harvest is come' (Mk iv. 29): and 'The harvest is the end of the world: and the reapers are the angels' (Mt. xiii. 39).

'One seated on a white cloud, like to a son of man and having on his head a coronet of gold,' reproduces the prophecy in the Gospels about the Son of Man coming in the clouds of heaven[1]. That it is put here and not at the

[1] It is 'a cloud' as in Luke. The ideas from Matthew and Mark might be common property in the Church, but this once more looks like dependence on Luke.

coming to found the Holy Jerusalem confirms the interpretation of that state as an unobtrusive, if effective, rule, and not as a visible city, for it means that then such a spectacular coming did not suit John's idea of what was taking place, whereas now it does.

Yet even here it is doubtful whether we have Jesus Himself or only His angelic representative, who wears His emblems because he is to use His standard and exercise His discernment of the good. The reasons for this doubt are: (1) Jesus is nowhere else in the book connected with works of power, but always with God's method of saving men by the testimony of service and sacrifice, even though His method is also the final victory and the final judgment; (2) The one who follows is called 'another angel,' and in the Gospels the reapers are the angels; and (3) Jesus would not gather the ordinary harvest of the earth and leave the vintage, its noblest fruit, to an angel from the altar, for, were He present, how could He leave the vine, which, in accord with the use of this figure for Israel in the Old Testament, is the true Israel and, therefore, especially the martyrs?

(*e*) *The Last Judgment and the Final State*

This closes the story of the victory of the Rule of God over the world, and the conflict ends as it began with a sign in the heavens. This sign is 'great' as the last was, that is, above the visibly human and natural. It is the seven angels who have the last plagues which complete the judgment of God. If the identification of the hosts of the Second Woe with Gog and Magog be correct, the final blotting out of the powers of evil is by fire from heaven; and this interpretation is confirmed by the fact that the casting of Satan into the lake of fire to join his creatures, the beast and the false prophet, which takes place immediately after the destruction of Gog and Magog, could only take place at this point, as Satan is the leader of the hosts in the second woe. Yet the sign shows all this to be past[1].

[1] This sign in heaven seems to mark the final consummation. In that case the seven angels are the angels of the woes, those who stand before God, and the woes are the plagues, and *seven* is a gloss.

Another vision at once declares the end and the justification of this judgment of the earth. The hosts of those who have overcome are seen standing beside a sea of glass mingled with fire. This is the heavenly sea which is before the throne of God, and which signifies the separation of His holiness. That they are still on this side of it is to mark that they have not yet attained their final perfection. Yet they have already entered into rest. They have harps, the symbol of harmony and peace, in their hands; and they sing the song of Moses and of the Lamb, which both alike ascribe all praise and obedience and worship to the Almighty. But, as the thought of his purpose is ever with the writer, the special victory which has tested them is the victory over idolatry, described according to its special form in his own time, as making offerings to the imperial image. Yet it is universalised by the interpretation he puts on the inscription, as belonging to the whole era of the World-empire[1].

§ XXVII. All things are now ready for the end, and John sees a great white throne, the symbol of righteous judgment, and Him that sat upon it, which is his usual way of speaking of his vision of God.

The idea of a final judgment was probably universal both in the Judaism and Christianity of his time, and needs no further explanation, yet he may have thought of Ps. ix. 7, 8: 'He hath prepared his throne for judgment, and he shall judge the world in righteousness,' while 'one seated on a throne' and the 'opening of the books' are from Daniel.

'The sea' from which the dead come cannot, for several reasons, be the ordinary sea. (1) Before God's face the old earth and heaven have already fled and no place is found for them, and the sea is part of the earth which is no more. (2) Only bodies could come from the sea, and they could not go with Hades, the place only of the departed soul. Moreover, the whole description shows that it is disembodied souls that

[1] The interpretation of the number of the name already given, as the turning of the letters of Caesar into the number of the years of the rule of the world-empires, is even more clearly applicable here than in the first reference, and the absence of the 'and' between the inscription and the number shows that the number is not something new and different, but merely the interpretation of the name.

come before God for judgment. (3) The saints also come to receive their final award, and they are neither in the sea nor Hades.

Suggestions have been made for emending the word, but in the present order of the text it is explained as being the heavenly sea, just described as the place of the departed saints. 'The Sea gave up the dead that were by it[1]' means that from it come those who have died in the Lord; and it goes with Hades, from whence come the souls of all the rest. Even Hades cannot be a final award, as if all in it were already lost, else another judgment would be superfluous; and the saints require to come for their final purification, as well as their final award, because only after the Last Judgment does the Sea of separation between them and God pass away.

The sea which is not any more (xxi. 2) must also be this heavenly sea, and not, however many pathetic utterances the idea of the passing of 'the unplumbed, salt, estranging sea' may have inspired, the sea of earth. It is the sublimer conception of the passing of all separation from the holiness of God, even that which still existed for the blessed dead.

A new kind of heavens and a new kind of earth appear. Not even they come down from heaven, but apparently God speaks as of old and they come to be and this time wholly good. Only the new rule so descends, which is another confirmation of the former contention regarding the Holy Jerusalem, that it is not material visible things which descend from heaven, but the Divine Rule which was already embodied in a small company offering its witness amid trial and persecution. This Rule was renewed and extended in the Millennial City, but was still imperfect. Now it descends from heaven afresh, wholly made new, its adornment as a bride complete, to be henceforth the tabernacle of God with men, where, in a new kind of realisation of His presence, all things will be for them made new. Nor will God merely wipe away the tears from men's eyes, but grief and complaint and burden are not to be at all, which would seem to mean, not merely any more among the saints, but anywhere in

[1] This is one more instance of the witness borne by the present arrangement to the remarkable soundness of the text.

God's world—'For all things are made new.' It ends with God Himself being the alpha and the omega, the beginning and the end. This may have a meaning something like Paul's: 'Then shall he deliver up the kingdom to the Father, that God may be all in all' (1 Cor. xv. 24 and 28).

The rest seems to be directed again to John's contemporaries. No one in heaven thirsts, but men in the present distress are assured of receiving the water of life freely, and they are encouraged to victory over idolatry by the assurance of inheriting all things and being to God sons, while they are warned against every kind of idolatry and insincerity by the second death, which above any death man can inflict on them, is to be shunned.

NOTES

I. ΒΑΣΑΝΙΣΜΟΣ

The primary meaning of the word is testing gold with a touchstone. It was widened to any kind of testing and this remained the ordinary meaning. Then it came to have the special meaning of trial by torture, a meaning extending from trouble to torment. Yet the ordinary meaning of testing remained, just as the meaning of 'question' remained, though 'The Question' came also to be used for trial by torture. The usage everywhere in the book could be 'tried so as by fire,' except in Ch. ix. 5 (§ XXIII) where it is defined by being 'as of scorpions.' Just because of this definition, this does not determine the meaning elsewhere. The full meaning would be, tested and found wanting and blotted out of God's universe. That the smoke goes up for ever and ever as explained by Is. xxxiv. 10 would signify an eternal memorial, and not an eternal torment. The idea of the lake of fire as the annihilation of all that cannot be taken up into the Rule of God would agree with its use for ending abstract evils like the false religious teaching, the World-empire, and death and Hades, as well as obdurately evil persons. This would again agree with the statement that all sorrow and evil cease from God's universe after the final judgment.

II. THE HEAVENLY REPRESENTATIVES

The living creatures depend on Ezekiel, and Ezekiel may very probably have drawn his description from Babylonian mythological figures which represent the four corners of the earth: but that does not decide what they meant for Ezekiel and much less what they meant for John. Perhaps it is of some consequence that John divides among the four the likenesses which Ezekiel ascribes to all, because he does the opposite with Daniel's four beasts, and fuses the characteristics of each into one. As that proceeding was important for his way of conceiving World-empire as one, this separation may be significant of an intended distinction between the four living creatures. That they continue to represent nature in some form seems probable, because: (1) They come forward when events are to happen by what we should call natural causes. (2) Their adoration is clearly based on the nature psalms. (3) The call of their representative to 'Come and see' before the sealing of the saints is at once explained if John had the same thought of nature waiting and travailing for the manifestation of the Children of God as Paul cherished.

That they do not represent the corners of the earth, as has been maintained, is plain for three reasons: (1) It is angels not living creatures who appear there. (2) In heaven it is the horns of the altar which correspond with the corners of the earth, and not the living creatures. (3) If the reference in § XXIV (ix. 13) is rightly interpreted, the corners are not, in John's view, places where God is specially manifested. To this we may add that the description of the eyes and even of the praise of the living creatures does not seem appropriate to mere parts of the earth. They rather mark nature as a whole, which is the probable meaning in Ezekiel. The fact that the vials, which are put into the hands of the angels by the representative of the living creatures, are poured out upon the earth, the waters, the sun to burn by fire, and the air, may afford the explanation of the distinction introduced into this by John, because it may mean that they represent the elements of nature. Nor, in that case, are the descriptions wholly inexplicable. The ox plainly stands for the earth he tills, and an eagle for the air in which he flies. The lion for fire which devours is also possible; and water with John is the symbol of fruitfulness and the likeness of man of God's way of working good; and, though less in accord with John's way of thinking, there is the description of a man 'as unstable as water.'

That they are in the midst of the throne and round about the throne is dogma, not picture, and would seem to mean that they belong to God's essential mind as well as do His bidding, while being full of eyes before and behind certainly presupposes a conception of nature very different from a merely mechanical order, and is in accord with Ps. civ. 4, 'who maketh winds his messengers and flaming fire his ministers,' and may possibly mean that nature regards both what God has done and what He will do.

Mythological explanations of the twenty-four elders as astral deities are still less convincing. (1) There is really no proof that the Jews of John's time entertained such ideas. (2) It is not in accord with the usual furniture of heaven in Revelation, which consists of heavenly representatives of earthly things, the living creatures as above explained, a tent of witness, an altar with horns, thrones, all of them symbolic. (3) An elder is the ordinary name for a representative both in the Old Testament and the New, and, as we have the Church represented in the Holy Jerusalem by the names of the twelve tribes and of the twelve apostles of the Lamb, that the twenty-four are its representatives would seem reasonably probable.

The glassy sea is a combination of the sea in the Temple and Ezekiel's firmament like terrible crystal, over which is seen the sapphire throne. The change from the firmament overhead to the sea at his feet is due to John's position as a spectator in heaven, but both seem to mean the separation of God's holiness.

'The seven torches which are His seven spirits' seems to be without any certain O.T. model to determine the meaning. In the Messages the eyes of one like to a Son of Man are also as a flame of fire, but there he simply has the spirits, and this is associated with having the stars. This may help to confirm the view that the idea originated from the seven planets, but that sheds no light on John's view, who almost certainly thought of no such connexion. Having the spirits, and his eyes being the spirits may, however, be the same, as it may mean that God's spirits were eyes to Him to look into men's hearts. This would connect them with the eyes of God's glory which men's evil provokes (Is. iii. 8), and with the Seven which are the eyes of the Lord, which run to and fro through the whole earth (Zech. iv. 10), which rejoice in good, and apparently are against evil, and with 2 Chron. xvi. 9: 'the eyes of the Lord which run to and fro throughout the whole earth, to show himself strong on behalf of those whose heart is perfect toward him.'

The Lamb 'in the midst of the throne' must also be dogma, not picture. Obviously it must mean that Christ's way of service is of the essence of God's rule. In some sense it must express the idea in Colossians that in him dwelleth all the fullness of the Godhead bodily. As the idea of the Christ and the World-rule is also in Colossians, it is possible that John knew the Epistle, but both might depend on common ideas. Yet there is nothing to express that the Lamb is an agent of God's rule as with the living creatures who are round about the throne, and this goes with the doubt which has been raised, in interpreting the book, whether the Christ ever appears in acts of power or judgment. He is the Lion of the tribe of Judah as well as the Lamb slain, but this may only mean that His sacrifice is so essentially of God's method of rule as to be the true victorious power. He fights against anarchy, but Daniel describes this as overthrown without hands, that is by moral force.

The more difficult question is, What is the relation of this figure to Jesus? Is it simply Jesus or, like the other figures, a heavenly representative of what Jesus manifests on earth, but which is also, though less perfectly, incarnated in the saints? As the saints are still upon earth, we might expect Jesus to be with them. But that might not have troubled John, and the nature of His presence in the Holy Jerusalem is in any case difficult to determine. Yet it is clear that John drew a very clear line between the divine principle incarnate in Jesus and his fellow-servant who might not be worshipped.

III. THE WOES

That there are only three woes is made certain by the precision of the result when the first four are omitted. The three sections then consist of 33 lines each, with precisely two words over, which are the first ἕπτα in viii. 6 and λοιπῶν in *v*. 13. And this is confirmed (1) by the 'thirds' which are destroyed in the first four, which seems to have no meaning except as an attempt to compensate for 'three' found in the original text, (2) by the style of these woes, which is of a feebleness quite unlike the author's own work, and (3) by the first woe destroying (viii. 7) the very things which in the fifth woe are not to be hurt (ix. 4).

Yet it is difficult to suppose that the editor found only three angels and three woes, numbered one, two, three, and deliberately changed them to seven, and put four woes of his own before the true woes, and changed the numbers of the latter to five, six, seven. The difficulty is further increased by the reference to 'the days of the voice of the seventh angel' in § V, x. 7. As this follows in the editor's arrangement, he may have had sufficient perspicacity to see that John's third was his seventh, and have changed the number accordingly, but this is most unlikely.

The explanation, as usual, is to be found in the Old Testament. The description of the angels as standing before God is from Zech. vi. 5, where they are also four and probably identified with the four winds. This makes it plain that the first four angels are those who are already standing at the four corners of the earth. Thus with the three now introduced, the angels are seven. In accord with Zechariah, they have all come from standing before the Lord of the whole earth, and are now upon earth, to do His final work in it. This explains why, though there are only three woes, they are introduced by the fifth, sixth and seventh angels. Then we have only to suppose that the editor supplied what he took to be an omission, in the same way as he supplied the openings of the intervening seals, which the author simply assumes.

The explanation has the further advantage that it enables us to explain the peculiar construction in ix. 14, 15, and to get rid of a kind of repetition which is characteristic of the editor, but which has no parallel in the work of the author. We have only to change *ἕκτῳ* into *πρώτῳ* and suppose that *λέγοντα* has been made to agree with the wrong subject. This way of addressing all the angels through their leader or representative is parallel with the way in which one living creature acts for all four. Then, if the real angels are thus distinguished, the four bound winds may be called angels or messengers in accord with 'He maketh the winds his messengers' (Ps. civ. 4). This is the more likely that they have been prepared for this hour. Yet it is at least possible that the very frequently used word *ἄγγελοι* has been substituted by a transcriber's error for *ἄνεμοι*. In any case they are the same as the 'winds' and the 'nations' which are in the four corners of the earth.

For EU product safety concerns, contact us at Calle de José Abascal, 56–1°, 28003 Madrid, Spain or eugpsr@cambridge.org.

www.ingramcontent.com/pod-product-compliance
Ingram Content Group UK Ltd.
Pitfield, Milton Keynes, MK11 3LW, UK
UKHW020315140625
459647UK00018B/1887

* 9 7 8 1 1 0 7 5 0 5 3 9 1 *